T0334543

REAL ESTATE
THE BASICS

Real Estate: The Basics provides an easy-to-read introduction to the core concepts of the industry to students new to the subject or professionals changing direction within the sector.

The book encapsulates the key 'need to know' aspects of Real Estate including the 'language' of real estate; its value and contribution to countries' GDP; its primary purpose, whether as an asset or as a resource; valuation concepts; asset classes; basic concepts of land law, and of landlord and tenant law; the increased role and importance of sustainability and technology; and an overview of the wide range of professionals involved in the industry. Readers will come to appreciate how the different elements of the profession fit together, and the professional standards and practices that may apply.

Real Estate: The Basics will be helpful reading for anyone thinking about studying Real Estate, Property, or other Built Environment topics. It could be used to teach across a wide variety of courses, to provide an aide memoire to those who are already working in the industry, and to give those who are responsible for appointing and monitoring real estate advisers a greater understanding of the workings of the real estate sector.

Jan Wilcox is a Fellow of the Royal Institution of Chartered Surveyors and a Senior Fellow of the Higher Education Academy. She spent 20 years working, mainly in property asset management, for a variety of institutions, including Fenn Wright, Transport for London, the Crown Estate, Hammerson plc, and Merrill Lynch Investment Managers before moving into lecturing in higher education. She is now a Senior Lecturer in Real Estate at the University of Westminster, Senior Lecturer in Management at the University of Suffolk, and an examiner for the Institute of Residential Property Management. She is also co-author of *Property Asset Management, 4th Edition*, Routledge, 2018.

Jane Forsyth is a Chartered Surveyor, a former property solicitor, a Fellow of the Institute of Residential Property Management, and an accredited landlord. She has 30 years' experience in the real estate sector including as director of her residential management business. Jane is now Associate Lecturer at Oxford Brookes University and Associate Tutor at the University College of Estate Management, UK. She also mentors RICS candidates and is an APC Assessor.

The Basics

The Basics is a highly successful series of accessible guidebooks which provide an overview of the fundamental principles of a subject area in a jargon-free and undaunting format.

Intended for students approaching a subject for the first time, the books both introduce the essentials of a subject and provide an ideal springboard for further study. With over 50 titles spanning subjects from artificial intelligence (AI) to women's studies, *The Basics* are an ideal starting point for students seeking to understand a subject area.

Each text comes with recommendations for further study and gradually introduces the complexities and nuances within a subject.

SUSTAINABILITY (SECOND EDITION)
PETER JACQUES

TRANSLATION
JULIANE HOUSE

TRANSNATIONAL LITERATURE
PAUL JAY

TOWN PLANNING
TONY HALL

WOMEN'S STUDIES (SECOND EDITION)
BONNIE G. SMITH

ENGLISH GRAMMAR
MICHAEL MCCARTHY

PRAGMATICS
BILLY CLARK

WORLD PREHISTORY
BRIAN M. FAGAN AND NADIA DURRANI

REAL ESTATE
JAN WILCOX AND JANE FORSYTH

For a full list of titles in this series, please visit www.routledge.com/The-Basics/book-series/B

REAL ESTATE

THE BASICS

Jan Wilcox
Jane Forsyth

Routledge
Taylor & Francis Group

LONDON AND NEW YORK

Cover image: © Getty Images

First published 2022
by Routledge
2 Park Square, Milton Park, Abingdon, Oxon OX14 4RN

and by Routledge
605 Third Avenue, New York, NY 10158

Routledge is an imprint of the Taylor & Francis Group, an informa business

© 2022 Jan Wilcox & Jane Forsyth

British Library Cataloguing-in-Publication Data
A catalogue record for this book is available from the British Library

Library of Congress Cataloging-in-Publication Data
Names: Wilcox, Jan, author. | Forsyth, Jane (Accredited landlord) author.
Title: Real estate : the basics / Jan Wilcox, Jane Forsyth.
Description: New York, NY : Routledge, 2022. | Series: The basics | Includes
    bibliographical references and index.
Identifiers: LCCN 2021039199 (print) | LCCN 2021039200 (ebook) |
    ISBN 9780367725488 (hardback) | ISBN 9780367725433 (paperback) |
    ISBN 9781003155256 (ebook)
Subjects: LCSH: Real estate business.
Classification: LCC HD1375 .W536 2022 (print) | LCC HD1375 (ebook) |
    DDC 332.63/24—dc23
LC record available at https://lccn.loc.gov/2021039199
LC ebook record available at https://lccn.loc.gov/2021039200

ISBN: 978-0-367-72548-8 (hbk)
ISBN: 978-0-367-72543-3 (pbk)
ISBN: 978-1-003-15525-6 (ebk)

DOI: 10.1201/9781003155256

Typeset in Bembo
by Apex CoVantage, LLC

CONTENTS

ABBREVIATIONS

AGA	Authorised Guarantee Agreement
AONB	Areas of Outstanding Natural Beauty
APC	Assessment of Professional Competence
APM	Association for Project Management
ARHM	Association of Retirement Housing Managers
ARLA	Association of Residential Letting Agents
ARMA	Association of Residential Managing Agents
AssocRICS	Associate of the Royal Institution of Chartered Surveyors
AST	Assured Shorthold Tenancy
AVM	Automated Valuation Model
BIM	Building Information Modelling
BRE	Building Research Establishment
BREEAM	Building Research Establishment Environmental Assessment Method
CAD	Computer Aided Design
CICES	Chartered Institution of Civil Engineering Surveyors
CIH	Chartered Institute of Housing
CIL	Community Infrastructure Levy
CILEX	Chartered Institute of Legal Executives
CIOB	Chartered Institute of Building
CLC	Council for Licensed Conveyancers
CLRA	Commonhold and Leasehold Reform Act 2002
CPD	Continuing Professional Development
CSR	Corporate Social Responsibility
DCF	Discounted Cash Flow
EMEA	Europe, Middle East and Asia

EPC	Energy Performance Certificate
ESG	Environmental, Social and Governance
FCA	Financial Conduct Authority
FMOP	Fair Maintainable Operating Profit
FMT	Fair Maintainable Turnover
FRI	Full Repairing and Insuring
FRICS	Fellow of the Royal Institution of Chartered Surveyors
GDP	Gross Domestic Product
GDPR	General Data Protection Regulation
GDV	Gross Development Value
GEA	Gross External Area
GIA	Gross Internal Area
GIS	Geographic Information Systems
GLAA	Gangmasters and Labour Abuse Authority
HETAS	Heating Equipment Testing and Approval Scheme
HMO	House in Multiple Occupation
HSE	Health and Safety Executive
ICE	Institution of Civil Engineers
ICO	Information Commissioner's Office
ICT	Information and Communication Technology
IESC	International Ethics Standards Coalition
IFRS	International Financial Reporting Standards
IPMA	International Project Management Association
IPMS	International Property Measurement Standards
IRI	Internal Repairing and Insuring
IRR	Internal Rate of Return
IRPM	Institute of Residential Property Management
ISE	Institution of Structural Engineers
IVS	International Valuation Standards
IVSC	International Valuation Standards Council
IWFM	Institute of Workplace and Facilities Management
JCT	Joint Contracts Tribunal
LEASE	Leasehold Advisory Service
LEED	Leadership in Energy and Environmental Design
LRA	Land Registration Act 2002
LRHUDA	Leasehold Reform, Housing & Urban Development Act 1993
LTA 1985	Landlord and Tenant Act 1985

LTV	Loan-to-value
MRICS	Member of the Royal Institution of Chartered Surveyors
MRTPI	Member of the Royal Town Planning Institute
NAEA	National Association of Estate Agents
NAPIT	National Association of Professional Inspectors and Testers
NIA	Net Internal Area
NICEIC	National Inspection Council for Electrical Installation Contracting
NPPF	National Planning Policy Framework
NPV	Net Present Value
NRLA	National Residential Landlords Association
NTSELAT	National Trading Standards Estate and Letting Agency Team
OECD	Organisation for Economic Co-operation and Development
PII	Professional Indemnity Insurance
PITT	Possession, Interest, Title, Time
PMI	Project Management Institute
REIT	Real Estate Investment Trust
REO	Reasonably Efficient Operator
RIBA	Royal Institute of British Architects
RICS	Royal Institution of Chartered Surveyors
RPSA	Residential Property Surveyors Association
RTMCo	Right to Manage Company
RTPI	Royal Town Planning Institute
SDLT	Stamp Duty Land Tax
SSSI	Site of Special Scientific Interest
TEY	True Equivalent Yield
TFA	Tenant Fees Act 2019
UPRN	Unique Property Reference Number

TABLE OF CASES

TABLE OF STATUTES

FIGURES

ACKNOWLEDGEMENTS

From Jan: Thanks to Celena and Jamilla for your unwavering support and encouragement in everything.

From Jane: Thanks to my family for your support, and especially to David Schermer for your patience, support, and interest throughout. Thanks to Jill Cripps for your time and for your very helpful feedback on the legal chapters.

From us both: Thanks to Ed Needle for commissioning the book, Patrick Hetherington for his regular 'nags', and to Ian Hornett, fellow author, for volunteering to read the final draft.

INTRODUCTION

WHAT IS THIS BOOK ABOUT?

Every human being has a connection with real estate throughout their lives. This includes, for example, the hospitals we are born in; the farms that grow the food we consume; the schools we attend; the homes we live in; the offices we work in; the stores we shop in; the restaurants we eat in; the gyms we exercise in; the hotels we holiday in; or, for the less fortunate, the ground we sleep on. This diversity in real estate cannot be covered in one book, so this book aims to provide an overview of the 'need to know' aspects with guidance on where to find out more.

With increased globalisation, the traditional property industry has evolved into the Real Estate industry. The industry has expanded in size, complexity, and importance – as both an asset class and a field of study. It is a significant store of value accounting for 21% of the UK's total net wealth[1] and representing more than 3.5 times total global GDP.[2] In the UK, over 11% of those in employment are in construction and real estate–related industries.[3] Globally, it is estimated that 70% of wealth is held in land and property assets.[4]

It is a fascinating industry and one that has provided us with, collectively, over 70 years of lived experience – and a good living.

WHO IS THIS BOOK FOR?

This book aims to introduce the core concepts of the industry to those new to it, or who may be changing direction within the

DOI: 10.1201/9781003155256-1

sector. It might also provide an aide-memoire, of key concepts and terminology, to those who are already working within the field. For those who are suddenly given responsibility for appointing and monitoring real estate advisers, it may provide a greater understanding of the workings of the sector.

After so many years working in the industry, we tend to forget that some of the terminology is confusing or ambiguous to our students, particularly those from overseas and non-cognate students. Basic concepts, familiar to old hands like us, may be alien to novices. The default position is to 'Google' the answer, but it can be difficult to assess which are reliable sources and they are often written by non-subject specialist authors. When Jan was teaching Property Transactions, one of her students asked for clarification on some terminology. Subsequently, the idea for this book was mentioned to some students, who said: '*I wish you had done it before*', and '*Such a good idea, I could have done with that when I went into agency*'. We hope it will help future students.

Jane, who had qualified as a solicitor, decided late in her career to re-train as a chartered surveyor. She agreed to co-author this book, as it is the book that she wished had been available when she started her studies and was gaining experience in new areas.

In common with most professions, there is a tendency to specialise at an early stage. One of Jan's contacts, who has been qualified for over 30 years and asset manages a valuable nationwide portfolio, confessed the other day that they always struggled with remembering the different types of property yield. This book will provide a quick reference for individuals like that, and others who have specialised, who want a more holistic overview of the industry.

WHAT MIGHT YOU LEARN FROM THIS BOOK?

This book should help you to understand the basic concepts relating to the real estate industry and will provide recommendations for further resources where you may require more detailed information. It should help you to grasp the way that each aspect interacts with the other and the importance of each specialism to the overall industry. It will provide a quick reference guide and building blocks for the basis of your learning going forward.

WHAT THIS BOOK WILL NOT DO?

It will not teach you everything you need to know about real estate. Real estate is a vast, and wide-ranging, industry and our aim is to provide you with a basic introduction to its key elements. This book should provide you with the basics together with some guidance on where to find out more. To succeed in our profession there is a need to continue learning throughout your career, and often to work alongside other specialists. Ours is a profession that starts with building basic knowledge. It then combines the acquisition of more detailed, specialist knowledge, with work experience, to achieve the required level of professional expertise. Personal relationships are likely to be important to successful Real Estate careers and these should be nurtured together with the acquisition of up-to-date knowledge and skills as the industry continues to evolve.

The book is based on UK practice, regulations and policy, and English law. It is impossible to cover the full range of international variations. It should however become clear that in certain areas, such as valuation and measurement, there is a continued focus on standardisation to achieve consistency across all countries.

HOW IS THIS BOOK ORGANISED?

This book attempts to present the 'need to know' elements of real estate in an accessible form. It is intended to identify, explore, and synthesise the key elements that combine to shape our unique industry.

Chapter 1 has introduced the importance of real estate, the purpose of this book, and what it will, and will not, do.

Chapter 2 considers the definition of real estate and its contributions to the wider economy. It also identifies the key groups of owners of real estate.

Chapter 3 outlines the diverse nature of real estate ranging through the standard commercial and residential types of property, to the less common such as wind and solar farms, seabed, and coastline.

Chapter 4 contemplates real estate as an investment producing income, capital gains, or both. This chapter includes a brief overview of the main methods of investing in real estate.

Chapter 5 reflects on how a variety of organisations use real estate as a resource to facilitate the operation of their core business.

Chapter 6 outlines the wide range of people involved in the real estate industry. This includes the diversity under the generic designation 'chartered surveyors' which embraces, amongst others, registered valuers, quantity surveyors, property managers, a range of agents, minerals surveyors, and land surveyors. It also includes other professionals such as architects, solicitors, and accountants without whom those working in the real estate industry could not successfully carry out their roles.

Chapter 7 is the first of three chapters to focus on law relating to real estate. This chapter provides an outline of key aspects of real estate law that underpin the industry and aspects of practice relating to real estate.

Chapter 8 builds upon the content of Chapter 7 to explicitly debate the landlord and tenant relationship and statutes and case law relating to this.

Chapter 9 is the last of the law chapters that focuses on interests in real estate beyond simply freehold and leasehold such as easements, wayleaves, and other rights.

Chapter 10 considers some of the most common types of property transactions that take place including leasehold and freehold, disposals, and acquisitions. The duties of an agent, methods of sale, the importance of heads of terms, marketing, and negotiation are also covered.

Chapter 11 provides an overview of the key aspects of value in relation to real estate and the core purposes, concepts, and terminology of valuation. The basis and main purposes of valuation are outlined together with the scope and purpose of the Red Book, and the content of valuation reports.

Chapter 12 outlines the process of carrying out a valuation and describes the five main methods. Definitions and explanations of the rate of return and commonly used yields are put forward. Detailed valuation methodology and numerical examples are not supplied but references to detailed specific valuation texts are provided.

Chapter 13 offers insights into the achievement of effective real estate management. This is achieved by a blend of technical knowledge and interpersonal skills. The chapter provides a framework of the technical aspects of the role together with an indication of the problem-solving approach required to solve the wide range of situations encountered by property managers.

Finally, Chapter 14 looks to the future, touching upon some of the recent developments in the field such as the increasing emphasis on sustainability, health and safety, diversity and inclusion, and ethical aspects.

HOW SHOULD YOU USE THIS BOOK?

This book should be kept close by to refer to whenever you come across some terminology, or real estate aspects, you are unfamiliar with or need a reminder of. We encourage you to keep it with you throughout your studies and annotate it, and add to it, so it stays relevant and useful to you. If there is anything fundamental you believe is missing, please let us know and we will endeavour to cover it in the next edition.

NOTES

1 British Property Federation (BPF) (undated) Online. Available from: www.bpf.org.uk/about-real-estate

2 Savills (2018) Online. Available from: www.savills.com/impacts/market-trends/8-things-you-need-to-know-about-the-value-of-global-real-estate.html

3 Office for National Statistics (ONS) (2021) *Emp 13: Employment by Industry* 18 May Online. Available from: www.ons.gov.uk/employmentandlabourmarket/peopleinwork/employmentandemployeetypes/datasets/employmentbyindustryemp13

4 RICS (2020) 'Peter Pereira Grey to Lead Independent Valuation Review' 29 September Online. Available from: www.rics.org/uk/news-insight/latest-news/press/press-releases/peter-pereira-gray-to-lead-independent-valuation-review/

REAL ESTATE IN CONTEXT

WHAT IS REAL ESTATE?

When writing the fourth edition of *Property Asset Management* (Scarrett & Wilcox 2018), we debated whether the title should be updated to Real Estate Asset Management but felt that 'Real Estate' was a US term rather than a UK term. As you can see from the title of this text, this time we agreed that Real Estate was the term to use, but were we right? Probably not, as this book covers both property and real estate. However, the two terms often appear to be used interchangeably, presumably in response to globalisation whereby the major international real estate consultancies needed a term that applied across all regions. There is however a subtle difference between real estate and property.

The RICS Red Book[1] defines real estate as:

> *Land and all things that are a natural part of the land (e.g. trees, minerals) and things that have been attached to the land (e.g. buildings and site improvements) and all permanent building attachments (e.g. mechanical and electrical plant providing services to a building), that are both below and above the ground.*

Property however is defined by the IVS[2] as:

> *A legal concept, encompassing all the interests, rights, and benefits related to property ownership.*

Real estate refers to tangible land; it is a physical object and includes any resources attached to it such as buildings. Property, however,

DOI: 10.1201/9781003155256-2

includes intangible rights connected with ownership such as rights of way and easements. These are legal concepts which will be discussed in Chapter 9. This is a fairly specialist point, and, over time, real estate has come to be considered to include both real estate and property. A recent example of this was the RICS Independent Valuation Review, the press release for which, in 2020, referred to both 'valuations of property assets' and 'real estate investment valuation practices'.[3]

Real estate and property include a wide diversity of interests. Real estate includes tangible buildings on land such as offices, houses, retail units, leisure properties, and farms. It also includes a wide range of other tangible constructions such as telephone masts, electricity substations, wind and solar farms, and sewage treatment works. The diversity of real estate will be discussed in more detail in Chapter 3.

Property includes intangible rights above and below land such as rights of way allowing access over a piece of land belonging to another, and rights to light. Land also needs to be clearly defined as there is, for example, a difference between the ownership of the foreshore (the area between low and high tide) and the seabed.

WHY IS REAL ESTATE SO IMPORTANT?

As mentioned in Chapter 1, real estate makes a significant contribution to a country's wealth with an estimated 70% of global wealth being held in land and property assets.[4] Real estate also provides a meaningful proportion of a country's tax revenue. In the UK, property taxes are higher than anywhere else in the world, as measured by the Organisation for Economic Co-operation and Development (OECD), a group of 37 developed nations. In the UK property taxes accounted for 12.4% of total taxation in 2019 and contributed 4.1% of GDP.[5] Property taxes in the UK are approximately double the levels in the average OECD country. The construction and real estate industries also account for over 11% of those in employment in the UK.[6]

In addition to acting as a store of value and a generator of tax, real estate is also a resource that can be developed and used by individuals and organisations to satisfy their needs.

Every individual needs a place to live in. This ranges from extensive detached houses in multiple countries to simply a doorway or subway that provides the homeless with some protection from the elements. Properties may be owned or rented or even simply constructed illegally on a piece of land as seen in the slums of India and the favelas in Brazil.

Every organisation needs a place from which to run their business although, in some cases, this may increasingly be carried out from home. Places in which businesses are carried out, away from the home, encompass a wide range, including industrial units for manufacturing goods; retail units for selling goods; hotels offering rooms; and offices as a central place for administrative work. All these premises are acquired to support the objectives of the organisation. The demand for real estate, however, changes over time in response to external factors.

In addition to providing places to live and work, real estate contributes towards infrastructure, provides community benefits, and delivers a sense of place. In the UK, local authority planning departments are responsible for exercising control over the development of land and buildings for an appropriate use that benefits both the local community and the wider economy. They aim to ensure that the right sort of development occurs in the right place which involves a system of statutes and approved plans working together to optimise the use of the land. This includes not only granting permission for development but also protecting regions such as areas of outstanding natural beauty (AONB). Most countries have a form of planning system but, in less developed countries, these planning systems are not fully effective. This is demonstrated by the slums and favelas where individuals erect their own homes using substandard materials on land where ownership is often unclear and there is insufficient infrastructure to support them.

HOW HAS THE REAL ESTATE MARKET EVOLVED?

To answer this question, we need to establish when the market started and the answer to this is perception-based and requires answering many other questions. When were the first buildings constructed? Were the origins of buildings the caves occupied by Neanderthal Man or were they the mudbrick houses that Neolithic people lived in? This is where the definition of real estate we covered at the beginning of the chapter becomes important.

We can probably agree that Neanderthal Man's caves are '*a natural part of the land*' and that the Neolithic people lived in '*things that have been attached to the land (e.g. buildings)*'. However, was this the start of the real estate market? A market requires the exchange of goods and services, and it may be that possession of these homes was bartered for food or utensils but there was no formal market structure. Perhaps this is where we need to look back at the definition of property as '*a legal concept, encompassing all the interests, rights, and benefits related to property ownership*'. For a market to fully develop, this intangible legal concept of ownership needed to be added to the tangible building.

The basis of current land ownership, and therefore the real estate market, in the UK could be considered to have started after the Norman Conquest in 1066.[7] Although there had previously been a system of land in exchange for duties this became more formal. Following his coronation, William the Conqueror claimed that all land and buildings now belonged to him. He then divided this land between the Church, his appointed barons, and himself. King William's confiscation of all land introduced feudalism and primogeniture. This system provided the beginnings of a real estate market as land ownership was awarded to barons who had fought for the King. Tenants of the owners provided agricultural or military service and villeins (also known as peasants or serfs) worked directly for their landlords. Primogeniture ensured that the land was passed on to the first-born son, which meant that the large estates were preserved over long periods of time.

This underlying ownership of the Crown continues today so that in the absence of any proof of ownership, land will revert to the Crown. By 1760 the estate had been substantially reduced, in both size and value, so an agreement was reached with King George III whereby the estate would be managed in exchange for a fixed annual payment known as the Civil List, with any surplus going to the Government. The Crown Estate Acts of 1956 and 1961 formed the Crown Estate, which continues to operate today and pays the revenue to the Government who then allocates a proportion of the revenue to the Monarch.[8] This payment is now known as the Sovereign Grant.

For the general population the structured system of land ownership made it possible, for those with sufficient assets, to purchase land and buildings. The system also allowed for the raising of finance on real estate assets. Building societies started up in the 1770s making mortgages for individuals, and organisations, more widely available. Financing for real estate continues to evolve as do types of land ownership and this will be covered in more detail in Chapter 14.

Different types of property have also gone through dramatic changes to meet society's needs. Houses, for example, used to be where people both lived and worked. The start of the global Covid-19 pandemic in 2020 has led to a return to home working, for those that were office based, which has in turn impacted on the office market.

Although a form of office, in terms of an area where official business takes place, has been around probably since Roman times, it was not until the 18th century that office buildings started being constructed specifically to deal with the extensive paperwork generated as a result of increasing levels of trade.

The advent of electric light, the invention of the telephone, and the development of more sophisticated construction techniques in the 19th century led to the development of multi-storey office buildings. In the 20th century, offices then moved from individual rooms, through open plan, cubicles and then to a combination of configurations.

The rapid development of technology facilitated work away from the office which then needed to offer other facilities such as restaurants, coffee shops, gyms, and informal meeting spaces to encourage social interaction. Companies have embraced hot desking whereby they can occupy smaller spaces with employees working partly from the office and partly from home or other places.

Technological and sociocultural development has also led to the creation of new types of real estate such as data centres, solar energy farms, and wind farms. It has also led to the development of new types of real estate ownership such as Real Estate Investment Trusts (REITs) and tokenisation (see Chapter 4).

The start of the global Covid-19 pandemic in 2020 accelerated the pace of change as most business had to shut their offices completely, during the government-imposed lockdown, and embrace home working. At the time of writing, it appears that office requirements are reducing and that the demand for housing, away from city centres, with dedicated home office space is increasing. With less of a need to commute to an office, this will, in turn, impact on the demand for housing in city centres. Combined with the continued rise in Internet shopping and the number of retail failures reducing the demand for retail units, it will be interesting to see how the cities of the future evolve.

WHAT IS THE ECONOMIC THEORY BEHIND THE MARKET?

The real estate market is created by an exchange, in this case of land, buildings, interests, rights or benefits – for money. Like all markets, price is derived from the balance between demand and supply. Basic economic theory dictates that where the level of demand is equal to the supply of real estate, an equilibrium price is achieved. However, the real estate market is an imperfect market.

Farmers' markets are often cited as examples of a perfect market. A busy farmers' market displays four characteristics of a perfect market:

- There are many sellers and buyers;
- The products are virtually identical;
- Both buyers and sellers can see the products and the asking prices;
- Sellers can enter and leave the market as they wish.

Contrast these characteristics with those of the real estate market where:

- There are few buyers and sellers and they can be difficult to identify;
- All real estate interests are unique;
- Many interests are not openly sold, information is not freely shared, and information can be interpreted differently;
- It can be difficult to sell some assets, and can take a long time, particularly in a falling market;
- It can be challenging to find the specific premises required meaning that compromises or alterations may be needed;
- Transaction costs are high.

In addition, real estate can be owned as an asset for investment purposes or as resource for occupational use linked to the operation of the business (see Chapters 4 and 5). It can be purchased outright, or it can be leased. There is no central marketplace although the proliferation of websites such as Rightmove and Zoopla has improved the free flow of information. A further difficulty with the real estate market is the long lead-in times. An office block, for example, cannot be constructed quickly. The time taken for purchasing, clearing a site (if necessary), designing a scheme, obtaining planning permission, and constructing a new building is considerable and during this time levels of demand, and specification requirements, might have changed significantly. The real estate market is susceptible to the stage in the economic cycle, to market confidence, and to other environmental factors including interest rates and government intervention, in the form of both taxation and planning constraints.

WHAT FACTORS IMPACT THE REAL ESTATE MARKET?

A basic PESTEL analysis of the real estate market can be used to highlight some of the key elements that will have impact on it. PESTEL is a framework that focuses on the Political, Economic, Sociocultural, Technological, Environmental, and Legal factors that have impact on the operation of an industry or organisation. This analysis is not exhaustive as the PESTEL framework, by its very nature, can be subjective, but it does pinpoint some of the major factors to be aware of.

POLITICAL

Government policy can have a major impact on the functioning of the real estate market. This can include the political situation in a particular country. For example, the transfer of sovereignty over Hong Kong from the UK to China in 1997 led to an influx of Hong Kong investors wanting to purchase real estate in more stable political climates such as the UK and the US. Similarly, the land reforms in Zimbabwe during President Mugabe's administration resulted in instability and unpredictability in the real estate market leading to investment in other countries.

Government policy can also lead to temporary changes in the market and impacts on both the residential and commercial markets. In the UK, this has included actions, in the residential market, such as the Stamp Duty Land Tax (SDLT) holiday introduced from July 2020 whereby properties purchased for up to £500,000 were exempt from SDLT with the intention of stimulating the housing market during the global Covid-19 pandemic. This appeared to have the desired effect with house price sales rising by 14.5% the month it was introduced and 15.6% the following month.[9] Construction output was also reported to have been boosted by 30% but this must be considered in the context of all construction having stopped during the first lockdown. The chancellor extended the SDLT holiday until 30 June 2021 followed by a tapered rate of support until 30 September 2021. This policy has resurrected the debate about whether SDLT should be abolished altogether.

The government also intervened in the English residential market under the hastily prepared Coronavirus Act 2020 to protect tenants from eviction by extending the notice period required by landlords to at least six months which is likely to have impacted on investor demand for buy-to-let properties in the short term. Commercial tenants were protected from eviction for an initial period that was then extended until 25 March 2022. This has impacted on the profitability and value of commercial property investment companies who are now expected to work with tenants to come to an agreement on how to deal with the arrears that have built up.

Government intervention in the market has also been used to correct other specific issues. For example, in the UK, the Grenfell Tower disaster in 2017 occurred when a 24-storey residential tower in North Kensington caught fire in the middle of the night. The fire, which was caused by a faulty fridge freezer, started in a flat on the fourth floor and rapidly spread to the rest of the building causing 72 deaths and many injuries. The first report into the enquiry highlighted a problem with the exterior cladding that did not comply with regulations.

Since this disaster there has been an increased focus on fire safety in buildings over 18 m high, that is beyond the reach of fire service equipment. Inspections have been carried out and many buildings do not comply. This has resulted in additional service charge costs to cover 24-hour fire wardens whilst arrangements for the replacement of defective cladding are made. Many residents are unable to sell their flats until these works are complete and they are unable to afford the very high costs. The RICS agreed an industry-wide valuation process to help with the sale of these properties which includes an EWS1 (External Wall System) form to be completed recording the status of the building. Although not a statutory requirement most mortgage companies will not lend without one in place. The government has therefore intervened and in March 2020 launched a £1.6 billion fund[10] to remediate unsafe cladding where the owners are unable to do so. This was subsequently increased in February 2021 by a further £3.5 billion bringing it to a total of £5.1 billion. This is intended to assist those leaseholders trapped in unsellable flats.

In the commercial real estate market, in both the UK and the US, with similar schemes in other countries, another example of government intervention was the formation of enterprise zones where tax concessions and support are provided to encourage the redevelopment of rundown areas. In these places, real estate is used to act as a catalyst for job creation and productivity. A similar provision was freeports, sited around shipping ports or airports, where concessionary tax arrangements encourage trade, construction, and job creation. There were a few freeports in the UK between 1984 and 2012 but these no longer exist. In 2021 eight further low-tax freeports in England were identified with the same objectives of encouraging trade, private investment, construction, and job creation.

Planning controls are used by governments in the UK and abroad and they are frequently reviewed, and revised, to respond to changes in the market. A recent example is the introduction of a new planning class in England, Class E. This came into effect from 1 September 2020 under the Town and Country Planning (Use Classes) (Amendment) (England) Regulations 2020. These regulations also introduced new classes F1 and F2, which relate to learning institutions and local community use, respectively.

The introduction of Class E was the government's response to the need to repurpose town centres and high streets following the fall in demand for retail buildings caused initially by the increase in

Internet shopping and accelerated by the global Covid-19 pandemic. Class E brings retail (with the exception of small local convenience stores); professional and financial services; restaurants, cafes, public houses, and hot food takeaways; offices, research and development, and light industrial; medical and health services; crèches, day nurseries, and day centres; indoor sports, fitness, and gym uses; all under one new use class. This means that use can be changed from any of the uses within this group, to any other one within the group, without additional planning consent, provided that the lease allows it, and that other aspects such as listed building consent and Building Regulations are complied with.

ECONOMIC

The state of the economy will clearly impact on the real estate industry, but it is an interdependent relationship; the real estate market also has impacts on the economy. For example, the rise in residential sales due to the SDLT holiday mentioned earlier helped to protect nearly 750,000 jobs in the sector.[11] In uncertain economic conditions, there is often a move towards investment in the real estate market due to its tangibility and relative stability.

The global, national, and local economy will all have an impact on real estate occupier decisions and investment performance. Pressures such as the Covid-19 pandemic have led to reductions in GDP worldwide. This has led to an overall reduction in total returns in the real estate market. However, a more detailed analysis is needed. Certain sectors such as restaurants, hotels, and retail have declined but others, such as online retailing, and ICT, have boomed during lockdown with a resultant high demand for warehousing and distribution units and data centres.

The main economic indicators, such as interest rates and employment, will also impact on the real estate sector. A rise in interest rates will mean that the cost of borrowing, for both commercial developers and residential purchasers, will increase, which tends to dampen the market. Similarly, a rising rate of unemployment adversely impacts on consumer confidence, so they are less likely to spend money on goods and services, or move house, reducing the volume of housing transactions, both sales and lettings.

SOCIOCULTURAL AND DEMOGRAPHIC

The shift towards online shopping is just one sociocultural development. Another recent one in developed countries has been the shift towards working from home which was accelerated by the Covid-19 pandemic lockdowns. This has led to reduced demand for traditional office space and residential units in city locations and an increased demand for houses further away from central business districts containing dedicated office space. The difficulty with these changing requirements is the time taken to supply these changing needs.

Demographic changes also have impact on the residential and commercial real estate markets. The aging population, together with increasing life expectancy, is leading to an increased demand for housing to suit the elderly such as sheltered and supported housing where additional assistance is provided to enable the elderly to continue living independently.

In the commercial sector, the relative increases in wealth in developed countries have led to increasing demand for holidays offering hotels and leisure facilities. In the UK, where the manufacturing sector accounts for only approximately 20% of employment[12] the demand for industrial properties has been shrinking.

TECHNOLOGICAL

Apart from the obvious impact in terms of the increased ability to work from home mentioned earlier, technology has also impacted the industry in terms of construction. For example, homes are now being constructed in Mexico using 3D printing technology making it possible to construct a detached home in less than 24 hours for under $4,000.[13]

Artificial intelligence (AI) is being used for sophisticated building management whereby, for example windows are automatically opened in response to the detection of an increase in temperature in a room.

Modular, or pre-fabricated, buildings, where the parts of a building are constructed off-site and assembled onsite, are becoming more common for offices and industrial units as well as residential.

Improvements in engineering knowledge and construction techniques have also facilitated the building of ever taller buildings. For many years, the Burj Al Khalifah was the tallest man-made structure in the world at 828 m, but this will soon be exceeded. The Jeddah tower is intended to be 1,000 metres tall and was due to be completed in 2020 but, at the time of writing, is running behind schedule.

ENVIRONMENTAL

Sustainability has gained increasing importance over the past few decades with the real estate industry now embracing sustainability from initial development plans, through construction, to completion and occupation. The impact of sustainable measures on the value of real estate is, as yet, inconclusive. As time goes by, and sustainability becomes essential, and a legal requirement, rather than just something that is perceived as 'nice to have' it is likely to add value. Sustainability will be discussed in more detail in Chapter 14.

Environmental issues, although focused around similar themes, will vary geographically. For example, concrete is considered an environmentally unfriendly material due to the use of energy, water, and raw materials extracted for its production. The process of creating concrete also emits carbon dioxide which is considered to add to global warming. It is also difficult to recycle and its impermeable nature has been thought to cause flooding. However, it must be considered in the light of the alternatives available and the area in which it is being constructed. For example, the tall towers in the UAE and Saudi Arabia are constructed of concrete and steel. Although concrete is perceived as environmentally unfriendly due to the energy and water used in its production this has to be balanced against the supply of one of the main ingredients of concrete – sand – that is in plentiful supply in these areas.

Environmental guidance is in place in all developed countries with a view to improving the sustainable credentials of the construction and real estate industry. There are a wide variety of 'green badging' systems around the world. BREEAM (Building Research Establishment Environmental Assessment Method) is most commonly used in the UK but the RICS promote their SKA rating which is a method of environmental assessment led, and owned, by the RICS, which aims to assist with improving the sustainability of fit outs of, currently, office and retail premises. Worldwide,

BREEAM and LEED (Leadership in Energy and Environmental Design) are the most widely used building rating systems, but some countries have also developed their own. These rating systems are not legal requirements but are an optional framework against which buildings can be assessed, and certified, in terms of their sustainability, efficiency, and running costs.

LEGAL

There are also legal requirements in relation to environmental issues. An example of these is the Energy Performance Certificate (EPC) introduced in England and Wales in 2007 and now used throughout the UK. EPCs measure the energy efficiency of both commercial and residential buildings on a range from A to G with A being very efficient and G very inefficient. From April 2020 residential properties with a rating below E can no longer be let. This will apply to all commercial tenancies from April 2023. Works must be carried out to improve their ratings to a minimum of E. The EPC provides a guide on the cost of running the building and the level of carbon dioxide emissions. It also highlights potential energy efficiency improvements together with the likely cost savings they will achieve. EPCs are valid for 10 years from the date they are prepared, and it is a legal requirement for one to be produced before marketing, virtually all properties for sale or rent.

There are a range of other legal factors affecting the real estate market, but one that is likely to have a major impact on the English residential leasehold market is the proposal for one of the biggest reforms to English property law in 40 years resulting from investigations and recommendations by the Law Commission. The Housing Secretary announced in January 2021 that leaseholders will be granted the right to extend their leases by a maximum term of 990 years (currently 90 years for flats and 50 years for houses) at zero ground rent (currently high charges can be incurred by residents to extend their leases). The government is also establishing a Commonhold Council with the aim of encouraging the market to increase the take-up of commonhold.

Commonhold was introduced by the Commonhold and Leasehold Reform Act 2002, and was designed to allow residents in multi-occupancy developments to own a share of the freehold, together with a share of the commonhold which owns and manages the common parts of the property. This aimed to give residents greater security and a more valuable asset, as it does not fall in value, like leaseholds do, as the remainder of the lease gets shorter. Commonhold came into effect on 27 September 2004 under the Commonhold Regulations 2004 but take-up has been very limited in England and Wales, although the approach is more prevalent in other countries, such as Australia's strata system and the US condominium system. There are estimated to be 4.5 million leasehold homes in England, 69% flats and 31% houses.[14] Some developers had begun to sell new build leaseholds with ground rents doubling every 10 years representing a secure income stream for the developer but an increasingly expensive, and wasting, asset for the resident. In contrast, there are estimated to be less than 20 commonholds in England and Wales,[15] that is only approximately one commonhold for each year since the legislation was introduced. Primary legislation, that is new statutes covering these areas, is unlikely to be in place before 2023. The Leasehold Reform (Ground Rent) Bill was introduced in the House of Lords on 12 May 2021 and future legislation is currently being developed.[16]

Having considered a selection of the main factors impacting on the real estate market, it is then useful to consider, in the light of these external factors, how it compares with other competing investment opportunities.

HOW DOES REAL ESTATE COMPARE WITH OTHER INVESTMENT OPPORTUNITIES?

A detailed discussion of complex financial instruments is beyond the scope of this book; however, a comparison of real estate with the most common alternative investment opportunities helps to highlight its distinguishing characteristics. The most popular forms of investment are, arguably:

- Cash
- Commodities
- Collectibles
- Cryptocurrencies
- Bonds or fixed income securities

- Stocks and shares
- Investment funds
- Pensions

Each of these investment opportunities has distinctive characteristics making them appeal to different types of investor.

Cash has traditionally been considered a very secure investment producing stable returns. However, in the current low interest environment, there is a cost to holding cash as its returns are lower than the rate of inflation; therefore, in real terms, it loses value. Most investors are likely to hold a certain amount of cash as it can be spent immediately without having to wait to liquidate assets. Over time, all other things being equal, real estate is likely to generate returns that outstrip those achievable from holding cash.

Commodities include natural resources such as gold, oil, or coffee beans. They can provide diversification in an investment portfolio. For personal investors, gold can provide a method of investment that is easily liquidated and can be passed on without tax liabilities. In many cultures, gold is gifted at weddings partly as a way of displaying wealth but also as a way of keeping wealth close and providing a quick source of funds if needed. The limited supply of gold means that it will always have some value. Similarly, real estate will nearly always have some value. Even if the property on the land is derelict the land will always have some value. There can however be occasions where a property could have a negative value. This might occur where, for example, extensive repairs are required but, in this instance, the property owner would probably consider substantial refurbishment or redevelopment to improve its value.

Collectibles are investments in items that are likely to increase in value over time. They include items such as antiques, fine wine, coins, art, and even some children's toys. The value of collectibles will depend on the rarity of the item, market demand, and the condition they are in. Some collectibles, such as antique furniture or art, not only provide a store of value, and potentially a financial gain, but can also be enjoyed. Valuations are very dependent on levels of demand and supply and being forced to sell in a hurry can erode returns. Compared to real estate investment, collectibles can be more challenging to value as they are not governed by the same level of valuation guidelines and professional standards.

Cryptocurrencies are virtual currencies that use digital files as money. They are unregulated, trading outside government or other financial system controls, making them very volatile. The first cryptocurrency was bitcoin which was released to the public in 2009[17] based on blockchain technology. Since this time, many competitors have entered the market and, although the overall trend in prices is upward, there have been dramatic swings in values. This means that if investors need funds quickly, they can suffer large losses, or potentially lose all their investment. Although certain classes of real estate can also undergo dramatic falls, or increases in value, these tend to occur over weeks, months, or even years, rather than in minutes as with cryptocurrencies.

Bonds or fixed income securities are issued by governments or corporations and are basically loans at a fixed rate of interest for a fixed term. The rate of interest reflects the risk of the borrower not repaying the loan at expiry. Bonds provide an income return via the fixed rate of interest and may also generate a capital return if sold at a higher price than that paid. Bonds are perceived as more secure than stocks and shares; therefore, the returns tend to be lower. Although the returns are lower than might be achieved when investing in real estate, they tend to provide a steady stream of income providing some stability as part of a diversified portfolio. There is, however, a risk that the relatively low returns may be eroded, or extinguished, by inflation and bonds, like real estate, can be difficult to sell quickly.

Stocks and shares are small parts of a company being purchased by an investor. Investing in a company, by purchasing shares, means that the owner will benefit from profits made by the company that are paid as dividends. If a company is successful in the long term, then share prices will increase and the investor can realise a profit by selling the shares. However, a poorly performing company may stop paying dividends and may ultimately fail, going into liquidation, which will mean the investor will end up with nothing. A major advantage of investing in stocks and shares, over real estate, is that they can be bought and sold within minutes, but the market can be quite volatile in the way it reacts to external events. For example, the US Dow Jones Industrial average fell by 23% and the FTSE100 fell by 25%[18] in response to the first coronavirus lockdown.

Investment funds provide a way of avoiding some of the risk of investing in stocks and shares, particularly for smaller investors. Investment funds invest in shares based on the expert knowledge of those that run the funds. They then sell units in these funds to investors. This enables investors to spread their risk across a wider range of companies. Most funds will have a theme in terms of geographical focus, or size, or type, of company. For example, there are some property funds which enable investors to participate in the real estate market spreading their risk across a range of different assets. However, during the global Covid-19 pandemic in 2020/21 many of these funds suspended dealing, as they were unable to raise money quickly enough due to a combination of valuation uncertainty and the time it takes to sell property. This left investors unable to access their money for periods of over a year; some funds have now closed completely.

Pensions, although not perhaps an investment choice in the sense of the other options outlined in this section, the amount of money invested in them, beyond the legal minimum, is discretionary investment. In developed countries, pensions have evolved, over the past century, in response to pressures such as the aging population and increased life expectancy. Historically pension companies invested money provided by employers and employees into fairly low risk assets such as bonds and large, well-established, financially sound stocks known as 'blue chip'. Today however, pension funds are chasing higher returns and are investing more widely in a range of shares and in real estate, either directly or via REITs. It is also no longer a legal requirement, in many developed countries, to buy an annuity with your pension to provide a regular income in retirement; it is now possible to access portions of the pensions at different times. For the real estate market, the impact of changes in pension regulation is that a greater proportion of pension money is invested in it. At the end of 2018 an average of 2.7% of global pension fund assets were invested in land and buildings ranging from 0 in multiple countries up to 11.9% in Finland.[19]

This review of the most popular forms of investment demonstrates that even though they are considered as alternative options to direct real estate investments, many of them include real estate to add diversity to their portfolios.

WHAT ARE REAL ESTATE'S KEY CHARACTERISTICS AS AN INVESTMENT?

Despite the imperfections of the real estate market, outlined in the section on economic theory, it remains a popular investment choice. Comparing real estate as an investment with the other popular investment options outlined earlier, it offers:

- Some protection from (commonly described as a hedge against) inflation as, when there is inflation, and the economy is expanding, rents also tend to rise keeping pace with inflation;
- Reduced volatility due to imperfections of the market;
- The ability to control the amount and timing of costs, to an extent;
- The opportunity to offset costs against income to reduce tax liabilities;
- The prospect of adding value by carrying out improvements;
- An asset against which finance can be raised;
- Diversification of an investment portfolio to reduce risk;
- A tangible asset that is nearly always likely to have some value;
- An increase in value, in the long term, as the supply of land is finite.

This generic list relates to real estate as a class of investment, but there is a huge diversity of land, buildings, and property rights that come under the overarching term 'Real Estate'. The diversity of real estate will be considered in Chapter 3.

WHAT ARE THE MAIN REASONS FOR OWNING REAL ESTATE?

As outlined earlier, one of the main reasons for owning real estate is for a financial return which can be either the income it produces and/or a capital gain. Real estate investment will be discussed in more detail in Chapter 4. There is also another reason for owning real estate: it is a resource for most businesses forming an essential part of its operation. This will be discussed in Chapter 5.

WHO OWNS REAL ESTATE?

The primary reasons for possessing real estate will vary depending on the key objectives of the owner. Real estate can be owned by a variety of different entities, including individuals, private sector companies, public sector organisations, not-for-profit organisations, landed estates, and trusts. Decisions on what type of ownership is required will need to be made, for example freehold, leasehold, or, in the residential sector, commonhold or shared ownership; they may even require a combination of different ownerships. The decision on what type of ownership is required will depend on the *purpose* of the ownership. In most cases this will be for investment, development, occupation, or a combination of these reasons.

NOTES

1 RICS (2019) *RICS Valuation: Global Standards* Online. Available from: www.rics.org/uk/upholding-professional-standards/sector-standards/valuation/red-book/red-book-global/

2 IVS (2020) Available (to members, sponsor organisations and subscribers) from: www.ivsc.org/standards/international-valuation-standards/IVS

3 RICS (2020) 'Peter Pereira Grey to Lead Independent Valuation Review' Online. Available from: www.rics.org/uk/news-insight/latest-news/press/press-releases/peter-pereira-gray-to-lead-independent-valuation-review/

4 RICS (2020) 'Peter Pereira Grey to Lead Independent Valuation Review' Online. Available from: www.rics.org/uk/news-insight/latest-news/press/press-releases/peter-pereira-gray-to-lead-independent-valuation-review/

5 OECD (2020) *Tax on Property (Indicator)* https://doi.org/10.1787/213673fa-en

6 Office for National Statistics (ONS) (2020) Online. Available from: www.ons.gov.uk/employmentandlabourmarket/peopleinwork/employmentand employeetypes/datasets/broadindustrygroupsicbusinessregisterandemployment surveybrestable1

7 Scarrett, D and Wilcox, J (2018) *Property Asset Management* 4th Edition Abingdon, Oxon: Routledge

8 The Crown Estate (no date) *Our History* Online. Available from: www.thecrownestate.co.uk/en-gb/our-business/our-history/

9 HM Treasury (2020) 'House Sales Rise Following Introduction of Stamp Duty Holiday Supporting Nearly 750000 Jobs' Online. Available from:

www.gov.uk/government/news/house-sales-rise-following-introduction-of-stamp-duty-holiday-supporting-nearly-750000-jobs

10 Ministry of Housing, Communities and Local Government (2020) 'Building Safety Fund for the Remediation of Non-ACM Cladding Systems (England Only)' Online. Available from: https://assets.publishing.service.gov.uk/government/uploads/system/uploads/attachment_data/file/945257/BSF_Non-ACM_Cladding_Prospectus.pdf

11 See note 9

12 See note 6

13 Newstory (undated) *Introducing the World's First Community of 3D Printed Homes* Online. Available from: https://newstorycharity.org/3d-community/

14 Wilson, W and Barton, C (2021) 'Leasehold and Commonhold Reform' Briefing Paper Number 8047, 7 February Online. Available from: https://researchbriefings.files.parliament.uk/documents/CBP-8047/CBP-8047.pdf

15 The Law Commission (2020) 'Reinvigorating Commonhold: The Alternative to Leasehold Ownership: Summary' 21 July Law Com No 394 (Summary) Online. Available from: https://s3-eu-west-2.amazonaws.com/lawcom-prod-storage-11jsxou24uy7q/uploads/2020/07/Commonhold-Summary-final-N16.pdf

16 House of Commons Library, Constituency Casework (2021) Leasehold Reform in England and Wales: What's Happening and When? Tuesday 18 May Online. Available from: https://commonslibrary.parliament.uk/leasehold-reform-in-england-and-wales/

17 Chuen, D L K, Guo, L and Wang, Y (2018) 'Cryptocurrency: A New Investment Opportunity?' *The Journal of Alternative Investments* Winter 20 (3), 16–40 Online. https://doi.org/10.3905/jai.2018.20.3.016

18 BBC News (2020) 'Coronavirus: Stock Markets Suffer Worst Quarter since 1987' Online. Available from: www.bbc.co.uk/news/business-52113841

19 Oakley, M (2020) 'Real Estate Solutions for Pension Funds Impacts' *Savills* May Online. Available from: www.savills.com/impacts/social-change/real-estate-solutions-for-pension-funds

FURTHER INFORMATION

BREEAM www.breeam.com

EPC Energy Performance Certificates Guidance Available from: www.gov.uk/government/collections/energy-performance-certificates

Jowsey, E Ed. (2015) *Real Estate Concepts: A Handbook* Abingdon, Oxon: Routledge

LEED www.leed.usbgc.org

THE DIVERSITY OF REAL ESTATE

WHY ARE WE LOOKING AT THE DIVERSITY OF REAL ESTATE?

Diversity is about variety and, in the context of real estate, it is about the earth, its surface, and how the surface is used to meet society's needs. When thinking about diversity, it is helpful to recognise the range of lifestyles, cultures, legal, political, and economic systems that exist across the globe and the similarities and differences that exist between them. When we then consider the diversity of real estate, we also need to think about the airspace above the earth's surface and the ground beneath it. This links with Chapter 7 in which we consider what constitutes 'land'.

Understanding the diversity of real estate will help students and practitioners to appreciate the size and importance of the real estate sector, and the choices and opportunities that it presents. It also helps us to understand how diverse uses can be interlinked; sustainability, for example, is a global issue, relevant to all land uses and we discuss this further in Chapter 14. Real estate professionals need to develop the knowledge and skills required to practise with a diverse range of properties. For example, building surveyors need to understand different methods of construction and the defects associated with them. Valuers need to identify the building defects and property characteristics that may impact upon value. Property managers need to be aware of the maintenance needs of the type of real estate they are responsible for.

The diversity of real estate is reflected in the pathways (training routes) to chartered status offered by the RICS. There are currently

DOI: 10.1201/9781003155256-3

22 sector pathways covering the rural, residential, and commercial sectors, mineral management (mining and quarrying), and land and resources, amongst others. It is important for real estate professionals to specialise to ensure they have detailed knowledge, but this can be challenging at times. For example, management of mixed commercial and residential sites requires an understanding of both use-types.

Student assignments will typically be scenario-based, addressing the requirements of a specified property. You may be asked to write a marketing report for a commercial property to let or the task may require you to advise on the best method of sale for a dilapidated house, for example. APC candidates also need to demonstrate knowledge and experience of a variety of properties. It helps, therefore, to be aware of the diversity of real estate to develop a thorough understanding of the sector.

HOW MIGHT REAL ESTATE BE DIVERSE?

As we explain in Chapter 2, real estate is tangible; we can touch it and see it. We may even be able to hear it or smell it. It is a real, solid physical asset, whether that is a piece of land, a 'bricks and mortar' building, a phone mast, or a wind turbine. As a tangible asset, real estate may be substantial – a skyscraper, for example – or it may be flimsy and insubstantial in the case of a slum dwelling. It may be centuries old, or it may be temporary and portable. Real estate may be diverse, therefore, in terms of construction and design and in its maintenance and management requirements and the lifestyle, security and protection it offers its occupants.

Diversity can also apply to the scale of real estate assets in terms of both size and value. Think of the range of property you might encounter; a home might be a studio flat (flats are also sometimes called apartments) or a room in a shared house, or it may be a multi-million-pound mansion. The smallest asset we have dealt with professionally was an advertising hoarding worth £200 per annum ('per annum' means per year) and the largest transaction was the sale of a £70 million shopping centre.

Real estate is also diverse on a global, national, regional, and local scale. Diversity can not only arise between different types of real estate asset – agricultural, commercial, and residential for example – but it can also occur within asset classes. Therefore, an investor may acquire, say, a mix of residential and commercial assets, or they may focus on one asset class but acquire different types of assets within that class – for example, student lets and professional lets if investing in residential property. This reflects the value of diversification as a means of risk management as explained in Chapter 4.

Sometimes a single asset may have diverse uses, as we will see later in this chapter when we look at mixed-use developments. Diverse uses may apply to different parts of the building, such as a ground floor shop with offices or flats on the upper floors. Diversity may relate to the time of the day, week, or year. For example, a school will educate its pupils during the school day and during term-time, but it may hire its facilities for other community purposes during the evenings, weekends, or school holidays.

Land use may evolve in response to other changes, such as the construction of railways or the creation of employment such as coal mines or the exploitation of other natural resources. As we identify in Chapter 2, land use may be highly controlled in countries with clear, enforced planning policies. However, it can also be uncontrolled, evidenced by, for example the sprawl of vast slums and favelas, which contrast with the neatness of purpose-built towns and villages. In England, the creation of planned new towns, such as Telford, Milton Keynes, and Welwyn Garden City, are examples of how political strategy and planning policies can change land use and create new places. Port Sunlight, in the northwest of England, is an earlier example of a planned settlement. This village was purpose-built to house the employees of the Lever Brothers' soap factory and adopted diverse architectural styles to create an interesting environment. This contrasts with the 'cookie-cutter' approach sometimes taken to housing developments, characterised by a lack of diversity between homes.

A further interesting example – socially, environmentally, and politically – is the town of Pripyat in Ukraine (formerly part of the Soviet Union). Pripyat evidences large-scale land-use planning, built to house workers at the nearby Chernobyl nuclear power plant. It was abandoned and is now a contaminated environment following the nuclear disaster in 1986. From a town with a population of around 50,000 people[1] Pripyat is now overgrown and abandoned, but nature is reclaiming it and it is also now a, perhaps unlikely but extremely thought-provoking, tourist-destination demonstrating how the purposes to which we put real estate can adapt and evolve.

We mention earlier that real estate may be diverse in its design and construction. Buildings may be constructed on-site or prefabricated and transported to site in sections. They may be created by hand with minimal use of tools or by using modern machinery. They may encompass a range of materials, whether local or transported great distance: concrete, glass, marble, brick, stone, slate, steel frame with cladding, timber frame with wattle and daub, and adobe, are just a few examples.

WHY MIGHT REAL ESTATE NEED TO BE DIVERSE?

Real estate is diverse because it must meet a whole range of needs over a long period of time. Real estate also needs to adapt to reflect change. In the UK, many former industrial sites, such as factories, mills, and engineering or manufacturing sites, have new uses, perhaps residential, or mixed commercial and residential use, and new sectors and land uses may emerge – data centres and distribution warehouses, for example. We have years of experience managing converted commercial properties and have seen how the creative and imaginative conversion of disused and derelict buildings can revitalise not just the building, but also the surrounding areas, whilst still reflecting and celebrating their heritage. We have managed, amongst others, former workhouses, dairies, abattoirs, clothing factories, pubs, woollen mills, and engineering works. You may find it interesting to visit or research this type of site, as this will help you to understand the diversity of real estate. In Cheltenham, the former Kraft Foods UK head office is now luxury retirement living, using a combination of converted period buildings and new build. The Battersea Power Station redevelopment in London, Gloucester Quays, and Albert Docks in Liverpool are further examples of the need for real estate to adapt and diversify, but you may be aware of others within your local area, and you may already encounter these in practice.

Diversification can be controversial in that it may introduce new occupiers and users to an established area, changing the character of a community and putting pressure on local services. The 'studentification'[2] of areas within university towns and cities can cause tension with other residents. The use of residential properties as holiday homes and short-term lets can cause resentment amongst permanent residents due to pressure on house prices and the transient nature of the occupation. The alternative view is that this type of diversification can bring new visitors to an area and boost the economy if there are otherwise limited investment, employment, and business opportunities.

In some instances, real estate development may be asset-led. This means that the owner will find a market or a new market for a real estate asset, which they may already own. For example, farm diversification may involve utilising farm buildings for non-agricultural use. This contrasts with a market-led business, which identifies a gap in the market and builds or develops real estate to satisfy that demand. Hence a new hotel may be built next to an airport to satisfy that market, whereas a farm might diversify its business by converting existing farm buildings to holiday lets, business units, storage facilities, or long-term lets, to take a few examples from our local area.

PLANNING CONTROL AND DIVERSITY

We have mentioned that in some societies, land use is tightly controlled. In England, local plans are created by local authorities to set out planning policies in their area. These help to control development and are important when considering applications for planning permission.[3]

Land use is categorised into 'Use Classes' – the authorised purposes for which real estate may be used by its occupier. Changes to the authorised use may require permission from the local planning authority. The Town and Country Planning (Use Classes) Order 1987 (as amended) helps to demonstrate the legal framework around land use and reflects the diversity of real estate. Under this order, land use was (until recently) divided into the following Use Classes:

- A1 Shops;
- A2 Financial and professional services;
- A3 to A5 Food and drink;

- B1 Business (including offices and some light industrial processes);
- B2 General industrial;
- B8 Storage and distribution;
- C1 Hotels and guest houses;
- C2 Residential institutions, for example a nursing home, residential school or prison;
- C3 Dwelling houses (single households);
- C4 Houses in multiple occupation (with 3-6 unrelated occupiers);
- D1 Non-residential institutions, for example schools, museums, day nurseries, and health centres;
- D2 Assembly and leisure, for example a gym, swimming pool, or cinema.

In addition, some uses are known as 'sui generis', which means that they are in a group of their own and fall outside the listed Use Classes. These include large, shared houses (houses in multiple occupation with more than six residents), for example.

This list indicates the broad categories of use, but each category contains detailed provisions. It is not the purpose of this chapter to go into these further, as we are using them to illustrate the diversity of real estate and to provide an example of how land use may be subject to a strict legal framework. However, you can find out more by looking at the legislation listed at the end of the chapter and by looking at the online Planning Portal.

Use Classes were amended further by the Town and Country Planning (Use Classes) (Amendment) (England) Regulations 2020. These regulations introduced two new Use Classes: E (business, commercial, and service) and F (local community and learning). They also revoked three Use Classes, re-categorising some types of use with effect from 1 September 2020:

- Use Classes A and B1 were revoked;
- Use Classes A1, A2, A3, and B1 were changed to Class E (some shops selling essential goods now fall within Class F);
- Classes A4 and A5 become sui generis;
- Classes B2, B8, and C remained unchanged;

- Class D was revoked;
- Class D uses now fall within the new Classes E and F or are now sui generis.[4]

Planning is a complex and specialist area, and it is not the purpose of this chapter to consider it in further detail. However, it is useful to be aware that, again, the current classes include broad categories of use. This makes it easier to change the use of a building or for a building to be used for a variety of purposes, without needing to obtain planning permission. The intention behind this is to allow flexibility of use for town centres and struggling high streets, to help them to adapt to the changing environment.

Listed buildings are a further example of the diversity of real estate, recognising the historical or architectural significance of some buildings. Listing is categorised into Grade I for the most exceptional buildings, followed by Grade II*, through to Grade II (the most common). There are many examples of listed buildings including, in London, Buckingham Palace (Grade I), and Regent Street, where the facades are at least Grade II. Listing a building protects it and restricts the alterations that can be made to it.

The National Planning Policy Framework (NPPF) is the government's planning policy for England. The policy refers to effective land use and the conservation and enhancement of the natural and historic environment.[5] Awareness of this document is another useful way to develop understanding of the diversity of real estate, as it reflects the need to balance the variety of land uses that exist. We recommend that you keep up to date with changes to planning policy as this will also help you to appreciate how the built and natural environment evolves and diversifies.

Remember also that land law and landlord and tenant law are relevant to land use. It may be necessary to obtain both planning permission and mortgagee consent to a change of use of freehold and leasehold properties, but landlord consent may also be required for change of use of a leasehold property. Freehold properties may be subject to covenants (though generally less than a leasehold property) so use may be restricted and the agreement of the covenantee may be needed if change of use is being contemplated. As leasehold property is likely to have more restrictions on its use than freehold land, always check the lease for the authorised use when thinking about diversification in relation to property investment or management. For example, the use of long residential leasehold properties (typically flats) as holiday lets is likely to be in breach of the user clause in the lease. The authorised use of commercial premises may be expressed in relation to Use Class; although these changed recently, the old Use Classes are still relevant if they define the authorised use in a lease.

In the remainder of this chapter, we will outline land use in the UK and overseas. Our list is not exhaustive, so you may be able to think of other uses. However, our outline should help to develop your awareness of the diversity of the global real estate sector and the different ways in which diversity can manifest itself.

COMMERCIAL USE

Commercial real estate is a broad term, which represents a diverse range of asset type. It comprises our workplaces, and the premises from which business owners operate. Commercial land use has evolved over centuries, sometimes becoming closely associated with a locality. The modern business parks, high streets, and industrial estates with which we are familiar are preceded by centuries of diverse business and trade use. In Britain, the Romans had over 400 known potteries, with kilns, stores, and work sheds, some of which were located alongside other activities, such as iron smelting.[6] In Cornwall, tin and copper mines grew up, supporting populations and leading to the development of smelting facilities, so also supporting the coal-mining industry. As trade routes developed around the globe, commodities such as silk, salt, spices, gems, tin, and amber were traded by sea, overland, or by river and canal. Towns and cities grew alongside these industries, providing commercial facilities, such as ports and warehousing, as well as accommodation. In the UK in the 18th and 19th centuries, the Industrial Revolution saw significant changes in population spread and land use, with the growth of industry leading to the development of new industrial areas and the expansion of towns and cities as populations moved from rural areas to the towns and cities for work. In areas of the developing world, migration from rural to urban areas is still happening now. More recently, we have seen a technological revolution and corresponding changes to land use; Silicon Valley in California and Bangalore in India are examples of the recent emergence of a new, modern land use.

The construction of commercial buildings is diverse, reflecting this history. In our local areas, there are commercial buildings of traditional brick or stone construction and modern steel framed buildings, but you may be able to identify other types of construction in your locality. In some instances, commercial premises have been created from former homes; we have worked in Regency townhouses and villas converted into offices, for example.

We will cover some key commercial real estate types later; other business uses come under their own heading within this chapter.

DATA CENTRES

A data centre is a building used to house computing systems and data storage facilities. In view of the growing importance of technology and the extensive use of remote data storage it is no surprise that data centres are a relatively recent use of real estate. The nature of the building will need to reflect the sensitivity of its use; for example a high degree of security will be needed, together with a reliable power supply and suitable temperature and humidity control. A data centre must also be secure against environmental events such as earthquakes and flooding to reduce the risk of potentially serious disruption to service and of the potentially disastrous loss of data that could affect every aspect of modern society.

INDUSTRIAL USE

The word 'industry' can be a broad one, used to refer to an economic activity or sector – for example the 'insurance industry' and the 'tourism industry' are commonly used terms. However, for our purposes, we are referring to industry, and to industrial real estate, as the production or processing of raw materials and goods. We are therefore thinking of factories and manufacturing workshops, and other industrial uses, such as chemical treatment plants and oil refineries.

Industrial land use falls within Use Classes B2 (General Industrial) and E or may be sui generis. The location of industrial real estate is relevant to its Use Class; industrial processes that can be carried out in a residential area without detriment to the area come within Use Class E, whereas other uses not suitable for a residential location will be Class B or sui generis (i.e. in a class of their own). In view of this, some industries will be based in industrial zones away from residential areas whereas others will coexist with other uses and contribute to the diversity of real estate within a locality.

Other ancillary uses may be associated with industrial real estate. For example, a factory will need offices, and it may also need research facilities, storage, meeting, and training rooms. There may be other uses in the area to support the industrial use, such as transport hubs and cafes.

OFFICES

Offices come within Use Class E and are, again, the premises from which businesses operate, and at which we might work. They are typically used for administrative work. An office will not only be a real, physical building but it may also be virtual, offering an address at which a business is based even if it does not actually occupy those premises. Therefore, real estate may diversify to satisfy the needs of both occupiers and non-occupiers. For example, limited companies must have a registered office, but it is not unusual for this to be the address of a registered office provider, or accountant, rather than the actual physical offices of the company.

The nature of office use has diversified in recent years with the growth of more flexible working practices combined with improved technology and a more technologically capable workforce. Business centres offering virtual offices and hot desks, registered offices for companies (as we mention earlier), parking, and facilities such as rest areas, cafes, and meeting rooms for hire, have become more apparent in recent years, in a range of locations from town centres to out-of-town business parks. We have experience, however, of town–centre business centres offering office space, secretarial services, and meeting rooms for hire being converted back to their original residential use. New business centres in the area seem to be based in modern developments on the edge of town, on business parks close to good motorway communications and with ample parking; sometimes an issue with town centre working. Pre-pandemic, homeworking was already becoming more popular; hence demand for properties with home offices has increased in recent years. Following the global Covid-19 pandemic, it is likely that the office sector may see longer term change.

Offices may vary considerably in scale; they may comprise a small office above a high street shop, or they may be considerably larger, an example of the latter being the Google offices on the Kings Cross redevelopment, at 650,000 sq. ft.[7] (60,386 sq. m.).

STORAGE AND DISTRIBUTION CENTRES

Storage and distribution centres come within Use Class B8 and remain unchanged following the 2020 reclassification of land use. This is a growing sector, as more and more people shop online, requiring warehousing to store goods in readiness for prompt delivery and the distribution facilities close to transport links to enable that delivery. The logistics of this sector can be highly complex and may operate on a huge scale, reflected in the size of the some of the facilities required by national and international operators. Storage and distribution facilities are not just required for online businesses; they may also be essential for other sectors. Supermarkets, for example, need sophisticated delivery systems and large-scale distribution facilities to manage the supply of goods to their physical stores.

EDUCATIONAL INSTITUTIONS

Use Class F covers non-residential educational and training facilities, such as schools and colleges. Residential accommodation (boarding facilities) provided by schools falls within Use Class C. We have mentioned that real estate may have diverse uses, so accommodation may be available to students during term time but available for short-term rent by tourists or business travellers during holiday periods. Cambridge University ensures that students vacate their rooms during holidays for this reason enabling them to maximise income from their accommodation. Similarly, school facilities may be available to hire outside school hours – gyms and classrooms for evening classes, for example. Educational institutions may be publicly or privately owned.

HOSPITALITY AND LEISURE

The hospitality and leisure sectors provide a variety of services, reflected in diverse real estate needs.

Hotels, hostels, and guest houses provide accommodation other than for the purposes of a home and come within Use Class C. These facilities give us somewhere to stay, when travelling for business or leisure purposes. We may choose to use a hotel, a bed and breakfast, a guest house, motel, hostel (e.g. backpackers' hostels and youth hostels), or holiday accommodation. The real estate requirements of these services vary considerably as regards location, size, design, construction, and facilities. Location will reflect the market; airport hotels obviously need to be close to airports, business travellers need hotels close to good communications and business districts, whereas accommodation catering for tourists and leisure visitors needs to be close to attractions.

The leisure sector provides for our leisure activities, and it encompasses the diverse range of real estate in which we may spend our spare time. Again, some will be on a very large scale – theme parks, for example. Others may be much smaller; cinemas, bingo halls, casinos, nightclubs, and amusement arcades are just a few examples, all of which are sui generis.

Outdoor sports facilities and indoor or outdoor swimming pools are examples of the use of real estate for leisure purposes. These come within Use Class F, whereas indoor facilities such as gyms and other indoor recreational facilities are Class E. Some of these facilities may also fall within the public buildings section later.

Food and beverage outlets are another use of real estate; cafes and restaurants (Use Class E) and bars, pubs, and takeaways (sui generis). Some of these businesses were badly affected by the Covid-19 pandemic, but in general this has been a strong sector in recent years. You may have noticed the growing number of coffee shops in many towns. Food and beverage outlets have filled many buildings previously used for other purposes. In our local area, the former newspaper office became a wine bar, and the former court building became a bar and restaurant. As more people are banking online, many banks have closed and been converted to restaurants.

Relationships exist within the sector, for example hotels will usually have restaurants, pubs may also provide accommodation, leisure facilities will often cluster together; hence, we see cinemas and other leisure facilities located alongside restaurants, bars and hotels providing the range of facilities required by leisure users. Planning is also used to encourage this clustering, but the introduction of Class E use led to concerns about conflicting uses in certain areas. The 'permitted development' right to change from one use to another was therefore restricted by size of premises and length of use to try to avoid conflict.

Short-term holiday lets can be controversial, so we are now seeing steps taken to control this form of diversification. In London, for example, the Deregulation Act 2015 limits this type of use to a maximum of 90 days per year; planning permission may be required to let a property if the use exceeds this limit. Other cities, including Paris, Berlin, and Barcelona, have also introduced restrictions.

MIXED USE

Mixed use developments involve a combination of Use Classes on one site or in one locality. Typically, this will involve a mix of residential, leisure, and commercial use. For example, the regeneration of King's Cross in London encompasses 67 acres of former industrial land, redeveloped as a mix of 2,000 homes, 26 acres of public open space, educational facilities, shops, restaurants, leisure facilities, and offices.[8] Mixed-use real estate therefore centres upon a diverse range of uses to 'place-make', to create a community with all the facilities one associates with that.

The scale of some individual buildings allows a diverse mix of occupiers and uses. The Shard skyscraper in London, for example, describes itself as a vertical city containing offices, restaurants and bars, a hotel, and residential apartments.[9] A smaller scale example of mixed use is our local farm shop. This makes creative use of its real estate assets by providing a retail shop, play area, café, farmyard animal attractions, and pick your own fruit and eggs.

The diversity of real estate can also be seen within – as well as between – categories of use. A trading estate may be occupied by a variety of commercial, manufacturing, and service tenants, for example. A quick review of one of our local estates shows diverse uses such as the following:

- Post Office sorting office;
- Social housing provider offices;

- Manufacturing of electronic equipment, fabricated metal products, industrial; machinery, double glazing, and other products;
- Builder's yard and offices;
- Kitchen supplier showroom and workshop;
- Vehicle repair workshop;
- IT consultants' offices and customer service centre;
- Freight services depot;
- Storage and distribution facilities;
- Mechanical engineering works.

Mixed use can present the opportunity for innovative and creative design, as can be seen at CopenHill in Denmark. This waste management plant incorporates a ski slope, hiking trail, climbing wall, and other leisure facilities within the structure of the building.[10]

PUBLIC BUILDINGS

A public building can be defined as a building open to the public, for public use and owned and funded by public bodies such as local authorities. Use Class F covers local community and learning, so many public buildings come with this Use Class:

- Schools (we consider educational institutions separately, earlier);
- Libraries;
- Exhibition halls;
- Community halls;
- Museums;
- Art galleries;
- Places of worship;
- Law courts;
- Swimming pools and outdoor sports facilities.

For our purposes, we will also consider other buildings which provide key services to the public. Use Class E includes services, and covers indoor sports facilities, gyms, day nurseries and day centres, and medical and health centres.

Use Classes E and F therefore help to meet society's need for education, health, personal growth, spirituality, justice, and a sense of community.

Most types of real estate will include a variety of buildings within each class in terms of age, size, and design. In recent years many law courts in England have been closed and the buildings sold as some court services move online and as court facilities require modernisation. Our local county court is an interesting example. The court is now housed in a dockland redevelopment and the former period court building is now a bar and restaurant, as we mention earlier. Both buildings form part of the heritage of our built environment and both demonstrate how real estate needs to adapt and diversify.

A public service may not always have a fixed location. For example, tribunals may be held at a location close to the property concerned. We have attended tribunals in some unusual locations: an agricultural tribunal in a pub, and First-tier Tribunal (Property Chamber) hearings in a hotel and, more unusually, in a mock courtroom (complete with mannequins in Victorian dress) in a police museum. Clearly, therefore, a building's purpose may be diverse and change even day-to-day through temporary hire of premises for a specific use such as this.

Remember also that a building's primary use may require diverse ancillary facilities serving a variety of purposes. A hospital will serve its primary healthcare purpose, but it may also be used as a teaching facility for medical students. A church will often be located close to a vicarage, a church hall, and possibly also a church school. Similarly, a university campus usually includes retail, residential, healthcare, social and leisure facilities, and food outlets, to support the principal educational purpose of the real estate. It may also contain laboratories used for educational, academic, and commercial research and development purposes. Increasing numbers of universities are developing their land to build ancillary research, development, and offices for start-up businesses. Incentives are provided to occupiers who are then encouraged to work closely with the university and perhaps employ students.

RESIDENTIAL USE

We all need a home; hence, the residential sector is a significant area of practice for real estate professionals; in England alone as of 31 March 2019, there were an estimated 24.4 million homes.[11]

Homes are where we live and, increasingly, where we also work and study. They may be occupied by an individual, a couple, groups of friends or colleagues, a nuclear family, or a multi-generational extended family. Homes are where we feel we belong, with our families and friends, our neighbourhood, our identity, and our community. It is no surprise, therefore, that homes come in many forms, reflecting their political, economic, social, technological, environmental, and legal setting. Imagine the range of homes and the different lifestyles experienced by the residents of those homes. They may live in a slum or a favela, a hut within a village community, a modern or period house or flat, a purpose-built home, or one created from disused commercial or industrial real estate. The need for homes evolves – for example we have seen large Regency and Georgian townhouses converted into several flats for purchase or rental. In recent years, we have also seen the rejuvenation of derelict industrial properties – such as mills and factories – by conversion into homes, which reflect their history and their local heritage. This trend continues, with modern commercial spaces being converted to residential use in response to changes to working patterns and, in the UK, a housing shortage.

Residential use also reflects population changes; retirement housing reflects an aging population; student housing responds to the rise in the student population. In the UK, student accommodation reflects the tradition of going away to university and contrasts with some other cultures in which students traditionally attend university local to their family home.

So far, we have considered homes as a fixed point on the earth's surface. However, a home may be nomadic; moveable, to allow its residents to adapt to the environment.

The definition of a home can therefore be fluid. When we think of real estate, we tend to refer to land and the buildings on the land. But homes can, for example, be made from shipping containers or they can be insubstantial shelters. Contrast the tiny shacks that we have seen built on the roadside outside prosperous gated communities. The diversity of real estate often, therefore, reflects the unequal distribution of wealth.

Homes can also be above or beneath the land – a flat above ground floor level, for example, is a home created from the concept that a 'slice' of the airspace above the land is capable of legal ownership. Homes may be beneath the land – for example cave dwellings in Matmata, Tunisia, or in Coober Pedy, Australia. People may also live on water, in house boats, or in communities built on water, such as Thai stilt houses.

The concept of a home tends to be associated with an idea of permanency – of roots. However, residential use may also be temporary, short-term, or intermittent. For example, student accommodation may be purpose-built or converted halls of residence or it may be a shared house, occupied during term-time only or for the entirety of the academic year. Providers may be the educational institution itself, large-scale investors, or smaller scale private-rented sector investors, who understand that there will be a turnover of occupants and possible void periods during the year.

This idea of permanency also has a wider application. For millions of refugees from conflict or natural disaster, their 'home', in so far as it is the place in which they are living, may be a tent or a temporary structure within a refugee camp. An asylum seeker may reside temporarily in an asylum centre. These places accommodate people and provide us with another example of the diversity of real estate. We have mentioned that we all need a home; for many this is not the reality and 'home' may be insecure and transient, in bed and breakfast accommodation, a homeless shelter, a squat, or on the streets.

As we have seen, the global population resides in a huge range of real estate. In the UK, we are focused on permanent, immovable buildings, although there are other types. Our homes are owned – freehold or long-leasehold – or they may be rented in the private sector or in social housing. As we have seen in Chapters 4 and 6, investors in real estate may focus on a particular type of asset within the diverse range of real estate investment available. However, they may also specialise within a particular type of asset. In the residential sector, investors may focus on ground rent investments, private-rented sector tenancies, or Houses in Multiple Occupation (HMOs), for example. Alternatively, an investor may decide to diversify, to minimise their risk, so an investor may own a mix of residential assets – perhaps a range of sizes, areas, types, individual and multi-occupancy – in a mix of markets; professional lets and student lets perhaps.

In England, residential use falls within Use Class C or it may be sui generis.

RETAIL USE

The retail sector is the sale of products to the public. These sales will usually be small scale, rather than bulk. Retail relates to consumers; the consumers of goods acquire those products for their personal – rather than business – use. So, when you go into a shop to buy clothes to wear, or as a gift for a friend or family member, you will probably just buy one or two, or perhaps a few, items, and you will do so as a consumer.

Retail differs from wholesale, in that wholesale is the sale of larger quantities of products to another business, either for their own use or for retail sale to the public.

Once again, we see a diversity of real estate used for retail purposes:

* Makeshift, or more permanent, roadside stalls;
* Markets, perhaps roadside or in market squares, in the street or in market halls;
* Corner-shops;
* Small local concentrations of retail shops;
* High streets;
* Retail arcades;
* Designer outlets such as Bicester Village in Oxfordshire;
* Supermarkets;
* Retail parks;
* Large shopping complexes – the vast Dubai Mall is one of the biggest malls in the world at over 1 million sq. m. (12,000,000 sq. ft.) with over 1,200 stores and over 200 food and beverage outlets.[12] More local examples include the Bullring in Birmingham, Meadowhall in Sheffield, Liverpool One and Westfield in Stratford, East London.

In England, shops were within Use Class A, but they have now been reclassed as E or F, depending on their size and location.

Retail has long been a relatively safe real estate asset, attractive to investors and pension funds, but it is now common to see empty retail units in once-prime locations. The retail sector in the UK has had a troubled few years, with the collapse of some very large household names and store closures, including the loss of anchor tenants (key tenants that attract people to the site) in some locations. The growing popularity of online shopping combined with the Covid-19 pandemic has had a major impact; the proportion of expenditure online rose from 19.5% in January 2020 to 35.2% in January 2021.[13]

From a real estate perspective, retail needs to adapt, so premises also need to evolve, possibly to enable diversification and change of use; for example, as mentioned in Chapter 5, we are aware of plans to redevelop one large former department store into lecture halls for medical students, and another one is to be turned into an indoor trampoline centre.

RURAL LAND USE

The rural sector is another important area of work for surveyors. Agricultural land in the UK constitutes around 17.6 million hectares, accounting for approximately 72% of land area, with woodland and forests covering a further 3.2 million hectares.[14] These are interesting statistics, as there is perhaps a perception in the UK that we are a small, overcrowded country, where space is at a premium. A 2017 survey by Ipsos MORI revealed that the public believed that on average, 47% of the UK's land is densely built up.[15] The survey was in response to the Royal Statistical Society's Statistic of the Year for 2017, which revealed that, in fact, only 0.1% of the UK's land is densely built up, with only 5.4% of land built upon.[16] This demonstrates the extent and significance of rural land use, and is reflected in its diversity, as we will see in this section.

Firstly, we will consider farming, to include:

- Pasture (grazing);
- Livestock rearing and production;
- Arable (the production of crops for human or animal consumption);
- Orchards (fruit production);
- Horticulture (production of herbs, fruits and vegetables);
- Paddy fields (rice production);

- Viticulture (the production of grapes for eating or juice);
- Viniculture (growing grapes for wine);
- Aquaculture (freshwater fish and water plants).

Rural land use may often become part of the identity of the local area and a key part of the local economy. In England, the Vale of Evesham in Worcestershire is an example of a local focus on horticulture. This has evolved over the years with local settlements adopting it as a symbol of their heritage. The flag for Worcestershire includes the symbol of three black pears, associated with the county. The coat of arms for the town of Pershore includes two plums, again reflecting the historic land use and produce of the area.

However, rural land use is broader than food production; it might also cover areas that produce non-food items such as:

- Arboriculture (the cultivation and care of individual trees, generally for amenity) and silviculture (the care and cultivation of woodland);[17]
- Osiers used for basket weaving;
- Horticulture (production of garden and ornamental plants and flowers);
- Water reeds (harvested for use as thatch – in England, the Norfolk Broads are a source of reeds, but reeds are also produced from reed beds in river areas in China, Romania, and Ukraine amongst other countries[18]);
- Wool production, as well as leather, skins, and fur;
- Tobacco;
- Cotton.

The scale of agricultural real estate varies considerably. Compare, for example, small-scale subsistence farming with, historically, the huge collective farms of the Soviet Union, and currently, with the vast cattle and sheep stations of Australia. Nomadic cultures graze their livestock on the open plains and steppes of, for example, Mongolia, in a manner that contrasts considerably with the relatively small, enclosed fields and terraces associated with much global agriculture. The role of agricultural real estate may therefore be to support a family. Alternatively, use may be commercial – produce to trade or for financial gain – or it may be a combination of these; perhaps the land supports its occupiers, with produce left over to sell. It follows that rural land use requires a range of buildings to facilitate these functions.

We have seen that rural land use is often associated with a product. However, productive land may not only be more diverse than this, for example parkland grazed by deer is both visually appealing and designed for recreational use by its owners or their guests and visitors, but it may also be productive if it yields venison for its owners' consumption or for commercial sale as part of the management of that land.

Equestrian use involves pasture, stabling, and related buildings. This real estate may be used for private recreational purposes or for business use, to generate an income from a range of activities from breeding, teaching, training, trekking, trail riding, racing, or competition facilities.

Rural areas may include 'managed wilderness' – areas that we may consider to be 'wild', but which reflect agricultural use or active management to retain natural features. For example, the Lake District of England is characterised by its famous Herdwick sheep; their grazing and management helps to shape the natural environment of the region. The appeal of the area to walkers and tourists demonstrates a symbiosis of agricultural use and recreational use.

Planning policy impacts considerably on rural land use as it must control development and protect greenbelt and wilderness areas. Hence in the UK we have strict controls on development in designated protected environments – our national parks, AONBs, Sites of Special Scientific Interest (SSSIs), and Conservation Areas.

SEABED AND FORESHORE

The seabed and foreshore (the area between the average high and low tides) are both perhaps easily overlooked when we think about real estate. However, these are important, productive real estate assets, used for a range of purposes, for example:

- Aquaculture (such as oyster beds and growing and harvesting other seafood including seaweed);
- Fishing;
- Marinas, ports, and harbours;

- Leisure, including the Victorian seaside piers typical of many UK seaside resorts;
- Offshore wind farms (areas of the seabed may be leased as wind-turbine sites);
- Wave and tidal energy;
- Mining and mineral extraction;
- Seabed telecommunications cables;
- Oil and gas pipelines.

The Crown Estate owns the seabed that surrounds the UK, up to the limit of 12 nautical miles, together with a substantial part of the foreshore. The remaining UK foreshore is in a mix of public and private ownership with the National Trust owning over 780 miles of it (see Chapter 5).

AND FINALLY – SOME OTHER USES

When we think of real estate in the broad, global, context, it is clear that there are so many ways of using real estate. We do not go into these in detail in this chapter and we have probably not listed them all; you may be able to identify other uses. We list a few more types of real estate use later so that you are aware of them in relation to the diversity of real estate and of their potential relevance to your studies and practice:

- Solar farms – these may be small scale, on private land or roofs and gardens or large-scale;
- Wind farms;
- Phone masts;
- Ancient monuments and archaeological sites;
- Public monuments;
- Historic buildings and estates – for example National Trust properties;
- Power plants;
- Waste disposal facilities;
- Rivers, lakes, and lochs;
- Canals and towpaths;
- Abattoirs;
- Tanneries and rendering plants;

- Wilderness and wildlife reserves;
- Mining and minerals;
- Quarries;
- Car parks;
- Bridges;
- Public parks;
- Transport – highways, toll roads, bus stops and stations, train, tram and metro networks, airports;
- Fuel stations.

It can be seen from this chapter that real estate is diverse. It is diverse geographically, and within and between asset classes, reflecting the huge variety of real estate uses. It is also diverse in terms of design and construction, reflecting its age, location, and purpose. Understanding the diversity of real estate will support your career in real estate and any further studies. Awareness of an asset's heritage and of diverse uses through its history can enhance appreciation and understanding of the sector. You may decide to specialise, or you may deal with a range of real estate assets. For example, valuers often focus on either commercial or residential property, but will often also specialise in the valuation of particular types of property within these categories. It is important that real estate professionals deal only with the types of real estate that are within their area of expertise, as moving beyond it could result in mistakes and negligence claims.

We recommend that you have a look at the sources of information listed at the end of this chapter if you would like to develop your understanding of this topic. Another simple way of developing this understanding is to observe your local environment. Consider street and building names as these often reflect the heritage of a property or an area. Look at the design and construction of the buildings. Some will deteriorate over time whereas others will be enhanced by age, as new materials become weathered to blend in with the natural and built environment. Identify the services people need to access and observe where people live, work, study, shop, eat, and relax; the range of land and buildings involved to meet these needs demonstrates the diversity of real estate and the scope to study and practise within the sector. Most importantly ensure that you remain alert to changes and developments in the diversity of real estate; the workplaces and high streets of the future, for example, are likely to significantly differ from those that exist today and we are already seeing these changes start to take shape.

In the next two chapters, we first consider real estate in terms of an asset, for the income it produces, and the capital value it can create and hold. We then consider real estate as a resource where it is integral to the main business of an organisation.

NOTES

1 World Population Review (undated) *Chernobyl Population 2021* Online. Available from: https://worldpopulationreview.com/world-cities/chernobyl-population

2 Smith, D (2005) 'Patterns and Processes of "Studentification" in Leeds' *The Regional Review* 12, 14–16

3 Planning Portal (undated) *About the Planning System Local Plans* Online. Available from: www.planningportal.co.uk/info/200127/planning/102/about_the_planning_system/3

4 Planning Portal (undated) *Change of Use Use Classes* Online. Available from: www.planningportal.co.uk/info/200130/common_projects/9/change_of_use

5 Ministry of Housing, Communities and Local Government (2021) *National Planning Policy Framework* Online. Available from: www.gov.uk/guidance/national-planning-policy-framework/2-achieving-sustainable-development

6 Historic England (2017) *Rossington Bridge Roman Potteries* Online. Available from: https://historicengland.org.uk/listing/the-list/list-entry/1004787

7 King's Cross (undated) *Google* Online. Available from: www.kingscross.co.uk/google

8 King's Cross (undated) *The Mix* Online. Available from: www.kingscross.co.uk/mix

9 The Shard (2021) *A Vertical City* Online. Available from: www.the-shard.com/shard/a-vertical-city/

10 Visit Copenhagen (undated) *Copenhill* Online. Available from: www.visitcopenhagen.com/copenhagen/planning/copenhill-gdk1088237

11 Ministry of Housing, Communities and Local Government (2020) *Dwelling Stock Estimates: 31 March 2019, England* Online. Available from: www.gov.uk/government/statistics/dwelling-stock-estimates-in-england-2019

12 Burj Khalifa (undated) *The Dubai Mall* Online. Available from: www.burjkhalifa.ae/en/downtown-dubai/the-dubai-mall/

13 Office for National Statistics (2021) *Retail Sales, Great Britain: January 2021* Online. Available from: www.ons.gov.uk/businessindustryandtrade/retailindustry/bulletins/retailsales/january2021

14 Norton, E (2019) 'Current Agricultural Land Use in the UK' *Savills* Online. Available from: www.savills.co.uk/research_articles/229130/274017-0

15 Ipsos MORI (2018) *Public Hugely Overestimate How Much Land in the UK Is Densely Built Up* Online. Available from: www.ipsos.com/ipsos-mori/en-uk/public-hugely-overestimate-how-much-land-uk-densely-built

16 Royal Statistical Society (2017) 'The Royal Statistical Society Announces Statistic of the Year 2017' *Press Release* Online. Available from: https://rss.org. uk/RSS/media/File-library/News/Press%20release/18-12-2017-THE-RSS-ANNOUNCES-ITS-STATISTIC-OF-THE-YEAR-FOR-2017. pdf

17 Forest Research (2021) *Silviculture* Online. Available from: www.forest research.gov.uk/tools-and-resources/fthr/biomass-energy-resources/fuel/ woodfuel-production-and-supply/woodfuel-production/forestry-for-woodfuel-and-timber/silviculture/

18 Thatch Advice Centre (undated) *Water Reed* Online. Available from: www. thatchadvicecentre.co.uk/thatch-information/thatching-materials/water-reed

FURTHER INFORMATION

Hall, T (2019) *Town Planning: The Basics* Abingdon, Oxon: Routledge

WEBSITES

Airbnb www.airbnb.co.uk/help/article/1379/responsible-hosting-in-the-united-kingdom#cities

Historic England https://historicengland.org.uk/listing/what-is-designation/listed-buildings/

Historic England https://historicengland.org.uk/listing/what-is-designation/local/conservation-areas/

National Association for Areas of Outstanding Natural Beauty https://land scapesforlife.org.uk

National Planning Policy Framework www.gov.uk/guidance/national-planning-policy-framework

Natural England www.gov.uk/guidance/protected-areas-sites-of-special-scientific-interest

Planning Portal www.planningportal.co.uk/info/200130/common_projects/9/change_of_use

RICS Sector Pathways www.rics.org/uk/surveying-profession/join-rics/sector-pathways/

Royal Town Planning Institute www.rtpi.org.uk

Town and Country Planning Association www.tcpa.org.uk

REAL ESTATE AS AN ASSET

WHY HOLD REAL ESTATE?

Those acquiring real estate usually do so with one of two main purposes in mind, holding it:

- As an asset with a view to the generation of income, holding or building value, or some other future benefit; or
- As a resource that is used as a factor of production and drawn upon to enable the organisation to function effectively.

This chapter focuses on real estate as an asset and the next chapter on real estate as a resource. In a few cases, it will be held as both providing greater levels of control over the premises and tax efficiency.

WHY INVEST IN REAL ESTATE?

As discussed in Chapter 2, real estate offers various benefits to investors when compared with alternative opportunities. The choice of what sort of asset to invest in is ultimately a decision about the balance between potential risks and likely rewards. Real estate can offer investors a relatively stable store of value in a tangible asset (against which finance can be raised); a hedge against inflation (i.e. it protects the investor from the decreased purchasing power that results from rising prices of goods and services as rents can be regularly reviewed); tax benefits; the generation of a regular income; and the ability to control the amount and timing of costs. It can also provide the opportunity for owners to make a statement. An example of this

DOI: 10.1201/9781003155256-4

is Sheikh Mohammed's real estate developments in Dubai, including, amongst many others, the world's tallest tower, the world's largest shopping mall (depending on how it is measured), and the world's highest tennis court. Finally, real estate can be used for social and environmental benefit. For example, in the UK, the Church Commissioners set up a housing commission which reported, in 2021, that a significant proportion of their approximately 200,000 acres of land could be used to build affordable housing.[1] This could help with the housing crisis if issues, concerning the regulations surrounding charity law whereby disposal must be at the highest achievable price, can be overcome. The reasons for investing in real estate will have impact on how an investor decides to invest, either directly or indirectly.

HOW CAN YOU INVEST IN REAL ESTATE?

Direct real estate investment involves the purchase of the whole, or part, of a specific property interest, in one asset, or a group of assets. Direct investment in one asset is riskier for an investor, than investing in a portfolio of assets. Investing in just one asset means that the investor is susceptible to changes in that one market whereas investing in a portfolio helps to diversify the risk. Direct investment offers greater control over decision-making with the investor choosing exactly what type of building they want, in what location, with what use, what tenant, and what type of interest, for example freehold or leasehold. Direct investors will also make the final decision on what to pay for the asset.

Indirect investment in real estate enables investors to diversify risk. Indirect investment involves the purchase of shares, stocks, or bonds in a listed property company, or a REIT, such as Landsec, British Land and Hammerson in the UK, Evergrande Real Estate in China, Brookfield Asset Management in Canada, and Blackstone in the US. The values of the total assets owned by these companies demonstrate the sheer size of the real estate industry. In the UK, in 2020, Landsec's total asset value was £12.8 billion[2] (approximately $18 billion) and Evergrande Real Estate's was $273.8 billion (approximately £196 billion).[3] Indirect investment in these companies allows investors to benefit from the performance of a wide range of asset classes, despite investing a relatively modest sum, and those that have converted to REITs benefit from tax advantages.

Indirect investment can also include property index derivatives where returns are linked to indices, such as those produced by MCSI,[4] and property investment bonds. Bonds are issued by, usually, development and investment companies, to fund specific projects. They are effectively a loan secured against the properties. Bonds tend to be a short term, usually three to five-year, alternative to bank borrowing which can be more costly and restrictive. All these methods of indirect investment allow investors with very small amounts of capital to gain some exposure to the real estate market therefore experiencing less of a risk because of the limited amount of capital spent.

Tokenisation is an emerging trend in relation to indirect real estate investment whereby a real estate asset is divided up into shares and these are sold using blockchain technology. They are tokens that represent a share of the asset and, if the asset appreciates in value, the price of the tokens rises. Tokenisation is a response to the high entry costs discussed later. As real estate tokens are backed by actual properties, they are less risky, and less volatile, than other cryptocurrencies.

TRENDS IN DIRECT REAL ESTATE INVESTMENT

When we first dealt with property in the mid–1980s, direct investment tended to be focused on commercial buildings such as offices, shops, industrial, and leisure property. Investors were able to purchase freehold properties with standard 25-year leases subject to five yearly upward only rent reviews. The higher the quality of the tenant, in terms of their likely ability to pay rent and outgoings over the lease term, the higher the price paid for the property was likely to be. This is conventionally referred to as 'covenant strength' and a well-established plc is considered to have a greater covenant strength than a start-up. Today leases have become shorter and rent reviews can be upward or downward. There has also been an increase in the number of leases with break clauses to build in flexibility.

The choice of asset classes has also continued to evolve in response to external environmental factors. Chapter 3 provides an overview of the diversity of real estate and the real estate market. It is now possible to invest in wind and solar farms and data centres neither of which existed when we first entered our professions.

A relatively recent trend in the UK has been the growth of buy-to-let and build-to-rent properties. The buy-to-let market grew as Assured Shorthold Tenancies (ASTs) were introduced under the Housing Act 1988. This made it easier for landlords to gain possession of their properties and they could be let at market rents. This encouraged further investment and specialist financial products, such as mortgages for buy-to-rent properties, were offered in the 1990s. Former economist, Rob Thomas, published a report in 2015 highlighting that over an 18-year period, and based on a specialist mortgage with a 25% deposit, the returns on buy-to-let, outstripped those from all the other main asset classes (see Figure 4.1). £1,000 invested in buy-to-let with a 25% deposit would have been worth £14,897 at the end of 2014 compared to cash at £1,959 equating to compound annual returns of 16.2% and 3.8%, respectively.

The report goes on to predict that the value of £1,000 invested in buy-to-let at the end of 2014 will be £1,814 (with no mortgage)

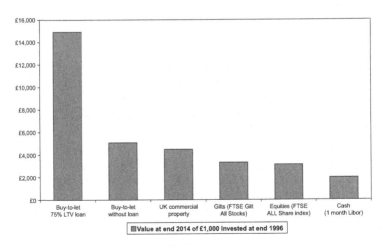

Figure 4.1 How £1,000 invested in buy-to-let outperformed other investments 1996 to 2014

Source: Rob Thomas, The Wriglesworth Consultancy (2015)[6]

and £2,874 (with a 75% mortgage) by the end of 2024. These equate to compound annual returns of 6.1% and 11.1%, respectively, over the ten-year period. However, these were based on 'as neutral as possible assumptions', made prior to the global pandemic, which included inflation averaging 2%; real household income growth of 2%; house prices growing at 4% a year; and base rate rising gradually to reach 3.75% by 2022. House prices are reported to have increased by 8.5% to the year ending December 2020 (the highest growth rate since October 2014)[5] and, at the same date, interest rates remained at their historic low of 0.1% making the predictions unreliable.

The current low interest environment, that has existed in the UK since the financial crisis in 2008, has fuelled demand for buy-to-let as a way of achieving both rental and capital returns that exceed those available on alternative investments such as cash savings and bonds. Government intervention in this market is however beginning to act as a bit of a deterrent with SDLT on buy-to-let properties being set at a 3% surcharge since 1 April 2016 and rumours of licencing requirements for landlords in England and Scotland in the future. Wales already requires landlords to be licensed under the Rent Smart Wales scheme.

The demand for housing in the UK still outstrips the supply and increasing numbers are having to rent privately. The private-rented sector is now the second largest tenure in the UK for the first time since the 1960s[7] due to the widening gap between house prices and median salaries. In England in 2020 full-time employees could typically expect to spend 7.8 times their workplace-based earnings on purchasing their homes. In Wales, in 2020 the figure was approximately 5.9 times earnings.[8] Figure 4.2 shows the trends in tenure in England over the past 40 years. It does not specifically cover those properties that are shared ownership. These are usually housing association properties where the purchaser is unable to afford to get a mortgage on the full price of the property; therefore they purchase a part and continue to rent a part.

The increased demand for private-rented housing has led to the emergence of new developments known as build-to-rent. These newly constructed developments are professionally managed and designed specifically for renting. They include purpose-built communal spaces such as gardens, gyms, offices, and meeting spaces. They

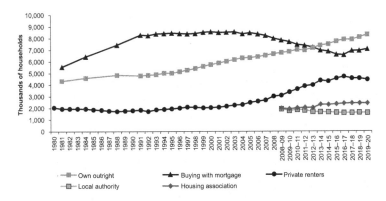

Figure 4.2 Trends in tenure in England 1980 to 2020

Source: English Housing Survey[9]

usually have a concierge service or onsite manager and will often offer longer tenancies than the standard one-year Assured Shorthold that most buy-to-let properties offer. They tend to charge higher rents than buy-to-let properties to reflect the additional services offered. There were estimated to be 195,600 build-to-rent homes planned, under construction, or operational across the UK in 2021.[10]

Internationally, there has been significant growth in investment in data centres and demand is likely to have increased during the global pandemic. Data centres have been one of the top-performing asset classes in REITs worldwide and four of the ten best performing REITs worldwide during the global pandemic were data centre REITs.[11]

It is important for investors to keep a close eye on trends in the real estate investment market as the performance of asset classes can change quite quickly as new classes emerge and external environmental factors have impact on existing asset classes. As previously mentioned, retail properties have been adversely impacted by the combination of online retailing and the global pandemic. The same two factors have led to increased demand for, and therefore returns from, warehousing and distribution units. It is clear that real estate investment covers a wide range of different opportunities and the investor needs to decide whether to invest directly or indirectly which will depend on a number of different factors but ultimately comes down to the availability of capital and the appetite for risk.

Despite the numerous benefits of owning real estate, there are also specific drawbacks to choosing to invest in real estate rather than any of the other alternatives outlined in Chapter 2. Indirect investment reduces the impact of these drawbacks which will be more pronounced if investing directly.

WHAT ARE THE DRAWBACKS OF DIRECTLY INVESTING IN REAL ESTATE?

Although the benefits of investing in real estate summarised earlier provide an incentive to choose real estate over other alternatives, there are some key drawbacks to investing directly in real estate.

HIGH ENTRY COSTS

To avoid high entry costs, indirect investment in REITs, shares, or tokenisation makes it possible to invest smaller sums in real estate. Direct investment, in whole real estate assets, such as an office or shopping centre, can be very expensive. In 2020, even when the market was suppressed due to the Covid-19 pandemic, in the UK, Landsec exchanged contracts for the sale of 389,615 sq. ft. (36,196 sq. m.) of office buildings 1&2 New Ludgate, in the City of London, to Sun Venture for £552 million (approximately $771 million)[12] Internationally, what has been described as the largest private real estate deal in history took place in 2019 when Blackstone agreed to buy Singapore-based GLP's US warehouse portfolio for $18.7 billion (approximately £13.4 billion) including debt.[13] The value of these deals limits the number of potential purchasers due to the relatively small number of organisations with access to that level of finance. For larger, more valuable assets, such as shopping centres, it has become common for organisations to form strategic partnerships, or joint ventures, to invest in, and manage, them.

ILLIQUIDITY

This high level of entry costs, which include not only the purchase price but also the legal fees, agents' fees, and then ongoing management costs, mean that not only is it difficult to raise the money to enter the real estate market in the first place, but also that it can take a considerable period of time to dispose of the asset due to the limited number of potential purchasers with access to this level of finance. This illiquidity is a common criticism of the real estate market and, as mentioned in Chapter 2, many funds suspended dealing for periods of over a year leaving investors unable to access their money. To satisfy the level of withdrawals (also known as redemptions) would have required very quick sales of the assets within the funds. Selling quickly, or 'forced sale values', would have been much lower than the recorded values. The asset managers running the fund have the responsibility of managing purchases and sales in such a way that they maximise value and minimise costs and they will have planned holding periods to achieve this. Indirect investment is usually more liquid than direct investment other than in exceptional circumstances such as the global Covid-19 pandemic.

MANAGEMENT COSTS

Real estate requires active management to ensure that costs are controlled and value for money is achieved. These costs will vary depending on the type of asset. Multi-tenanted offices with lifts, a concierge service, gymnasium, and catering facilities will require a considerable amount of management time and expense to ensure that the services provided are of optimum quality whilst providing value for money. Similarly shopping centres will usually have a dedicated centre manager or centre director running a team including, amongst others, cleaners, maintenance operatives, car parking attendants, and window cleaners. They are needed to ensure that the centre is safe and clean for customers. These management costs are likely to be mostly recoverable through the service charge, but a high service charge can be off-putting to potential tenants and may reduce the amount they are prepared to pay in rent. Service charges will be discussed in more detail in Chapter 13. Smaller investments such as single shops, with one occupier, are likely to require less intensive management.

COSTS OF REPAIR, MAINTENANCE, AND REFURBISHMENT

Most multi-tenanted properties will have a service charge in place to cover the cost of repairs and maintenance, but direct investors will have to manage service charges in accordance with the relevant professional statements (see Chapter 13). Although most investors will wish to transfer the responsibility for repairs and maintenance to tenants, in some cases, such as listed buildings, or those that form part of a landlord's wider holding, the lease granted might be internal and repairing only leaving the responsibility of repairing and maintaining the asset with the investor. Rental levels will reflect the likely costs of the agreed obligations.

With residential tenancies for example, the landlord is normally responsible for the exterior of the building and the tenants for the interior. The repairing obligations are likely to differ between long leasehold and ASTs. With long leaseholds the landlord will usually be responsible for all repairs and maintenance of the exterior, structure, services, and installations with the tenants paying their share of these costs via a service charge. The interior is likely to be the responsibility of the tenant. With ASTs the landlord tends to be responsible for all repairs with the tenant's obligation simply being not to cause any damage or commit waste.

This means that a residential investor, with tenants on ASTs, will need to arrange, manage, and pay for external repairs, either directly or through an agent. They will also need to check that their tenants are maintaining the interior in accordance with the terms of the lease. In one of our own properties, the tenants who were only in place for a year and a half, on a standard AST, caused over £10,000 worth of damage to the interior before they vacated which the deposit of £2,000 (all of which the Deposit Protection Service agreed should be paid to us) did not cover.

Direct investment properties also become dated over time and require refurbishment to meet the demands of the current market. For example, offices used to have perimeter trunking, but this is now considered rather inflexible, and occupiers expect raised floors to suit a variety of flexible interior layouts. Carrying out major refurbishments can be expensive in terms of not only the cost of the works but also the cost of having the premises empty, and non-income producing, whilst the works are carried out.

VOID PERIODS

In addition to periods when works are being carried out, void periods may occur when tenants vacate at lease expiry or go into administration. The period between one tenant vacating and another one moving in will be a period when no rental income is received. This will have an adverse impact on the overall yield generated by the asset. When reletting, the investor is also likely to have to offer some form of incentive (see Chapter 10) which will further reduce the yield achievable.

GOVERNMENT INTERVENTION

A final factor that can have an impact on overall returns from investments in real estate is government intervention, discussed in Chapter 2. This can take the form of, as previously mentioned, in the residential market, imposing additional SDLT on buy-to-let investments; withdrawing tax relief on mortgage payments; extending an SDLT holiday and extending the ban on eviction of tenants that had not paid their rent during the global Covid-19 pandemic (which has been difficult for landlords to manage); or proposals for leasehold reform including setting future residential ground rents to zero.

In the commercial market, the new planning class E may have impact on property values, both on the individual property itself and changes in use on surrounding properties. There are also government interventions in the form of both standard enterprise zones, and in 2019, a £10 million fund was launched to establish University Enterprise Zones. These aim to encourage universities to engage with Local Enterprise Partnerships and to develop space for small businesses. They offer business support packages, specialist facilities, and expert knowledge. The new freeports declared in 2021 (see Chapter 2) provide similar encouragement for private investment in real estate.

The drawbacks, and benefits, of investing in real estate are reflected by the anticipated returns. In Chapter 2 we considered some of the most common alternatives to real estate investment. The Wealth Report[14] suggests that the highest percentage increase in values over 2020 related to Hermes handbags with a rise of 17%; the second year running it topped the Luxury Investment Index. Luxury investment tends, however, to be much more volatile than real estate, but real estate is less secure than money simply held in bonds or a bank deposit account. The returns achieved are therefore likely to fall somewhere between these extremes and factors impacting on levels of return will be discussed in Chapter 12.

WHO INVESTS IN REAL ESTATE?

Having considered the benefits and drawbacks of investing in real estate and the various ways of investing in real estate, the next question is, who are the investors in real estate? These fall into two main groups: pure investors and investor/developers. Pure investors range from individuals to major multinational companies.

At entry level, an individual investor might, for example, hold a few units in an REIT, a few shares in a property company, or perhaps a buy-to-let property. At the other end of the spectrum, a major multinational may directly hold a wide variety of real estate worth billions of dollars. Both types of investor will have decided that real estate will provide them with the returns they require on their money, but these requirements may differ. For example, pension funds are likely to require regular income in terms of rental income to enable them to pay pensions. They will also require an increase in value of the properties to provide a hedge against inflation and ensure that the assets they are invested in continue to appreciate at a greater rate than money held, for example, in a building society account would. A buy-to-let investor will also be hoping to achieve an income stream but is likely to accept that this will be interrupted by void periods, costs of repair, and refurbishment. They will also be hoping for capital appreciation but may suffer from market downturns, particularly if these occur at the time the investor needs to dispose of the interest. Whatever the type, or size, of investor, as we demonstrated in Figure 4.1, how the investment is financed, and how long it is held for, will have impact on the level of return.

HOW CAN REAL ESTATE INVESTMENT BE FINANCED?

The approach to financing will obviously depend on the type of investor and the type of asset being invested in. In most cases, financing a real estate purchase will require a sizeable amount of borrowing. A principle that can sometimes be difficult to understand is that the returns from real estate investment can be improved by borrowing. Figure 4.1 shows that a buy-to-let investor borrowing 75% of the purchase price achieved a return of 16.2% whereas the same investment purchased with cash achieved a far smaller return of only 9.4%. The same principle applies to large commercial assets. On the face of it this seems to make no sense; surely it would be better to purchase outright if you were able to do so as then you do not have to pay interest and arrangement fees to the lender? However, the principle of gearing explains why this is not the case.

Gearing is the term used to explain the relationship between debt and equity, that is money borrowed and the borrower's own money. In the example provided in Figure 4.1, the buy-to-let investor has a gearing ratio, also expressed as loan-to-value (LTV), of 75%. They are borrowing 75%, in this case on a mortgage, and putting down a 25% deposit which is either money they already hold, or it may be borrowed from elsewhere. In some cases, the lender will restrict the amount available for a loan depending on market conditions. In the late 1980s, when we first entered the housing market, it was common to obtain a 95% mortgage, without suffering a higher rate of interest. One of us purchased our first house on a mortgage which was seven times our annual salary; this reflected the rising market at that time. Following the 2008 crash these high LTV mortgages were withdrawn from the market. In the 2021 March budget, the government intervened to guarantee loans if the buyer defaults encouraging building societies to again offer 95% mortgages.

The same principles apply to commercial loans on investment or development properties. A commercial lender will consider the type of property and its 'prospects' in terms of its ability to generate a regular steady and increasing income for the owner. The lender will also bear in mind market conditions and the ease of sale should the existing owners fail to make their loan repayments. In an uncertain market the lender is likely to offer a smaller LTV ratio than in a rising market.

The basic relationship between gearing and returns is that the higher the gearing, that is the higher the amount of money borrowed in relation to the value of the asset, the better the return, provided the investment is increasing in value over time at a faster rate than the rising interest rates. This is because, despite the payments of interest and arrangement fees to the lender, if the investment has increased in value at a rate that exceeds the interest rate payable, the LTV will decrease. This can be illustrated by a simple example.

Take the case of a £10 million office investment where the lender is prepared to offer a 70% LTV and the investor intends to hold it for 5 years before resale. Say the office market is showing annual growth of 8% and the lender is prepared to offer finance at 7% (see Figure 4.3).

Re-running the figures with all assumptions remaining the same, but the lender now being prepared to offer an increased LTV of 90%, would mean the investor only having to find an initial £1 million stake and borrowing the remaining £9 million. This increases the return considerably (see Figure 4.4).

These examples demonstrate how the higher the LTV, in a rising market with the right differential between loan rates and growth rates, the higher the return. This mathematical principle

---

70% LTV

Cost of asset	£10,000,000
Amount borrowed	£ 7,000,000
Five years' worth of interest payments at 7%	£ 2,817,862
At end of five years investor repays	£ 9,817,862
During period of ownership asset has increased in value by 8% per annum to	£14,693,281
Deduct loan repayment from market value =	£ 4,875,419
Deduct original deposit	£ 3,000,000
Profit on investment over the five-year period =	£ 1,875,419

Return on investor's original stake of £3m = £1,875,419/£3,000,000 = 62.5%
An annual return of approximately 10.2%

Figure 4.3 Loan to value of 70% calculation

90% LTV

Cost of asset	£10,000,000
Amount borrowed	£ 9,000,000
Five years' worth of interest payments at 7%	£ 3,622,966
At end of five years investor repays	£12,622,966
During period of ownership asset has increased in value by 8% per annum to	£14,693,281
Deduct loan repayment from market value =	£ 2,070,315
Deduct original deposit	£ 1,000,000
Profit on investment over the five-year period =	£ 1,070,315

Return on investor's original stake of £1m = £1,070,315/£1,000,000 = 107%
An annual return of approximately 15.66%

Figure 4.4 Loan to value of 90% calculation

helped former math teachers, Judith and Fergus Wilson to build a buy-to-let portfolio of 1,000 properties in Kent in the UK.[15] As house prices continued to rise, the Wilsons withdrew equity and re-mortgaged to buy more houses against a background of falling interest rates. However, a falling market with rising interest rates would reverse the outcomes so the decision on the level of gearing requires a view of future trends and a balance between risk and reward.

WHO FINANCES REAL ESTATE PURCHASES?

Most sizeable real estate purchases will involve borrowing in some form. As outlined earlier, the impact of gearing on returns is likely to lead to a sizeable proportion of the total funds required being borrowed. Lenders will vary depending on the size, and type, of the loan. Smaller loans tend to come from banks and mortgage companies with larger loans being provided by pension funds and insurance companies often through partnerships with investors or developers. To spread the risk, on larger schemes, lending will often be obtained from a syndicate of financial institutions. Lenders will require a valuation of the interest (see Chapters 11 and 12) based on which they will decide what level of gearing is appropriate under existing, and potential future, market conditions. The amount, and the cost, of borrowing will reflect the lender's opinion of the ability of the lender to repay the loan. A modern office building let to a high-quality tenant on a long-term lease is likely to be easier, and cheaper, to finance than a speculative office development. Financing of real estate purchases is usually based on the premise that the value of the asset is likely to appreciate during the period of ownership. This appreciation can be due to a rising market or specific actions that the investor can take to add value to the asset.

HOW CAN VALUE BE ADDED TO A REAL ESTATE ASSET?

There are various ways of adding value to an existing asset. These include purchasing cheaply, buying off-plan, proactive asset management, refurbishment, and redevelopment. Each of these will be briefly considered.

PURCHASING CHEAPLY

The meaning of 'cheaply' is entirely subjective and can only be applied in relation to alternative investment options. There are, however, some common situations where it is possible to purchase real estate at a lower price than market value. These include purchasing at auction where there are bargains to be had for those that can carry out sufficient research and are able to fund the required deposit which is payable immediately, when the hammer falls. Auction properties are often in a poor condition, so care must be taken to ensure that cost estimation is thorough and accurate.

It is also possible to purchase at lower than market value if the seller is desperate to sell and the purchaser can proceed quickly. Purchasing at the start of a growth cycle can, retrospectively, look like purchasing cheaply, and this requires the identification of an area that is likely to grow. Knowing the market helps with this as does knowing those operating within the market. Some of the most successful purchases we have made have been those that came about as a result of knowing people operating in the market with whom we had developed good working relationships. These purchases were 'off market', that is completed without the asset being fully exposed to the market, making it possible to agree the deal without competition from other potential purchasers.

BUYING OFF PLAN

Buying off market refers to the purchase of an asset that has not been exposed to the market. Buying off plan is however another method of real estate investment that builds on the principles of gearing outlined earlier. Buying off plan uses small amounts of initial outlay to achieve high returns, in the right market conditions. This is commonly seen in the residential market where, particularly with buy-to-let, investors will put down a deposit on a flat, or several flats, at the beginning of a development when the developer is keen to start generating cash. The purchaser knows that they do not need to pay in full until the development is complete. If prices appreciate, and the timing is right, the investor may be able to sell on the flat without ever having to complete on the purchase and pay for it in full. This is colloquially known as 'flipping', where the contract is simply transferred to the new purchaser and the original investor makes a profit. Alternatively, they may decide to complete on the purchase and then sell on to consolidate any gains. However, this is dependent on market conditions and, if there is a sudden downturn, significant losses can be incurred.

This can also happen, although it is less common, in the commercial market due to its smaller size and increased complexity. We are aware of situations where developers have purchased a site for retail development and after holding it for six months in a rising market decided to sell it on without developing it out due to the increase in value that could be consolidated by selling on with no risk. Receiving this return on their initial investment gave them the ability to proceed with an alternative scheme more quickly.

PROACTIVE ASSET MANAGEMENT

Effective real estate management will be covered in detail in Chapter 13 where it is defined as protecting the value and function of an asset using resources to manage the asset efficiently to achieve the client's objectives. Proactive asset management goes beyond effective and efficient property management as it involves taking a wider view of how the asset fits into any existing portfolio and identifying ways of increasing its value. The methods of achieving this will obviously vary widely depending on the type of real estate concerned.

Some examples from our own experience include office premises where surrender and regrants were agreed to consolidate leases on three different spaces into one lease for a much larger unit. It was also possible to phase the move to enable the tenant to continue to trade throughout and for the landlord to minimise the void periods and maintain an income stream. Surrender and regrants are an agreement between landlord and tenant to simultaneously surrender an existing lease and enter a new lease. This will be discussed in more detail in Chapter 5. Another example related to a retail warehousing park, adjacent to a light industrial park, where the potential for acquiring a small parcel of land joining the two estates was identified. This then made it possible to gain planning permission for retail warehousing on the industrial estate increasing its value dramatically. A final example relates to shopping centres, where proactive asset management has involved relocating tenants into different sized units to release other units to combine into a suitable size for waiting prospective tenants. It also included identifying a large amount of unused storage space where planning permission was gained for a gym and a light refurbishment was carried out to make the space suitable for this use.

REFURBISHMENT

This relates to renovation works carried out to an existing asset to improve its value. It can include anything from a simple external clean through internal redecoration to major structural work. It is important for investors to have a planned maintenance programme (see Chapter 13) to ensure that the asset remains fit for purpose and maintains its value. Proactive asset management will include identifying where refurbishment works might improve the asset's value. In our experience, this has included fairly straightforward improvements such as putting up a barrier to the car park of leisure premises then resurfacing the car parking, outlining the spaces and then being able to grant car parking licences for spare spaces generating additional income. If an asset has become incapable of refurbishment due to major deterioration, changes in requirements, or a more valuable alternative use then it can be redeveloped.

REDEVELOPMENT

Redevelopment can take the form of construction on a cleared site for a variety of asset classes. Some investors may not even develop their land holdings but may decide to sell them on to other developers, if they can achieve a profit without any risk and it fits their objectives. Development can also involve assembling a site, demolishing existing buildings, and rebuilding new ones. Development might also take the form of adapting existing structures for an alternative use. This happened after 2013 when permitted development rights were introduced by the UK government in 2013 in an attempt to address the housing shortage. This led to many former office buildings being converted to residential use.

The introduction of the new Class E Commercial, Business and Service use in 2020 now permits change of use between retail, industrial, warehousing, office, and leisure which is likely to lead to more redevelopment, and refurbishment, in pursuit of the most valuable use.

Real estate development can be very risky because of the time the development cycle takes. The development process involves a series of steps from inception to completion:

1 Identification of a potential site which could be either one that is in poor condition and is likely to have a more valuable use, or

   recognition of an increase in demand for a certain type of real
   estate which leads the search for a suitable site.

2 Investigation of the site and surrounding area and preliminary
   discussions with the local planning authority.

3 Appointment of professional advisors such as a project manager,
   architect, planner, engineer, etc.

4 Carrying out of a feasibility study and viability assessments to
   include residual appraisals and sensitivity analysis incorporating
   financial and programming aspects of the development. A feasibility study is a formal analysis that incorporates all relevant
   factors that will have an impact on the successful completion of
   a development. A viability assessment takes this a stage further
   to assess whether the development is financially viable. Finally, a
   sensitivity analysis models the impact of small changes in inputs
   on the outcome, for example, changes in interest rates, or building costs helping to highlight the level of exposure to risk.

5 Exploration of physical, financial, and legal aspects relating to
   the site prior to completion of purchase, if not already acquired.

6 Carrying out a detailed design and firming up on the project
   timings and finalising finance.

7 Obtaining planning permission and Building Regulation consent for the scheme and agreeing any contributions to the local
   authority in terms of S.106 agreements or a Community Infrastructure Levy (CIL).

8 Awarding the main construction contracts.

9 Project managing the build through to completion.

10 Marketing, disposal, and management.

These steps are not always linear; it may be necessary to go back and
revisit design elements as the process evolves. The ten steps illustrate
how it can often take many years for the development process to
complete, during which time the market may have changed dramatically. For example, the global Covid-19 pandemic had a major
impact on the demand for offices that could not have been predicted at the time the feasibility analysis and viability assessments for
office developments were carried out.

   Developments, particularly the larger ones, are often carried out in
partnership to reduce the financial exposure and make use of specific
expertise. Organising the legal aspects of that partnership is another
time-consuming aspect of the process. Sometimes the partnership is

between funders and developers, particularly on larger schemes as this helps to diversify the risk. The Bluewater shopping centre in the UK, for example, is currently owned by a changing consortium of developers and investors. The Lend Lease Retail Partnership, who carried out the development, at the time of writing own only 25%, with the largest ownership being the 30% owned by Landsec, who also manage the development. There are also currently four other investors.[16] Some partnerships are formed through necessity, for example, the Shard development in London, owned by developers Sellar Property Group, looked uncertain, due to the global economic downturn, but when the State of Qatar stepped in and purchased 95% of the scheme in 2008 the future of the scheme was assured.[17] In other cases, partnerships may be formed for primarily strategic reasons. For example, when Hammerson were planning the Bull Ring Shopping Centre in Birmingham, Land Securities (now LandSec) were planning a similar development of the Martineau Galleries. Rather than compete, the Birmingham Alliance was formed, together with Henderson Investors, to develop the sites in a complementary fashion. It took over a year simply to agree the basis of the partnership and how it would operate before starting on the developments.

The length of time taken for developments is a challenge for developers as it can be difficult to time the development for when the property cycle is rising rather than falling. Certain steps can be taken to mitigate risks such as selling off-plan or agreeing pre-lets of commercial units, but sometimes the timing of these cycles can be difficult to predict which can lead to the failure of proposed schemes.

Whether value is added to an asset through development, through proactive asset management, or through effective and efficient property management, real estate owners need to be able to judge how their assets are performing. Asset performance will have an impact on investors' decisions on when to buy and sell, and whether to invest more money in the asset.

HOW CAN PERFORMANCE OF REAL ESTATE ASSETS BE MEASURED?

The first step in assessing real estate performance is to establish the objectives of the owner. Although we might assume that investors and developers are driven mainly by financial goals there can often be additional objectives that might be important to them. In the next chapter we will be considering real estate as a resource and, in that case, the objectives are likely to be more about value for money than overall returns. Some owners may be holding real estate as both an asset and a resource.

Most owners holding real estate as an asset will have the overriding objective of generating either capital or rental returns, or both. These are relatively straightforward quantitative measures that can be calculated (see Chapters 11 and 12) to establish how an individual asset, or portfolio of assets, has performed. However, measuring performance alone is not enough. Owners of real estate assets need to *analyse* the performance of their assets. For example, achieving a 5% return on an asset sounds quite attractive, but if all other assets in the same class are achieving 10% it sounds a lot less attractive. If inflation is running at 10% it also sounds a lot less attractive than if inflation is at 2%. It is therefore essential not only to measure performance but also to contextualise, and analyse, the returns to ensure that the assets are producing what is expected. To define 'what is expected' the asset manager will help to develop various targets in terms of not only capital and income returns but also metrics like void periods, cost reductions, or payback periods on investing further capital to add value to the asset.

Financial performance measurement therefore usually involves three stages:

- Calculation of overall returns from the asset;
- Quantification of changes in rent and capital values;
- Comparison of these quantitative measures with suitable benchmarks and alternative investment opportunities.

The type, and frequency, of performance measurement will depend on the individual investor. Our own experience demonstrates that REITs, and other property trusts, tend to be valued monthly so that the units held by investors can be accurately valued. Other investors will value quarterly, or even annually, depending on the size of the investor and the need for reporting to, for example, shareholders. The results of performance measurement will be considered in absolute terms by comparison with targets, and relative terms by comparison with benchmarks and indices.

Beyond financial performance, investors in real estate may also have additional objectives which might include those relating to sustainability, waste reduction, quality, stewardship, customer satisfaction, and employee performance. All larger organisations will have a Corporate Social Responsibility (CSR) statement, which is widely publicised, that covers these aspects. Each investor will have their own objectives, and balance of objectives, that they want to achieve with their assets. Performance measurement and analysis enables the asset owner to assess to what extent their agreed objectives are being achieved and what action needs to be taken to ensure that they remain on track to achieve them.

CAN REAL ESTATE HELD AS AN ASSET ALSO BE A RESOURCE?

This chapter has outlined the two main groups that invest in real estate as an asset: investors and investor/developers. There are however a small group that may utilise real estate as both an asset and a resource. We are aware of small businesses that own their office through their pension fund and then lease the space back to themselves. This is a legitimate, and tax efficient, way of holding real estate both as an asset and as a resource. Another example is the purchase of a property to live in for a few years in a capital city, with a view to moving out and letting it out as an income producing let property. There are however many real estate owners that use real estate purely as a resource and this will be covered in the next chapter.

NOTES

1 The Commission of the Archbishops of Canterbury and York on Housing, Church and Community (2021) 'Coming Home: Tackling the Housing Crisis Together' *Full Report* February Online. Available from: www.archbishopofcanterbury.org/sites/abc/files/2021-02/COE%20 4794%20%E2%80%93%C2%A0HCC%20Full%20Report%20 %E2%80%93%20V6.pdf

2 Landsec (2020) *Landsec Annual Report* Online. Available from: https:// landsec.com/annual-report-2020

3 McClary, S (2020) 'EG Global 100: World's Biggest Real-Estate Owning Companies Revealed' Online. Available from: www.egi.co.uk/news/the-top-100-global-real-estate%E2%80%91owning-companies/

4 MCSI Various Indices Online. Available from: www.msci.com/

5 Office for National Statistics (2021) *UK House Price Index: December 2020* Online. Available from: www.ons.gov.uk/economy/inflationandpriceindices/ bulletins/housepriceindex/december2020

6   Thomas, R (2015) *Buy-to-Let Comes of Age* April Sponsored by Landbay

7   Scarrett, D and Wilcox, J (2018) *Property Asset Management* 4th Edition Abingdon, Oxon: Routledge

8   Office for National Statistics (2020) *Housing Affordability in England and Wales: 2020* Online. Available from: www.ons.gov.uk/peoplepopulationand community/housing/bulletins/housingaffordabilityinenglandandwales/2020

9   English Housing Survey Headline Report (2019–20) Online. Available from: https://assets.publishing.service.gov.uk/government/uploads/system/ uploads/attachment_data/file/945013/2019-20_EHS_Headline_Report.pdf

10 Savills (2021) *Build to Rent Market Update-Q2 2021* Online. Available from: https://www.savills.co.uk/research_articles/229130/316529-0

11 JLL (2020) *Playing Defence: Investors Looking to Data Centres* 10 June Online. Available from: www.jll.co.uk/en/trends-and-insights/investor/playing-defence-investors-looking-to-data-centres

12 Landsec (2020) *Landsec Sells 1&2 New Ludgate for £552m to Sun Venture* 4 December Online. Available from: https://landsec.com/media/2020/ landsec-sells-1-2-new-ludgate-ps552m-sun-venture

13 Fontanella-Khan, J and Palma, S (2019) 'Blackstone Seals Record $18.7bn Private Real Estate deal' *The Financial Times* 3 June Online. Available from: www.ft.com/content/1738601e-8599-11e9-a028-86cea8523dc2

14 Knight Frank (2020) *The Wealth Report* Online. Available from: www. knightfrank.com/wealthreport/article/2020-03-03-the-luxury-investment-index-2020-discover-the-worlds-mostcoveted-items

15 Dunkley, E (2014) 'Anyone with Half a Brain Could Do Buy-to-Let' *The Financial Times* July 11 Online. Available from: www.ft.com/content/ 64112204-084e-11e4-9380-00144feab7de

16 Bluewater (undated) *Bluewater Shopping & Retail Destination* Online. Available from: https://Bluewater.co.uk/our-business/about-us

17 The Shard (undated) Available from: www.the-shard.com/about/

FURTHER READING

Baum, A (2015) *Real Estate Investment: A Strategic Approach* 3rd Edition Abingdon, Oxon: Routledge

Blackledge, M (2017) *Introducing Property Valuation* 2nd Edition Abingdon, Oxon: Routledge

Furfine, C (2020) *Practical Finance for Property Investment* Abingdon, Oxon: Routledge

Hartzell, D and Baum, A E (2021) *Real Estate Investment* 2nd Edition Chichester, West Sussex: John Wiley & Sons Ltd

Reed, R and Sims, S (2015) *Property Development* 6th Edition Abingdon, Oxon: Routledge

Scarrett, D and Wilcox, J (2018) *Property Asset Management* 4th Edition Abingdon, Oxon: Routledge

Wyatt, P (2013) *Property Valuation* 2nd Edition Chichester, West Sussex: John Wiley & Sons Ltd

5

REAL ESTATE AS A RESOURCE

WHY DO ORGANISATIONS NEED REAL ESTATE?

As we have seen in Chapter 3, there is a wide diversity of real estate and there is a correspondingly wide range of real estate needed for organisations to run their core businesses. Most organisations need land and buildings as a resource to enable them to carry out their operations. These premises are usually known as operational or corporate real estate and the two terms are often used interchangeably although there is, arguably, a subtle difference.

Operational real estate is property that is directly related to the provision of the services or goods supplied. For example, railway stations would be considered operational real estate as they form an integral part of the transport service offered. Corporate real estate has a slightly wider definition, including land and property used by an organisation for both operational purposes and corporate support activities. The headquarters office of the railway company, where various support activities such as finance, legal, and human resources are situated, would be an example of corporate real estate. Corporate real estate is used as an integral factor of production for whatever the organisation is creating and selling. The specific way in which the real estate contributes to organisational outcomes will depend on the activity carried out by the organisation.

WHAT ARE THE PURPOSES OF CORPORATE REAL ESTATE?

Most importantly, corporate real estate enables the business to achieve its core objectives. Without corporate real estate it can be

DOI: 10.1201/9781003155256-5

impossible to operate the business. Corporate real estate can facilitate any, or all, of:

- The provision of a product;
- The provision of a service;
- The financing of expansion;
- The protection and preservation of heritage assets.

During the Covid-19 pandemic, many services, such as banking and insurance, discovered that there was no need for staff to attend the office every day; they were able to work effectively from home. Many occupiers are therefore reducing the amount of office space they occupy. Not all businesses, however, can be run from home. A hotel business, for example, could not operate without premises providing bedrooms, eating areas, kitchens, meeting rooms, leisure facilities, car parking, etc. Food production must be carried out in manufacturing units that comply with the stringent health and safety laws surrounding this business.

The RICS has recognised the importance of corporate real estate by creating a specific pathway for it and offering additional qualifications in Corporate Real Estate and Facilities Management.[1]

THE PROVISION OF A PRODUCT

Looking at the manufacture of a relatively simple product, such as a chocolate bar, gives an indication of how integral to the successful operation of the business corporate real estate is. Let us take the example of Cadbury, a long-established confectionery company headquartered in the UK.

Cadbury was founded in 1824 when John Cadbury opened a grocer's shop in Bull Street, Birmingham, selling cocoa and drinking chocolate which, as a Quaker, he perceived as a healthy alternative to alcohol.[2] In 1831 he then bought a four-storey factory to start producing his products on a commercial scale. The business continued to expand and in 1847 moved to a new, larger factory. This had its own private canal spur linking it to the Birmingham Navigation canal, and from there to all the UK's major ports, making transportation more efficient and cost-effective. The growth in the business was facilitated by acquiring the corporate real estate that enabled him to reach both his suppliers and his markets.

When John Cadbury retired, and his sons took over the business, it was against a backdrop of failures of other cocoa manufacturers. They invested heavily in the business using new technology and starting mass production. The company outgrew its existing factory and the brothers acquired a site for their new factory. This 14.5 acre site, a few miles outside Birmingham, had good canal, train, and road links together with a water supply. In addition to the new factory, the brothers decided to construct a few houses for senior employees. The brothers called the new site Bournville. They later added a further 120 acres to it enabling them to construct a village of cottages for the workers, demarcating 10% of the site as gardens and green space. Interestingly, the houses were sold on 999-year leases, presumably to enable the Cadbury family to retain overall control of the estate, and mortgages were offered to the workers. They then constructed sports facilities, swimming pools, organised summer camps, work outings and religious meetings. These increased social benefits helped to preserve the family atmosphere and generated loyalty and commitment amongst the workers. The company continued to expand by increasing their range of products and merging with, or acquiring, other companies. In common with many worldwide brands, Cadbury expanded their operational real estate to produce their products abroad. There are factories throughout Europe and in Tasmania.

In 2010 the company became part of Kraft foods which then split the confectionary part into a new company called Mondelez International of which Cadbury is a subsidiary. The takeover generated concerns that all production would be moved abroad but investment in the Bournville factory continued, with £75 million invested in 2014, and a further £15 million in 2021 with a view to producing, in Bournveille, in 2022,[3] an additional 125 million Dairy Milk bars (that had previously been produced in Europe). This demonstrates a commitment to retaining production in the UK.

Holding real estate as a resource is a cost to the business impacting on the profitability. Real estate is usually the second highest cost to a business after staff. All opportunities to reduce the costs of corporate real estate, and maximise any income it might create, must therefore be exploited. Cadbury realised that they could monetise their factory tours and invested £6 million in creating Cadbury World next to the Bournville factory as a visitor attraction.

As can be seen, Cadbury, in common with most businesses, created their corporate real estate, over time, to maximise the efficiency of manufacturing and sales of their product. In Cadbury's case, they had a strong social conscience and wanted to create houses for their workers that were an improvement on their previous living conditions. This was not entirely altruistic as they also realised that happy, healthy, and loyal workers would be likely to work harder and faster than those living in poor conditions. This brief history demonstrates how the locational decisions for their corporate estate were based on proximity to infrastructure enabling them to import their raw materials such as milk, sugar, and cocoa beans and then export their confectionary around the world. This example of Cadbury highlights the importance of corporate real estate to help a manufacturing company expand in pursuit of increased profitability and success.

For Cadbury, and other manufacturing companies, to operate they need raw materials, and these raw materials are also produced using corporate real estate. In Cadbury's case the raw materials such as milk, sugar, and cocoa beans are produced in farms and factories around the world which are another form of corporate real estate. Other examples of operational real estate that provide products include wind and solar panel farms that produce power; mines and quarries that produce aggregate; and forests that provide wood and paper.

Manufacturing of products in the UK, and most developed countries, however accounts for only a small part of a country's GDP. GDP is a widely used measure of the size and health of a country's economy[4] and can be estimated by calculating the total value of all goods and services produced in the country. In the UK, service industries employ over 85%[5] of the workforce and account for over 80% of GDP. There are a very wide range of requirements for corporate real estate depending on the service that is provided.

THE PROVISION OF A SERVICE

In Chapter 3, the diversity of real estate was considered. This highlighted the wide range of corporate real estate utilised by organisations. For service industries, these include offices occupied by a range of businesses; hospitals providing health care; laboratories researching illnesses and developing drugs; hotels, leisure centres, restaurants, theatres, and transport networks.

Taking the example of the provision of a transport service in the UK, specifically the London Underground, demonstrates the importance of both operational and corporate real estate to successfully provide this service.

The London Underground, colloquially known as 'the Tube', was the world's first underground railway. The Metropolitan Railway opened on 10 January 1863, transporting both passengers and goods. Today the network transports passengers only. The Metropolitan Railway ran from Paddington to Farringdon stopping at six intermediate stations. At that time, the trains were steam locomotives; therefore the network could not go deep underground. Once electric trains were developed the tunnels went deeper and the underground stations were widely used by Londoners during the world wars for protection from air raids.

The Central London network was built first; then the network extended to Greater London and the surrounding counties. The London Underground currently comprises 11 lines and 270 stations. The impact of the network on real estate has been profound. The Docklands Light Railway, for example, opened in 1987 initially to service the redevelopment of the London docklands resulting in dramatic increases in the value of real estate in that area. The Docklands Light Railway then formed an integral part of the transport service for the 2012 London Olympic and Paralympic Games doubling its passenger numbers to achieve 100 million passenger journeys in the financial year 2012/13.[6]

Today Transport for London (TFL) is the integrated transport authority which is responsible for all transport in London not only the London Underground but also buses, taxis, trams, boats, coaches, and cycling. The transport strategy is developed by the Mayor of

London and has the key objective of encouraging more people to walk, cycle, and use green public transport.[7]

The operational real estate includes the tunnels, stations, land surrounding stations, car parking at some suburban stations, maintenance depots, staff accommodation, railway lines, offices, and residential and retail units. The corporate real estate includes the headquarters office in Docklands and the Surface Transport and Traffic Operations Centre in Blackfriars Road. This wide range of real estate, equating to a 5,700 acre estate[8], makes TFL one of London's biggest landowners.

As with Cadbury, holding real estate as a resource has a cost implication. Although in TFL's case there is not the same focus on profitability, there is a need to mitigate costs where possible to ensure that the estate contributes to the running costs of the service. Like Cadbury, TFL have created a visitor attraction in the form of the London Transport Museum. London Underground has also utilised space on stations and platforms for retail units and advertising hoardings, space above stations for offices and residential purposes, and even used the railway arches supporting the overground railways as industrial units. Property income for the accounting year ending July 2021 was over £100 million.[9] Although this is a very small part of TFL's overall income, it has helped to maximise the value of the operational estate. Historically, real estate that was not required operationally was sold off to bring in capital receipts. More recently, TFL set up a Property Partnerships Framework with a view to maximising the development potential of the operational estate. This involves working with a group of 13 companies and consortia, under a development framework, that is helping to supply homes, offices, and retail spaces on their existing landholdings and providing additional revenue.

For TFL their overarching objective is to use their operational real estate as a resource enabling them to provide a fit-for-purpose public transport network. However, there is the need to try to extract from that estate as much value as possible. In common with many local authorities, they identified that selling off surplus land does not create any income going forward. Developing operational real estate with expert partners can provide a longer-term income stream and help to maintain, and potentially increase, the proportion of organisational value attributable to corporate real estate.

Network Rail, unsurprisingly, takes a similar approach, in terms of maximising income from its operational real estate, as TFL. However, in 2019 it controversially sold its railway arches, on 150 years leases, to Telereal Trillium and Blackstone Property Partners (The Arch Company).[10] The portfolio comprised 5,261 units, mainly converted railway arches, that were not considered essential for running the railway, that is, not operational real estate. These units had been providing an income, in the year before the sale, of £83 million and this was projected to almost double over the ten-year period post-sale. The portfolio was sold for £1.46 billion. The reason the sale was controversial was concerns about existing tenants struggling with uncertainty and affordability. There were also suggestions that the sale involved a short-term gain in exchange for the long-term loss of a valuable asset and potential interference with the effective operation of the railway. However, the sale of 150-year leases, rather than freeholds, means that access for operational reasons, such as maintenance, can be achieved. More recently, to maximise operational real estate income, Network Rail identified the possibility of raising additional revenue from phone lines running adjacent to railway tracks. The right to upgrade cables and build mobile phone masts close to railway lines will be auctioned to private sector bidders and is anticipated to raise up to £1 billion.[11]

Other organisations using operational real estate to provide a service include central government who hold real estate assets such as the parliament buildings, tax and valuation offices, and prisons. Local government is responsible for a wide range of real estate providing services such as libraries, registry offices, leisure centres, town halls, toilets and, of course, housing. Essential services such as fire and rescue, police, education, and healthcare also require operational property to provide their services. Creative ways of both producing income from operational estates and reducing costs are explored by these organisations. One of our local council offices now incorporates a police station and leisure centre, maximising the use of the site and releasing land for redevelopment. Another recent example includes the Ministry of Defence installing solar farms on some of their operational estates to increase the use of renewable energy across the estate, reducing emissions and making sizeable efficiency savings.

The value of real estate that is publicly owned is estimated to be approximately £700 billion;[12] therefore, there has been an increasing focus on ensuring that operational portfolios are used optimally, effectively, efficiently, and are achieving value for money. This is evidenced by, for example, the formation of NHS Property under the Health and Social Care Act 2012. NHS Property currently has a portfolio of over 3,000 properties with a value of over £3 billion which accounts for approximately 10% of the total NHS Estate.[13] NHS Property Services was set up to try to ensure that the estate is run in a cost-effective and efficient way and that it provides the most suitable accommodation from which to dispense high-quality healthcare.

FINANCING OF EXPANSION

As discussed in Chapter 2, real estate provides an asset against which finance can be raised and corporate real estate is no different. Although the primary objective of the real estate as a resource is to facilitate the running of the core business, a strategic approach to corporate real estate can identify ways of optimising its use and contributing towards the profitability of the business.

This can take different forms, but usually involves either using corporate real estate as security to increase borrowing or carrying out sale and leasebacks. A sale and leaseback transaction involves the owner of operational real estate selling their interest to a purchaser and simultaneously completing a second contract to lease it back. This has advantages for both parties. The owner occupier can free up capital, gaining liquidity and realising an immediate cash injection to their business. This also avoids the costs and restrictions associated with conventional financing approaches. The owner occupier can negotiate favourable lease terms building in flexibility by incorporating break clauses, or shorter lease terms. There will also be balance sheet implications as owned properties will be stated as assets whereas some leases may be an operating expense which could have tax benefits. The purchaser can negotiate lease terms, including upward only rent reviews, and benefit from a secure income stream. The purchaser is also able to assess the covenant strength, or financial standing, of the tenant.

There have been a considerable number of sale and leasebacks recently including BP's £250 million sale of its headquarters offices in 2020; Brewdog's £10 million plus sale of its refrigerated beer warehouse; and Sainsbury's and Waitrose's sales of some of their supermarkets for over £50 million and over £70 million, respectively, in 2020. JLL report[14] that 2020 was a record year for disposals of corporate and owner-occupied properties with over 27 billion euros raised in the Europe, Middle East, and Asia (EMEA) region across 580 disposals. It is likely that this may be, in part, due to the Covid-19 pandemic putting companies' balance sheets under pressure and finance becoming more difficult and expensive to obtain. The types of assets undergoing sale and leaseback transactions include supermarkets, retail units, office headquarters, industrial and distribution units, data centres, and healthcare.

The example of Next PLC, a British multi-national clothing and homeware retailer, demonstrates how they have optimised their operational real estate using sale and leasebacks to release capital. A sale and leaseback will occur when a freehold owner occupier sells their freehold interest at the same time as taking an occupational lease. This means that they can remain in the property, operating their business as usual, but they can realise the value of the asset by selling the income stream that their lease will provide to an investor. The business operator can both realise cash and retain the asset that they need to successfully operate their business.

For Next plc, real estate is not necessarily a central part of their business as they carry out a considerable part of their trade online. They do, however, also use retail units, both town centre and out-of-town retail parks, to display their products for sale. They also need warehousing and distribution units to store stock for both the retail units and their online sales.

Next plc carried out a sale and leaseback on their head office and a warehouse complex and reported in their July 2020 half year accounts that this generated an income of £147 million.[15] This surplus cash was used to reduce their net debt. Although details of the leases have not been widely publicised it is likely that they will be long term 20 or 25-year leases that are attractive to institutional investors such as Aviva Investors who purchased the warehouse complex and BA Pension fund who purchased the head office. Both investors would have been attracted by the covenant strength of Next plc who have consistently performed well when benchmarked against their main competitors.

Sale and leasebacks of this type have quite an impact on the balance sheet of the organisation. The International Financial Reporting Standards (IFRS) issued IFRS 16 Leases which came into effect in 2019. This was intended to capture the value and liabilities of leases which were not recognised under the previous accounting rules. A lease now shows on a company's balance sheet as both an asset and a liability whereas previously it was possible to hold what were known as 'operating leases' off balance sheet, showing them only on profit and loss accounts as an outgoing. The change was brought into effect with the aim of making financial status more transparent and achieving easier comparison and benchmarking with other organisations. It makes comparison more straightforward between organisations that borrow to purchase freehold property, making mortgage payments, and those that lease, making rental payments. IFRS 16 only applies to public limited companies (PLCs) and international companies but it is likely to be expanded to apply to small and medium enterprises (SMEs) in the future. The IFRS estimate that, globally, listed companies have approximately $3 trillion worth of lease payments that are recognised under IFRS 16 but were not acknowledged under the previous accounting requirements.[16]

Next plc, like many other operators, identified the amount of capital that was tied up in their corporate real estate and used sale and leasebacks to release some of this capital so that they were then able to invest this back into their core business to achieve the levels of profitability expected by their shareholders. However, not all organisations are primarily motivated by profit. Some organisations have objectives beyond financial ones including strategic objectives such as sustainability, customer satisfaction, meeting stakeholder requirements and more.

PROTECTION AND PRESERVATION OF HERITAGE ASSETS

Some corporate real estate is held for reasons beyond those outlined earlier. Organisations such as the great London estates identify their responsibility for stewardship of their estate as one of their primary functions. This needs to be balanced with their core economic, environmental, and social objectives. The challenge is to combine preservation and protection of their historic estates with enhancements to maximise their potential in the future. One organisation with the primary focus of protection and preservation is the National Trust.

The National Trust is Europe's largest conservation charity. It was founded in 1895 with the aim of not just preserving historical sites but also of opening them up to the public to be more widely enjoyed.

The National Trust is responsible for managing real estate including over 780 miles of coastline, more than 250,000 hectares of land and over 500 historic houses, castles, ancient monuments, nature reserves, parks, and gardens. It also has responsibilities beyond real estate managing various works of art.[17] Although the core purpose of the National Trust is to preserve and protect historic buildings and green spaces in England, Wales, and Northern Ireland, there is still a requirement to create some income, where possible, to assist with the costs of running the charity.

This income is generated from a variety of sources including membership subscriptions, charges to visitors, legacies, donations, real estate income, investment returns, and profits from shops and restaurants. Donations come from various sources such as the National Lottery. In 2020 the total income generated from all sources was £681 million.[18]

Although it could be argued that real estate is held by the National Trust as an operational property, because it charges entry fees for visitors, and maintains the real estate in a condition that continues to attract visitors, creating income from the real estate is not its primary function. Most of the real estate it holds is held 'inalienably'. This means that it cannot be sold, compulsorily purchased, redeveloped, or substantially altered without government consent.

> The core objectives of the National Trust were set out in the National Trust Act 1907[19] which states that it was incorporated
>
> > *for the purposes of promoting the permanent preservation for the benefit of the nation of lands and tenements (including buildings) of beauty or historic interest and as regards lands for the preservation (so far as is practicable) of their natural aspect features and animal and plant life*
>
> Since 1907 various sections have been repealed or annulled by later Acts and Orders but this core purpose remains unchanged.

There are other holders of operational real estate that have a core objective of protecting and preserving the public realm. These include organisations such as English Heritage which is now a charity that cares for over 400 historic buildings, monuments, and sites; like the National Trust, its core focus is on conservation and stewardship.

There are also organisations in the not-for-profit sector that use their operational estate to create income to fund their core purpose. These include charities such as the Church Commissioners whose strategic focus is to support the Church of England's ministry and their £8.7 billion investment portfolio is used to facilitate the Church's growth, contribute to the common good, and reimagine ministry,[20] so it is effectively using real estate as an asset. However, the portfolio also includes corporate real estate in the form of accommodation for the clergy, as well as some historic cathedrals and churches that require preservation. Like the National Trust, the Church Commissioners are a charity and are accountable to the government. However, unlike the National Trust, it is possible for the Church Commissioners to sell closed churches that have a suitable alternative use. One of us previously lived in a converted former chapel and was also involved in leasing a former church as commercial premises. In our local area, former churches are now used as an antique centre and a restaurant.

There are also not-for-profit organisations that use operational real estate to help them to achieve their objectives. Most sizeable national charities such as Oxfam, the RSPCA, and Save the

Children have operational portfolios of charity shops to collect and re-sell second-hand goods; there are also local charities. In one of our hometowns, the local hospice operates three retail units in the town centre, and three out-of-town units selling furniture, clothing, and books. These charities focus on generating trading income from their real estate portfolios.

It can be seen therefore that corporate real estate can be managed to generate trading income, generate investment income, or to preserve and protect real estate with unique historic characteristics. There are however a few organisations that combine all of these objectives and all of the elements outlined in this chapter so far, that is the provision of a product; the provision of a service; the financing of expansion; and the protection and preservation of heritage assets.

HYBRID ORGANISATIONS

The Crown Estate provides an interesting example of a unique organisation that takes an innovative and creative approach to managing a wide variety of real estate interests whilst protecting their legacy and heritage. This organisation uses its real estate holdings to satisfy the full range of purposes of corporate real estate. The challenge for this organisation is to combine the generation of income from assets, with protection of their historic estate, and the operational element of some housing in Windsor Great Park being occupied by the Royal Family.

As outlined in Chapter 2, the Crown Estate creates revenue from its real estate portfolio. Surplus revenue has been paid to the Government since 1760. Under the provisions of the Sovereign Grant Act 2011,[21] the government now allocates a specific proportion of the revenue to the Monarch. The proportion allocated is based on a percentage of the profits made by the Crown Estate.

From this description, it appears that the Crown Estate holds real estate as an asset generating an income from it; therefore it is not operational or corporate real estate. However, it is not that clear-cut. The regional portfolio, comprised of retail and leisure destinations plus industrial and business parks, is an asset primarily held to generate profit. The Central London portfolio also generates profits.

However, there is a purpose, beyond simply a financial one, to holding this estate. Regent Street represents a large part of the Central London portfolio. Regent Street was designed by John Nash and constructed in 1819. The distinctive crescent and facades are all Grade II listed. This has made redevelopment challenging. The Crown Estate has worked hard not only to maximise the income from these assets but also to retain the unique heritage of the area. The requirement for stewardship of these assets takes the real estate beyond simply being an asset.

The portfolio also includes the Windsor Estate which is a working rural estate that includes Windsor Great Park. As a working rural estate, it has tenants and produces not only beef, pork, and lamb but also timber. Again, stewardship is an important consideration here. Countryside and environmental stewardship of rural land is also supported by a series of government grants and subsidies in the UK. The Windsor Estate includes residential property, some occupied by staff and some occupied by members of the Royal Family, which, arguably, makes it more of an operational estate. The Windsor Estate also hosts the annual Royal Windsor Horse Show[22] which was first staged during the second world war to raise income for the war effort and has continued since, although it now raises money for various charities.

The final part of the Crown Estate portfolio is comprised of the seabed and approximately half of the foreshore surrounding England, Wales, and Scotland. The seabed includes the land below the lowest tide out to 12 nautical miles, and the foreshore is the area between high and low tides. Income is generated through the installation of, for example, wind turbines, cables, and pipelines. Although this is an income-producing asset, there are wider stewardship requirements. Creating income from these assets must be achieved within the constraints of limiting any adverse impacts on the environment and preserving the natural beauty of these areas.

From this brief overview, it can be seen that the Crown Estate has a wide-ranging remit that includes operational elements where it provides accommodation for members of the Royal Family; a corporate real estate element where it occupies head offices that are managed by the Crown Estate; and a pure asset element that is designed to maximise income generation, and raise finance to facilitate the diversification of the portfolio.

The Crown Estate is an unusual organisation as it uses its portfolio for all the main purposes of holding corporate real estate outlined, in addition to being an income-producing asset. The estate provides products in the form of timber from Windsor Great Park and meat produced on tenanted farms and sold from the farm shop. It also provides a service in the form of accommodation for some members of the Royal family. It has been used to finance expansion when inviting partners to purchase a share in the Regent Street portfolio enabling it to invest in other real estate to diversify and reduce exposure and risk. Finally, under its stewardship approach it protects, preserves, and enhances the unique real estate within the portfolio.

ASSESSING THE PERFORMANCE OF CORPORATE REAL ESTATE

Real estate as an asset, as discussed in Chapter 4, generally measures performance in financial terms whether that is return on investment, increases in capital value, or some other measure that can be used to compare the asset with alternative investments. There are often other supplemental objectives relating to CSR, customer satisfaction, and employee performance. With corporate real estate there is not the same overriding objective of a financial return. For corporate real estate, the financial issue is more about value for money, making optimal use of resources, and combining effectiveness and efficiency. This raises the question of how these aspects can be measured. The RICS, in their Public Sector Management Guidelines,[23] provides advice on a delivery review that suggests there are four key areas to be reviewed. They are as follows:

- Property asset management processes;
- Performance of property assets in property terms;
- Performance of the property assets in business terms;
- Customer experience.

Although this relates purely to the public sector, these measures are also relevant to the private sector. The difficulty is in applying suitable measurements. For performance in property terms, these could include metrics like property costs as a percentage of total expenditure or per full-time member of staff. For performance in business terms, metrics could include worker and customer satisfaction or productivity levels. Each occupier would need to develop their own balanced scorecard[24] identifying and attempting to quantify non-financial measures in addition to financial ones. Benchmarking performance, over a defined period, is one way of demonstrating performance improvements.

REDUCING THE COSTS OF HOLDING CORPORATE REAL ESTATE

Although the balanced scorecard approach might emphasise objectives beyond purely financial ones, all organisations, private, public, and not-for-profit, will aim to reduce the costs of holding corporate real estate whilst maintaining the service it needs to offer. There are many ways of reducing cost; we have already considered sale and leasebacks which is a way of accessing capital from corporate real estate rather than borrowing from financial institutions. Costs can be reduced by maximising the potential of the estate, whether by selling assets as Network Rail have done, or by implementing sustainable measures, such as installing solar farms as the Ministry of Defence have done. More intensive use can be made of existing real estate by, for example, hot desking to reduce the amount of office space required. Partnerships can be formed as has been seen where coffee shops take space in bookshops and offices rather than having stand-alone units.

The scope for reducing costs and maximising income is limited only by the creativity and innovation of the occupiers and the open-mindedness of their landlords.

THE INCREASING IMPORTANCE OF CORPORATE REAL ESTATE

The global Covid-19 pandemic has highlighted the high proportion of most organisations' costs that are attributable to corporate real estate and the lack of flexibility offered in use and occupation, particularly if leasehold. There has been a shift in focus from real estate being an inflexible factor of production to a service that needs to respond to changing needs. The global pandemic highlighted the need for owner and occupier to work in partnership, rather than in conflict, to maximise profitability for both parties. Tenants were protected from eviction for non-payment of rent during the pandemic due to government action but came up with creative ways of producing some income to keep their businesses going, whether extending production of fashion items to face masks or moving production from perfume to hand sanitiser. Many hospitality units started producing food to take away and some local public houses installed small shops selling items to locals unable to travel.

At the time of writing, many organisations are reducing their office space requirements due to numbers of staff that have become used to working from home during lockdowns. Retail failures have led to an excess of vacant units. Repurposing of these units needs to be considered and creative uses such as former Debenhams units being converted to lecture halls for medical students in Gloucester and a trampolining centre in Wandsworth are being seen.

Corporate real estate will need to continue to evolve to respond to changes in the environment brought about by a combination of factors, most significantly advances in ICT that enable working from anywhere that there is a good WiFi connection, and the Covid-19 pandemic that has impacted on where, and how, we live and work. It is hoped that the relationship between real estate owner and occupier, and other parties involved in the provision and operation of corporate real estate, will continue on a more partnership-orientated basis even after government interventions have come to an end.

NOTES

1 RICS (2018) *Pathway Guide Corporate Real Estate* August Online. Available from: www.rics.org/globalassets/rics-website/media/qualify/pathway-guides/corporate-real-estate-pathway-guide-chartered-rics.pdf
2 Cadbury (undated) Online. Available from: www.cadbury.co.uk/our-story
3 BBC (2021) *More Cadbury Dairy Milk Production to Return to Bournville* 4 February Online. Available from: www.bbc.co.uk/news/uk-england-birmingham-55938419
4 Office for National Statistics (2016) 'What Is GDP?' Online. Available from: www.ons.gov.uk/economy/grossdomesticproductgdp/articles/whatisgdp/2016-11-21
5 Office for National Statistics (2020) 'Employees in the UK: 2019' Online. Available from: www.ons.gov.uk/employmentandlabourmarket/peopleinwork/employmentandemployeetypes/bulletins/businessregisterandemploymentsurveybresprovisionalresults/2019

6   Transport for London (undated) Online. Available from: https://tfl.gov.uk/corporate/about-tfl/culture-and-heritage/londons-transport-a-history/london-underground

7   Greater London Authority (2018) *Mayor's Transport Strategy* March Online. Available from: www.london.gov.uk/what-we-do/transport/our-vision-transport/mayors-transport-strategy-2018?intcmp=46686

8   See note 7

9   Transport for London (2020) *Annual Report and Statement of Accounts 2020/21* −28 July 2021 Online. Available from: https://content.tfl.gov.uk/tfl-annual-report-9-august-2021-acc.pdf

10 National Audit Office (2019) *Network Rail's Sale of Railway Arches* 2 May Online. Available from: www.nao.org.uk/press-release/network-rails-sale-of-railway-arches/

11 Network Rail (2021) 'Network Rail Invites £1bn Private Sector Investment in Telecoms Infrastructure to Upgrade Rail Network for Passengers' *Press Release* Monday 26 April Online. Available from: www.networkrailmediacentre.co.uk/news/network-rail-invites-gbp-1bn-private-sector-investment-in-telecoms-infrastructure-to-upgrade-rail-network-for-passengers

12 RICS (2012) *RICS Public Sector Property Asset Management Guidelines* 2nd Edition Online. Available from: www.rics.org/uk/upholding-professional-standards/sector-standards/real-estate/rics-public-sector-property-asset-management-guidelines-2nd-edition/

13 NHS Property Services (2020) *Annual Report and Accounts 2019/20* Online. Available from: www.property.nhs.uk/media/2937/annual-report-202021-final_comms-version.pdf

14 JLL (2021) *Raising Capital from Corporate Real Estate 2021 Update* Online. Available from: www.jll.co.uk/en/trends-and-insights/research/raising-capital-from-corporate-real-estate

15 Next PLC (2020) *Results for the Half Year Ending July 2020* Online. Available from: www.nextplc.co.uk/~/media/Files/N/Next-PLC-V2/documents/2020/websitepdf-july-20.pdf

16 IFRS (2019) Online. Available from: https://www.ifrs.org/news-and-events/news/2019/01/ifrs-16-is-now-effective/

17 The National Trust (undated) *About the National Trust* Online. Available from: www.nationaltrust.org.uk/features/about-the-national-trust

18 The National Trust (2020) *Annual Report 2019/20* Online. Available from: https://nt.global.ssl.fastly.net/documents/annual-report-201920.pdf

19 The National Trust Acts 1907–1971 (undated) Online. Available from: https://nt.global.ssl.fastly.net/documents/download-national-trust-acts-1907-1971-post-order-2005.pdf

20 The Church Commissioners for England (2020) *Supporting the Work and Mission of the Church of England: The Church Commissioners Annual Report 2019* Online. Available from: www.churchofengland.org/sites/default/files/2020-05/33295_CofE_AR19.pdf

21 HM Treasury (2021) *Sovereign Grant Act 2011: Guidance* Online. Available from: www.gov.uk/government/publications/sovereign-grant-act-2011-guidance/sovereign-grant-act-2011-guidance

22 The Royal Windsor Horse Show (undated) Online. Available from: https://rwhs.co.uk/royal-windsor-horse-show-history/

23 RICS (2012) *RICS Public Sector Property Asset Management Guidelines* 2nd Edition Online. Available from: www.rics.org/uk/upholding-professional-standards/sector-standards/real-estate/rics-public-sector-property-asset-management-guidelines-2nd-edition/

24 Kaplan, R S and Norton, D P (1992) 'The Balanced Scorecard: Measures That Drive Performance' *Harvard Business Review* January–February, 71–79

FURTHER READING

Chang, D (2015) *The Essential Guide to Corporate Real Estate* Atlanta, Georgia: CoreNet Global Inc

Hartzell, D and Baum, A E (2021) *Real Estate Investment* 2nd Edition Chichester, West Sussex: John Wiley & Sons Ltd

Haynes, B P, Nunnington, N, and Eccles, T (2017) *Corporate Real Estate Asset Management: Strategy and Implementation* 2nd Edition Abingdon, Oxon: Routledge

RICS (2012) *RICS Public Sector Property Asset Management Guidelines* 2nd Edition Conventry: RICS

Scarrett, D and Wilcox, J (2018) *Property Asset Management* 4th Edition Abingdon, Oxon: Routledge

6

REAL ESTATE PEOPLE

WHY DO WE NEED TO THINK ABOUT ROLES IN REAL ESTATE?

Real estate encompasses a wide range of valuable asset types so the study of real estate and professional practice within the sector requires extensive technical knowledge. However, real estate is also a 'people role' involving teams of specialist advisers; hence the Royal Institution of Chartered Surveyors (RICS), for example, assesses candidates on their understanding of communication and teamworking. For practitioners, awareness of the limits of one's own competency and knowing when to seek specialist advice is essential. This requires knowledge of the roles of other real estate professionals to understand how their contribution to the overall outcome is necessary to maximise efficiency and effectiveness.

When undertaking assessments or working in class, students may be asked to assume a role; you may need to imagine that you are a graduate surveyor advising the client on legal issues with a property, or an agent preparing a marketing report. Real estate students may therefore find it helpful to understand the application of their studies if they have an overview of professional roles and how these might relate to one another. For example, a common residential property transaction – the sale of a flat in a block – may require input from estate agents, valuers, building surveyors, legal professionals, the freeholder (landlord) and the freeholder's managers, and letting agents if the flat is sub-let.

We can see from this example that dealings with property can involve many people, whose roles complement one another to give

DOI: 10.1201/9781003155256-6

effect to the transaction or to achieve the client's objectives. In some instances, however, roles will be adversarial, for example valuers representing the landlord and tenant in a rent review or lease extension valuation may disagree on the value, in which case the matter may need to be referred to a dispute resolution process.

Professionals and stakeholders engaged in the real estate sector must comply with the law, the professional standards that apply to them, and the membership requirements of their professional bodies. These may encompass technical knowledge, a requirement to undertake continuing professional training or development (CPD), ethical standards, and conduct rules. Expertise must extend not just to their area of practice but also to general business requirements – knowledge of professional indemnity insurance (PII), negligence, employment and contract law, health and safety, anti-money-laundering requirements, complaints handling, and consumer protection legislation are examples. Students need to recognise the mandatory standards and the guidance that apply to real estate professionals; this information may be relevant to assignments, which require awareness of practice standards and the following sections should be read with this in mind.

Furthermore, real estate is an evolving sector; Chapter 14 will help you understand some of the current issues affecting real estate people. Chapter 3 provides more detail on the types of assets real estate people may be involved with.

CHARTERED SURVEYORS

The RICS is a professional body with over 134,000 trainees and professionals working in the built environment[1] so we will begin by considering the role of chartered surveyors.

WHO ARE THEY?

Chartered surveyors have attained Membership of the RICS (MRICS) having successfully completed the Assessment of Professional Competence (APC).

Qualification as a chartered surveyor requires a combination of experience, academic study, and professional training. Eligibility depends on whether the candidate has an RICS-accredited degree, a non-accredited degree, is working at a senior leadership level, or is a specialist or academic.

The RICS also offers an entry-level qualification conferring Associate status (AssocRICS). This requires experience, with or without an academic qualification, and provides a 'stand-alone' RICS qualification that may be of particular interest to those starting out in their careers. The associate qualification can also provide a stepping-stone to full MRICS designation subject to further training and experience.

Fellowship of the RICS (FRICS) is the highest level of membership, awarded to applicants who have made a particular contribution to the profession. Candidates need to demonstrate the required number of specified characteristics, for example service to the RICS, advancing or sharing knowledge or acting as a role model to others.[2]

It is also possible to become a student member of the RICS.

You can find out more information on the different levels of membership and the routes to becoming a chartered surveyor on the RICS website.

WHAT DO CHARTERED SURVEYORS DO?

Within the three RICS membership designations there are a multitude of competencies and specialisms. Surveyors will have selected a 'pathway' when training – for example, residential, valuation, commercial, building surveying – to reflect their knowledge and experience and their area of practice.

When you read the following sections, remember that chartered surveyors' work may encompass some of the other roles we consider: a chartered surveyor may work in the commercial or residential sectors and may be, for example, a letting agent, estate agent, property manager, valuer or building surveyor, or may fulfil more than one of these roles.

HOW ARE CHARTERED SURVEYORS REGULATED?

The RICS is the professional body that oversees the qualification of individual surveyors and the many practice standards that apply to them. This involvement begins at a very early stage of training;

RICS-accredited real estate degrees are a key component of education in the sector and often form the foundation of a career in real estate. The RICS requires members at all levels (AssocRICS, MRICS, and FRICS) to comply with its ethical standards and to undertake regular training in ethics. In addition, members must comply with conduct rules; breach of the RICS rules can lead to disciplinary action.

So far, we have considered individual chartered surveyors. However, the RICS also regulates firms of surveyors, which must comply with conduct rules for firms. RICS-regulated firms are also subject to audit (a detailed review of the firm's compliance with rules and standards) and could be disciplined in the event of non-compliance.

The RICS is a self-regulating professional body, which means that the organisation is responsible for setting its standards and for disciplining members who do not meet those standards. This contrasts with sectors in which standards and compliance are overseen by an external regulator. For example, the Financial Conduct Authority (FCA), which regulates the financial services industry in the UK. Whilst it is mandatory for some property professionals to join an ombudsman (redress) scheme, others may be able to join voluntarily.

WHAT LAWS AND PROFESSIONAL GUIDANCE APPLY TO CHARTERED SURVEYORS?

RICS documents are divided into:

- Mandatory standards and professional statements;
- Codes of practice, which may be mandatory or are recommended good practice;
- Guidance, which again recommends best practice.

It is important to understand that although compliance with recommended best practice may not be mandatory, if a surveyor is accused of negligence a court may take into account whether the surveyor followed best practice. Therefore, adhering to all standards and guidance can offer a defence to a negligence claim.

Students and trainee surveyors will need to be familiar with the specific laws, standards, and guidance that apply to study modules and to areas of professional practice as these may vary. Each RICS document defines its status as mandatory or best practice within the document. The use of 'must' in the document indicates a mandatory requirement; 'should' indicates best practice; other content is for information only. We find isurv extremely helpful; this is the RICS online information resource, which contains detailed guidance. Do look at isurv if your university or employer provides you with access. If you do not have an isurv subscription, much of the information is publicly available if you search online.

You can find out more information about chartered surveyors on the RICS website.

BUILDING SURVEYORS

WHO ARE THEY?

Building surveyors are specialist professionals who carry out detailed inspections and investigations of buildings to assess condition and identify defects. Many building surveyors will be RICS members, whether Associates, Members, or Fellows. There are other professional organisations for building surveyors; see the links to the Chartered Institute of Building (CIOB), Sava, and the Residential Property Surveyors Association (RPSA) at the end of this chapter.

WHAT DO BUILDING SURVEYORS DO?

Building surveyors undertake detailed inspections and investigations to assess the condition of a building. Surveys are carried out to different levels depending on the type of property, the purpose of the survey, and the needs of the client. For RICS surveyors, there are three levels, with level 1 being the most basic, level 2 intermediate, and level 3 the most detailed level of inspection and report. The CIOB, Sava, and RPSA surveyors also provide surveys – again, you can find out more via the links at the end of this chapter.

Typically, the surveyor will take a three-stage approach when investigating and reporting on à property defect:

- Diagnosis – what is the defect?
- Prognosis – what will happen if the defect is not repaired?
- Remedy – how can the defect be rectified?

However, the role of the building surveyor is not limited to the surveys mentioned earlier. Building surveyors may, for example, carry out snagging surveys for new-build homes, identifying defects to be reported to the developer for correction under warranty. They may prepare building maintenance programmes, manage construction and maintenance projects, deal with Party Wall etc. Act 1996 requirements and carry out schedules of dilapidations at lease expiry or schedules of condition at lease commencement.

It follows that building surveyors require an in-depth understanding of the construction techniques and materials used for different types of buildings and the types of defects – rising damp, penetrating damp, wet rot, dry rot, and cracking for example – that may afflict them. This is known as building pathology. Location will influence a building surveyor's knowledge, as it will reflect local building characteristics, which vary geographically. We have dealt with Regency- and Georgian-era properties concentrated in one town centre and period limestone buildings typical of another, nearby, town. Each type of building construction has its own maintenance requirements and common defects. Some specific construction defects even have their own name drawn from the location they are commonly found in. We came across Regent Street Disease which, although not only found in Regent Street, London, is common in the Portland stone-clad buildings found in this street. It relates to the corrosion-related damage to steel frames in stone or other masonry clad buildings.

Technical knowledge must be complemented by attention to detail and good observational skills to spot defects and to follow the trail of suspicion to identify the source of a problem. For example, the point at which rainwater penetrates a building may be some distance from the point at which the leak becomes apparent – hence a roofing defect may allow water to track from the roof through the structure of the building to show visible water ingress some metres away.

Building surveyors involved in construction and maintenance projects will need to understand procurement procedures, health and safety requirements, and contract law and to be familiar with construction contracts such as the Joint Contracts Tribunal (JCT) suite of contracts. The Building Research Establishment (BRE) is a useful source of training, guidance, and information on standards relevant to building surveyors – you can find links to the JCT and BRE at the end of this chapter.

HOW ARE BUILDING SURVEYORS REGULATED?

Self-regulation applies, so a surveyor will be subject to the membership rules, practice standards, and disciplinary procedures of their professional organisation. The RICS licenses surveyors with the necessary training and experience to carry out surveys. If a surveyor is also carrying out a valuation, the surveyor must also be a member of the RICS Valuer Registration Scheme (see the section on Valuers in this chapter for more information).

WHAT LAWS AND PROFESSIONAL GUIDANCE APPLY TO BUILDING SURVEYORS?

Building surveyors need to be aware of a range of laws: the Building Act 1984 (which enables the creation of Building Regulations); the Construction (Design and Management) Regulations 2015; the Party Wall etc. Act 1996; and the Control of Asbestos Regulations 2012 are examples although this is, by no means, an exhaustive list.

The RICS publishes an array of guidance and practice standards to assist building surveyors, for example:

- Surveys of Residential Property 3rd edition reissue 2017;
- Home survey standard 1st edition 2019;
- Party wall legislation and procedure 7th edition August 2019.

These are frequently updated to reflect new construction techniques and legislation so the RICS website should be checked for updates.

ESTATE AGENTS

WHO ARE ESTATE AGENTS?

Estate agents are those professionals dealing with the buying and selling of real estate on behalf of someone else. An estate agent might be a chartered surveyor; 'purchase and sale' is one of the recognised competencies for RICS training and assessment. Alternatively, an estate agent might have an NAEA Propertymark qualification.

The 'High Street' estate agent is still very common, offering a local presence and market knowledge, with a physical shop front displaying property for sale. However, recent years have seen the emergence of online agents offering a remote, virtual service.

WHAT DO ESTATE AGENTS DO?

The Estate Agents Act 1979 Section 1(1) defines estate agency as

> *things done by any person in the course of a business (including a business in which he is employed) pursuant to instructions received from another person (in this section referred to as 'the client') who wishes to dispose of or acquire an interest in land.*[3]

Agency may relate to commercial or residential properties.

Typically, an estate agent will act on behalf of their client seller and will:

- Carry out a market appraisal to advise the seller on the sale price, the target market, and the marketing strategy;
- Advise on the most appropriate method of sale, for example, private treaty, auction, or formal or informal tender;
- Market the property;
- Conduct viewings, which may be virtual or in person;
- Negotiate with prospective buyers;
- Conduct the auction or tender process if appropriate;
- Liaise between the parties until completion of the sale has taken place.

Marketing properties and negotiating between the buyer and the seller to complete the transaction is a pressured role, being 'sales-driven' and agents will have targets to meet, for example, a minimum number of sales completed in a month and a minimum number of new instructions gained. Agents need to know their local market and they need to be able to judge the appropriate asking price, a realistic sales price to achieve during negotiations and the appropriate method of sale in order to meet the client's objectives as regarding price and timescale. They also need to be able to communicate and negotiate with the parties during a sometimes very challenging and stressful process (see Chapter 10 for more details).

HOW ARE THEY REGULATED?

Estate agency is regulated by the Estate Agents Act 1979, which contains detailed provisions relating to the banning of unfit persons from carrying out estate agency work, handling client money, conflicts of interest, and redress schemes. The Act is enforced by the National Trading Standards Estate and Letting Agency Team (NTSELAT) led by Powys County Council, with Trading Standards departments of local authorities operating locally. This regulation does not cover the full extent of the agent's role and there is no requirement for licensing or qualifications, but the regulation of property agents is under review by the government and this may change. RICS and NAEA Propertymark members must comply with the requirements of their professional body.

By law, estate agent businesses must join an ombudsman service. This is a redress scheme authorised by NTSELAT under the Consumers, Estate Agents and Redress Act 2007, which offers redress in relation to consumer complaints about estate agents. The two approved schemes are the Property Ombudsman and the Property Redress Scheme. Estate agents must join one of them.

WHAT LAWS AND PROFESSIONAL GUIDANCE APPLY TO ESTATE AGENTS?

As we have seen, the Estate Agents Act 1979 is the key piece of legislation relating to the practice of estate agency. The RICS produces professional standards and guidance, including these mandatory professional statements with which RICS members must comply:

- Real Estate Agency and Brokerage 3rd edition August 2016;
- UK residential real estate agency 6th edition September 2017 (known as the Blue Book);
- UK commercial real estate agency 1st edition October 2016.

There may be more than one guidance document for each area of professional practice, and this can initially be confusing and overwhelming. It helps to understand that some guidance applies globally as the RICS is an international organisation, some will apply to a specific region – the UK, for example – and some will apply to specific specialisms. There is additional legislation on areas covering consumer protection and money laundering which estate agents need to comply with (see Chapters 10 and 14).

REAL ESTATE DEVELOPERS AND INVESTORS

WHO ARE THEY?

'Bricks and mortar' are generally regarded as a good investment in the UK, with its long history of real estate investment. Ownership of real estate has evolved over centuries, with monarchs conferring land on loyal followers who gained great wealth from the income that these estates generated as discussed in Chapter 2. The concept of the 'great estate' still exists today with some large swathes of land and buildings owned by both very old 'traditional' estates and more modern investors. Examples of the traditional estate include the Crown Estate, and the Grosvenor, Cadogan, Howard de Walden and Portman estates. The purpose of these estates varies but might provide income for family trusts, charities, or in the case of the Crown Estate, the Treasury.

Other more modern investors include Soho Estates, which owns real estate in the Soho area of London, pension funds that have started to invest in the residential sector having historically been investors in commercial property, and large regeneration projects such as at Kings Cross or the Queen Elizabeth Olympic Park in London. There is a crossover between property developers and investors, in that developers may acquire a site for redevelopment, but retain a long-term interest in the development, for investment purposes. For example, a developer may sell individual residential units on long leases and retain the freehold of the development to obtain an income from the ground rents payable under those leases.

We include landlords within this category, as their role will usually involve an element of investment in, and development of, real estate.

There are many different types of smaller investors in real estate. The 'accidental landlord', for example, may have decided to rent out their former home perhaps because the sales market is poor and they will be unable to realise enough capital on the sale, or perhaps they are moving away temporarily and want to have the option to return to their home. In these cases, the property becomes an income-generating asset that also provides a capital investment, but it was not originally acquired for this purpose. Other investors will have decided to invest in real estate as it can offer a capital gain as property prices rise over time, combined with a rental income. They may invest in residential buy-to-let properties or in office, retail, or industrial properties, student lets or holiday properties, for example.

WHAT DO PROPERTY DEVELOPERS AND INVESTORS DO?

Investors in real estate acquire land and property for investment purposes. Their objective is to generate an income from ground rents or market rents via a real estate asset which is likely to increase in capital value, or, alternatively, to make a profit from the sale of the asset. Typically, investors will become landlords in order to receive these rents from commercial lets, short-term residential lets such as Assured Shorthold Tenancies, or long residential leases for which the tenant not only has paid a premium (a full market price) but also pays a ground rent which will usually be a relatively low sum.

Investor landlords can minimise their liabilities and responsibilities to maximise the return they receive on their investment if tenants are responsible for the building maintenance and management costs, either directly or indirectly if they pay a service charge. It is usual for tenants under long residential leases to pay a service charge to cover these costs. Commercial tenants may take on a full repairing and insuring (FRI) lease, in which they are directly responsible for all maintenance, whether via a service charge or organised individually, or they may only be responsible for internal, non-structural, repairs under an internal repairing lease.

Landlords who let residential properties under Assured and Assured Shorthold Tenancies have statutory obligations regarding repairs and cannot delegate these functions to the tenant; these costs therefore need to be factored into the overall viability of the investment. It follows, therefore, that some landlords will be closely involved in the management and maintenance of their asset; they may do this themselves or they may appoint an agent to act on their behalf.

These investors also need to monitor their tenants' compliance with the lease terms to ensure the value of the asset is maintained. For example, a schedule of dilapidations may need to be drawn up to identify the works the tenant must do at the end of their lease if the tenant has repairing responsibilities under the lease.

Real estate developers acquire sites to develop for profit whether small or large scale. Examples include brownfield sites (unused former industrial or commercial sites) for renovation and sale or rental, greenfield sites acquired for development into housing, industrial estates, or business parks, and existing buildings for refurbishment or conversion to a different use – perhaps commercial to residential use.

Developers need to be able to identify development opportunities, be sufficiently financially astute to assess the level of risk, understand the property market in order to identify the target market, and have the expertise and funding to execute the project from start to finish. Developers will typically engage a wide range of professionals to achieve these aims: building surveyors; planning consultants; health and safety advisers; quantity surveyors; architects; trades people; estate and letting agents and property managers to name a few.

Similarly, investors need to be able to identify an investment opportunity that meets their objectives, whether this is to develop the asset to sell at a profit over a relatively short period of time or to gain a rental income from a long-term investment. They must therefore understand the financing and tax treatment of a real estate investment, be able to budget for maintenance and identify target markets, whether this is for sale or rental.

Identifying a good investment and retaining the income potential from an asset over a long period of time involves keeping up to date with market trends and the economic, social, political, technological, environmental, and legal drivers affecting real estate. Examples include changes in demographics, as evidenced by the UK's aging population giving rise to a need for retirement housing, and the expansion of the student market in recent years. Investors will reflect and adapt to these trends to minimise risk and maximise the return on their investment. Chapter 4 provides additional information on the investment market.

Investment in real estate is not generally regulated, but there are some exceptions. In Wales, residential landlords must register with Rent Smart Wales. In England, landlords of larger HMOs must be licensed by the local authority. An HMO is a shared dwelling, in which each tenant will have their own bedroom but will share facilities such as kitchen and, possibly, bathroom. Mandatory licensing applies to HMOs with five or more people in two or more households. Local authorities also have powers to extend licensing to landlords of smaller HMOs and individual lets, called selective and additional licensing schemes.

The National Residential Landlords Association (NRLA) runs a voluntary accreditation scheme for members who complete the required training and agree to comply with the Association's rules.

WHAT LAWS AND PROFESSIONAL GUIDANCE APPLY TO PROPERTY DEVELOPERS AND INVESTORS?

Investors must comply with the laws that apply to their properties and to the purpose for which the property is used. It is common for investors to be landlords, buying properties to let, whether under commercial leases, long residential leases, or short-term residential lets. You can find more information on the guidance applicable to lettings in the Letting Agent section of this chapter, and on landlord and tenant law in Chapter 8.

LETTING AGENTS

WHO ARE THEY?

Some letting agents will be chartered surveyors or they might have a qualification from another organisation, such as ARLA Propertymark or the Chartered Institute of Housing (CIH). The Institute of Residential Property Management (IRPM) also offers a build-to-rent qualification, for individuals engaged in this emerging sector.

As is the case with estate agents discussed earlier in this chapter, the 'High Street' letting agent is still very common, offering a local presence with a visible shop front and prominent displays of property available to let. However, recent years have seen the emergence of online agents offering a remote, virtual service. Some letting agents have also specialised in, for example, student lets.

The term 'letting agent' tends to be used in relation to residential lets. However, some agents will deal with commercial letting, covering offices, retail units, and industrial properties as well as mixed-use sites. These are commonly known as either commercial agents or, more specifically, office agents, retail agents, or industrial agents.

Letting agents act on behalf of the landlord and typically offer a choice of services from marketing the premises and finding a tenant, to setting up the tenancy, to full tenancy management. Their role might include:

- Carrying out a market appraisal for the landlord to advise on the rent, the target market and the marketing strategy;
- Marketing the property;
- Conducting viewings, which in response to the Covid-19 pandemic may be virtual or may be in person;
- Obtaining references for the tenant;
- Arranging a guarantee if required;
- In the case of residential tenancies, carrying out 'Right to Rent' checks under the Immigration Act 2014 to ensure the prospective tenant's immigration status allows the tenant to rent a property;
- Preparing the tenancy agreement and arranging signature;
- Arranging preparation of an inventory (possibly by an independent inventory clerk);
- Collecting the deposit and, for residential lets, registering the deposit with the appropriate deposit protection service;
- Managing the check-in when the tenancy starts;
- Collecting the rent and carrying out rent reviews;
- Arranging repairs and safety checks, for example, gas and electrical safety inspections;
- Monitoring compliance with tenant covenants and carrying out periodic property inspections;
- Managing the end of the tenancy, serving notice to terminate the tenancy if instructed to do so and, if required, participating

in eviction proceedings. End of tenancy tasks also include checking the condition of the property, obtaining all keys, and arranging return of the deposit after any agreed deductions.

Like estate agency sales discussed earlier in this chapter, marketing properties to let and finding tenants is also a pressured role, being very 'sales-driven' with targets to meet, for example a minimum number of lets completed in a month and a minimum number of new instructions gained. Letting agents therefore need to be good salespeople, whilst the management of lettings requires communication and negotiation skills, overlapping with the role of the property manager discussed under the separate heading.

Letting agents are instructed by the landlord; therefore, the landlord is the agent's client and the agent will owe a duty of care to that client. However, the end user is the tenant who lives in the landlord's property or runs their business from the landlord's premises, so the agent must be able to deal with potential conflicting interests. Sometimes those interests will coincide; for example, it will be in the interests of both the landlord and tenant to carry out essential repairs. Sometimes, however, the landlord may not want to pay for repairs or improvements that the tenant requests and this can cause conflict. The letting agent needs to understand the landlord's legal obligations regarding maintenance in order to advise the landlord and to deal with the tenant. The agent also needs to exercise their judgement to decide when specialist advice is needed, for example, legal advice in the case of evictions. During the Covid-19 pandemic, current at the time of writing, this task has been complicated by legal changes making the eviction of tenants more difficult to achieve.

HOW ARE LETTING AGENTS REGULATED?

At the time of writing, in 2021, residential letting agents are partially regulated in that the National Trading Standards Estate and Letting Agency Team (NTSELAT) enforces compliance with the Tenant Fees Act 2019 (see later for more information on the Act). Bristol City Council leads enforcement, which is carried out by local Trading Standards departments.

We mention that residential letting agents are partially regulated. This is because although there is some independent enforcement by

NTSELAT, there is currently no legal requirement for these agents to be licensed or qualified.

However, there are professional organisations that support member agents to maintain standards and compliance. Both ARLA Propertymark and the RICS offer qualifications relevant to lettings and as we have said, many chartered surveyors work in the lettings sector. RICS training and assessment covers several competencies that apply to letting – the principal competency is Leasing and Letting but others are also relevant – Inspection, Market Appraisal, Valuation, Measurement, Communication and Negotiation, and Legal and Regulatory Compliance, for instance. RICS Regulated Firms dealing with lettings must also comply with RICS standards and conduct rules.

Following the Enterprise and Regulatory Reform Act 2013, residential letting agents are required to join an ombudsman scheme offering free redress to consumers if the client is dissatisfied with the outcome of a complaint made to the agent regarding their service. There are two ombudsman schemes authorised by the Ministry of Housing, Communities and Local Government – The Property Ombudsman and the Property Redress Scheme – and agents must join one of them.

In Chapter 14 we will look at the regulation of residential property agents. At the time of writing there are government plans to introduce licensing, minimum standards of training and qualification, a code of practice and an independent regulator to enforce standards.

In Wales, the Rent Smart Wales training, registration, and licensing scheme applies to landlords and letting agents.

Chartered surveyors are a significant presence in the commercial sector and are subject to RICS self-regulation, with an obligation to comply with RICS standards and conduct rules.

WHAT LAWS AND PROFESSIONAL GUIDANCE APPLY TO THEM?

Letting agents need to comply with:

- The law relating to agents' own business practices, which are particularly rigorous in the residential sector: agents must belong to a client money protection scheme (this reimburses clients whose money is misappropriated by an agent), and the Tenant Fees Act 2019 (TFA) limits the type of payments that a residential tenant can be required to make. Following the TFA, landlords and agents can only charge tenants for certain authorised payments such as a default fee if the rent is paid late. Landlords and agents cannot charge tenants any fees relating to the creation or renewal of the tenancy or for obtaining references. The introduction of the TFA resulted in the loss of a significant income stream for agents who had previously charged fees to both landlords and tenants. Landlords have also been affected, potentially increasing costs, as they now have to absorb expenses such as tenant reference fees.

- Legislation covering the lettings that they arrange and manage, for example regarding the registration and protection of deposits received from residential tenants via a government-approved deposit protection scheme.

Professional guidance is available via member organisations such as the RICS and ARLA Propertymark. In the residential sector, the Private Rented Sector Code of Practice 2015 is approved by several industry bodies and the RICS publishes UK residential real estate agency 6th edition 2017; compliance with this is mandatory for RICS members acting for landlords and tenants.

For chartered surveyors dealing with commercial lettings, the RICS Code for leasing business premises 1st edition February 2020 is key – compliance with some sections of this is mandatory, other parts outline best practice guidance. Other RICS documents include Service charges in commercial property 1st edition September 2018. The key piece of legislation for commercial agents is the Landlord and Tenant Act 1954, which creates security of tenure for business tenants, prescribes procedures for the termination and renewal of commercial leases, and stipulates the grounds on which a commercial landlord can gain possession of their premises when the lease ends. You can read more about this in Chapter 8.

PROPERTY AND ASSET MANAGERS

WHO ARE THEY?

'Property manager' is an 'umbrella' term which covers those professionals engaged in the management of a wide range of real estate. This is reflected in the qualifications that a property manager might hold; a residential property manager might be a chartered surveyor, or possess CIH, IRPM, or ARLA Propertymark qualifications, for example.

WHAT IS THE DIFFERENCE BETWEEN A PROPERTY AND AN ASSET MANAGER?

A property manager is generally considered to be the individual directly responsible for managing a specific property, or group of properties, for the owner. An asset manager however takes a broader role considering the property in relation to whether it should be bought, sold, or works carried out to add value to it. The asset manager will consider how individual properties fit into an overall property portfolio developing long-term plans for its future retention or disposal. Larger individual properties might also have a building manager permanently based in the building with responsibility for the day-to-day running of the building, usually reporting to the property manager.

Property managers are often known by the collective term 'managing agents' when the property management work is subcontracted to a specialist company. Asset management is more commonly carried out in-house although it can be outsourced. Building management can be either in-house or outsourced.

WHAT DO PROPERTY MANAGERS DO?

Property managers may be directly employed by the owner of the real estate asset under management, or they may manage a property as the owner's agent.

Within the commercial sector a property manager might manage retail units (shopping centres or retail parks for example), industrial estates, or offices. In the residential sector they might manage blocks of flats, retirement homes, private sector rentals, social housing, or student accommodation, for example. The role of a property manager covers:

- Managing finances including preparation of service charge budgets, collecting rents and service charges and arranging preparation of annual accounts;

- Arranging insurance, reactive repairs, and cyclical maintenance;
- Appointing contractors (e.g. cleaners and gardeners) to ensure a satisfactory and cost-effective service;
- Arranging servicing of installations such as fire alarm systems and lifts;
- Compliance with safety requirements such as fire risk assessments and asbestos surveys;
- Compliance with lease covenants;
- Obtaining landlord's consent where required, for example to alterations or to sub-lets;
- Liaising between all parties including landlord, tenants, subtenants, and contractors to ensure the smooth running of the site.

As we have seen, real estate practice usually requires a mix of technical knowledge and communication skills and the property manager is no exception. Key to this role is the ability to read, understand, and interpret the legal language contained in leases and registers of title, to understand the respective rights and obligations of landlords and tenants. A property manager must also be able to budget and if they manage residential flats, they need an understanding of the complex law relating to service charges. They need good financial awareness in order to manage cash flow and they need to follow the statutory consultation procedure that can apply to major building works.

A manager needs to know the limits of their own and their team's expertise and be prepared to appoint and work alongside other professionals when needed. This bringing-together of different individuals with complementary skills is a fundamental aspect of property management. Property managers therefore need to work alongside a wide range of specialist advisers and contractors. Examples of these include:

- Building surveyors to assess the condition of a property for example to enable the manager to plan a maintenance programme and to check compliance with repairing covenants under a lease;
- Legal professionals, when managed properties are bought and sold or perhaps if legal action needs to be taken in relation to a breach of a covenant in a lease;

- Letting and estate agents, for example if units within a managed property are sublet or sold;
- Energy performance assessors, fire risk assessors, health and safety advisers, and asbestos surveyors to meet legal obligations;
- Insurers;
- A whole range of maintenance and servicing contractors; builders, plumbers, electricians, lift contractors, cleaners, gardeners, and caretakers to name a few;
- Property managers will also form the link between asset managers and individual building managers.

HOW ARE THEY REGULATED?

Property management is unregulated at the time of writing but as we have seen earlier individual property managers may possess industry qualifications and the organisations that employ them may belong to trade or professional bodies such as the RICS, ARLA Propertymark, the Association of Residential Managing Agents (ARMA), and the Association of Retirement Housing Managers (ARHM). These industry bodies have their own conduct rules and disciplinary processes and following the Enterprise and Regulatory Reform Act 2013, residential letting and managing agents must belong to a redress scheme.

WHAT LAWS AND PROFESSIONAL GUIDANCE APPLY TO THEM?

The laws and guidance that apply to property managers will depend on the type of real estate that they manage.

In the residential sector the following apply:

- RICS Service charge residential management Code 3rd edition 2016;
- RICS UK residential real estate agency 6th edition September 2017 (also known as the Blue Book);
- RICS Real estate management 3rd edition October 2016 (this also applies to the management of commercial property);
- Private Rented Sector Code of Practice 2015;
- ARHM Codes of Practice for England and Wales;

- Legislation includes the Housing Acts 1988, 1996 and 2004, the Homes (Fitness for Human Habitation) Act 2018, the Commonhold and Leasehold Reform Act 2002 and the Landlord and Tenant Acts 1985 and 1987.

And in the commercial sector:

- RICS Service charges in commercial property 1st edition September 2018;
- RICS Real estate management 3rd edition October 2016 (known as the Blue Book this also applies to the management of residential property);
- RICS Commercial Property Management in England and Wales, 2nd edition 2011;
- The Landlord and Tenant Act 1954 creates security of tenure for commercial leases; commercial agents need to be familiar with this key statute;

Chapters 8 and 13 contain more information on the law applicable to property management.

VALUERS

WHO ARE THEY?

Valuers are those RICS-qualified professionals who provide valuations of real estate for specified purposes, typically for sale, rental, lease extension, taxation, or mortgage. Valuers may be AssocRICS, MRICS, and FRICS but regardless of their level of RICS membership the valuer must also meet the RICS requirements for Registered Valuers, which we discuss further later.

WHAT DO VALUERS DO?

Valuers provide an estimated value of an asset on a specific date for a specific purpose, applying methods and bases of valuation in line with legal and regulatory requirements and professional guidance. These are explained in more detail later and in Chapters 11 and 12. Valuers practise across the real estate sector, and may specialise in residential, commercial, or agricultural real estate. They may also further specialise within their area of practice, for example office, retail, or industrial properties within the commercial sector, and secured lending valuations or lease-extension valuations within the residential sector.

The valuer must establish the client's objectives in order to provide the appropriate valuation report. The client may be, for example, a landlord or tenant seeking a rent review, a prospective purchaser, or a lender. The report will explain the rationale behind the value reached by the valuer; it will state any assumptions that the valuer has made in order to reach this value and it will make clear any material valuation uncertainty so that the client can make an informed decision as to whether to proceed with the transaction.

Valuation is one of the RICS pathways for qualification as a chartered surveyor, reflecting the skills and training required. A valuer must be observant and thorough when inspecting properties as part of the valuation. They must also have a good understanding of building pathology in order to identify defects that might affect value and those defects that may need to be referred to a building surveyor or other specialist (e.g. a structural engineer) for further investigation before a value can be established. Valuers also need to be able to measure a property accurately, applying International Property Measurement Standards (IPMS).

Some areas of valuation (e.g. lease extension and enfranchisement valuations) may lead to negotiation with other valuers to agree a value to enable a transaction to proceed – negotiation is another key RICS competency.

HOW ARE VALUERS REGULATED?

Valuers are regulated via the RICS Valuer Registration Scheme but are not required to join an ombudsman. Registered Valuers are those valuers who meet the RICS requirements for valuer competency and have signed up to the RICS's Valuer Registration Scheme.

WHAT LAWS AND PROFESSIONAL GUIDANCE APPLY TO VALUERS?

The key document for Registered Valuers is RICS Valuation – Global Standards, known as the Red Book, and the UK National

Supplement. These comprehensive and detailed documents combine mandatory standards and best practice guidance for a wide range of valuation types.

The RICS also publishes a whole raft of other guidance to assist valuers, for example:

- Comparable evidence in real estate valuation 1st edition October 2019;
- Bank lending valuations and mortgage lending value 1st edition March 2018;
- Valuation of residential leasehold properties for secured lending purposes England and Wales 1st edition May 2021;
- The valuation of buy-to-let and HMO properties 1st edition December 2016;
- Valuation of individual new-build homes 3rd edition December 2019;
- Reinstatement cost assessment of buildings 3rd edition February 2018.

Case law and legislation is also relevant to valuation. Analysis of case law is not the purpose of this chapter, but we will mention some key cases as they help explain the role of a valuer. *Smith v Bush 1990* and *Harris v Wyre Forest District Council 1990* confirm that a valuer carrying out a valuation for a lender also owes a duty of care to the borrower in an ordinary residential transaction. This principle contrasts with *Scullion v Bank of Scotland Plc 2011*, which established that a valuer carrying out a valuation for a lender does not owe a duty of care to the borrower in a buy-to-let transaction, as this is a commercial – rather than residential – transaction.

Some valuers might carry out statutory valuations for taxation purposes, for example Inheritance Tax Valuations (commonly known as probate valuations) and Capital Gains Tax valuations. Valuers need to understand the law as it applies to these; Section 160 of the Inheritance Tax Act 1984 and Section 272 of the Taxation of Chargeable Gains Act 1992 provide definitions of market value for these taxation purposes.

You will find more useful information on valuation in Chapters 11 and 12. Some current issues covered in Chapter 14 are particularly relevant to valuation as, for example fire safety has severely affected the valuation of high-rise buildings following the Grenfell Tower fire.

LEGAL PROFESSIONALS

Legal professionals perform a key role in real estate. They may be:

- Solicitors, who provide legal advice to clients and may represent them in legal proceedings. The Law Society is the professional body supporting solicitors and regulation is carried out by the Solicitors Regulation Authority;
- Barristers specialise in advocacy in court. The Bar Councils are the professional bodies for barristers, who are regulated by the Bar Standards Board;
- Legal executives and paralegals possess Chartered Institute of Legal Executives (CILEX) qualifications;
- Licensed conveyancers carry out property transactions (conveyancing) and are regulated by the Council for Licensed Conveyancers (CLC).

Solicitors and barristers have a broad, general training, and may specialise once they have qualified, whereas licensed conveyancers and CILEX members train as specialists and practise in that field of law.

LAST BUT NOT LEAST . . .

We have focused on the key positions in the private sector, but some real estate people work in the public sector, for local authorities and social housing providers. We have identified some key roles but there are many more. It is outside the scope of this chapter to consider these in detail, but we have listed some later; this is not an exhaustive list and you can carry out further research into their roles using the links at the end of this chapter if you need to.

ARCHITECTS

Architects design buildings and produce the plans necessary for construction or renovation. They may also oversee projects through to completion, working with contractors and other professionals as needed. The Royal Institute of British Architects (RIBA) is the professional body for architects.

AUCTIONEERS

Auctioneers carry out a specialist function that comes under the overarching mainstream estate agency heading. As a specialist function, dealing purely with auctions, it has additional requirements above and beyond the standard estate agency requirements. These mandatory requirements are set out in the RICS professional statement[4] and focus on standards, ethics, relationships, and money laundering due to the nature of the auction process whereby most auction contracts are unconditional, and exchange of contracts takes place at the auction without the possibility of any further investigations.

BUILDING INSPECTORS

Building inspectors ensure compliance with Building Regulations when buildings are constructed, converted, or renovated. They may be employed by the local authority building control department or a government-approved private firm registered with the Construction Industry Council Approved Inspectors Register.

FACILITIES MANAGERS

Facilities managers are responsible for the smooth running of a building including aspects such as maintenance, services, and security. The role is both operational and strategic and facilities managers will work closely with building managers, property managers, and asset managers. The facilities manager is responsible for ensuring that the buildings they are responsible for comply with the latest health and safety legislation and regulations. Their focus is on the efficient and effective running of the building balancing the needs of occupiers with those of the owners. Facilities managers are likely to be accredited by the Institute of Workplace and Facilities Management (IWFM) who are aiming for chartered status.

LAND SURVEYORS

Land surveyors, also commonly known as geomatics surveyors, are responsible for creating accurate maps and plans. They work on a diverse range of land and property including development sites, quarries, mines, offshore pipelines, and airports. The RICS, the CIOB, and the Chartered Institution of Civil Engineering Surveyors (CICES) can accredit land surveyors. Today land surveyors are becoming increasingly dependent on the use of technology including geographic information systems (GIS) computer-aided design (CAD) and drones.

The broad descriptor of land surveyors also includes: environmental surveyors who manage the use and development of land to minimise its environmental impact; rural surveyors who specialise in agricultural land and buildings in the countryside; minerals and waste surveyors who deal with the mining, use, and management of natural resources.

MECHANICAL AND ELECTRICAL ENGINEERS

These engineers specialise in mechanical and electrical systems in buildings such as lifts, air conditioning, and utility supplies. They work on both new buildings designing the necessary utilities and on existing buildings advising on updating to comply with legislative changes.

PLANNING CONSULTANTS

Planning consultants advise on planning issues and policy in relation to the use and development of land and buildings. They must understand the competing political, economic, social, technological, environmental, and legal factors affecting planning policy. They may, for example, advise a homeowner on planning permission for a house extension or a developer on planning aspects such as density, infrastructure, and parking provision requirements of a large housing or commercial development. Alternatively, they may be employed in a local authority planning department, where they are normally known as town planners, with responsibility for balancing the need to protect and preserve the environment with the requirement for economic growth and development. Planning and Development is an RICS pathway to chartered status and membership of the Royal Town Planning Institute (RTPI) confers Chartered Town Planner (MRTPI) status.

PARTY WALL SURVEYORS

Party wall surveyors deal with matters covered under the Party Wall etc. Act 1996. They generally deal with alterations to structures including not only walls but also floors, foundations, and chimney breasts. They provide a specialist role resolving disputes between neighbours and their primary duty is to enforce the provisions of the Act rather than to satisfy whichever party employs them.

PROJECT MANAGERS

Project managers are responsible for ensuring that specific projects are planned, organised, and completed in accordance with pre-agreed objectives within the approved time, cost, quality, scope, risk, and resources parameters. In the real estate industry most major construction projects will have a project manager with the responsibility for delivery. Project managers are usually members of the Association for Project Management (APM) in the UK and this achieved its Royal Charter in 2017. Internationally, project managers are likely to be members of the Project Management Institute (PMI) or the International Project Management Association (IPMA).

QUANTITY SURVEYORS

Quantity surveyors are involved with the management of awarding contracts for construction projects to achieve value and quality for the client. This includes costing, documentation, tendering, awarding, and administering contracts. They are also responsible for negotiating claims and variations during a contract. Quantity surveyors are usually members of the RICS or CIOB.

STRUCTURAL ENGINEERS

Structural engineers specialise in structural integrity in the construction, renovation, and maintenance of buildings, ensuring the ability of a structure to safely withstand the use for which it has been intended. They are likely to belong to the Institution of Structural Engineers (ISE) or the Institution of Civil Engineers (ICE).

TENANTS

Tenants are the end users of property as they have the right to possession under a lease. However, the tenant may be an investor rather than the actual occupier if the tenant sub-lets. For example, a tenant under a long residential lease may become a landlord by letting their property to a sub-tenant under an Assured Shorthold Tenancy. A tenant under a long commercial lease might also become a landlord by letting to a sub-tenant under a shorter lease.

A real estate professional might encounter – and be instructed by – residential and commercial tenants in agency, development, management, and valuation scenarios and it is important to understand the landlord and tenant relationship and the rights and obligations of each. You can find more information in Chapter 8.

AND MORE . . .

As we have said, the sector encompasses a myriad of roles, far too many to outline here in detail. Other essential members of the real estate team are likely to include:

- Health and safety advisers providing risk assessments and guidance on safety matters and legal obligations. Specialists include fire risk assessors and asbestos surveyors;
- Energy Performance Assessors, assessing building compliance with legal sustainability requirements and issuing the Energy Performance Certificates that are a legal requirement before marketing property interests;
- Contractors and service providers in a multitude of trades, some of whom are able to self-certify compliance with Building Regulations avoiding the need to separately apply for Building Regulation approval. These providers may be members of approved schemes such as the Gas Safe Register and the Heating Equipment Testing and Approvals Scheme (HETAS).

The skills and knowledge particular to each role outlined in this chapter piece together to form the jigsaw that makes up the real estate sector. The real estate people considered here evidence the breadth of skill and expertise that characterise the sector. It is this coming together of the real estate community that can make real estate practice such an interesting and challenging field to study and in which to practise.

NOTES

1 RICS (undated) *About Us* Online. Available from: www.rics.org/uk/about-rics/

2 RICS (undated) *Become an RICS Fellow (FRICS)* Online. Available from: www.rics.org/uk/surveying-profession/career-progression/become-an-rics-fellow-frics/

3 Estate Agents Act 1979: London: The Stationery Office

4 RICS (2018) *Auctioneers Selling Real Estate* 7th Edition London: The Royal Institution of Chartered Surveyors Available from: www.rics.org/globalassets/rics-website/media/upholding-professional-standards/sector-standards/real-estate/auctioneers-selling-real-estate-7th-edition-rics.pdf

FURTHER INFORMATION

Lemen, J (2022) *How to Become a Chartered Surveyor* 1st Edition Abingdon, Oxon: Routledge

WEBSITES

Association of Project Managers https://apm.org.uk

Association of Residential Managing Agents https://arma.org.uk

Association of Retirement Housing Managers www.arhm.org

Bristol City Council National Trading Standards Estate and Letting Agency Team www.bristol.gov.uk/web/ntselat

Building Regulations www.gov.uk/housing-local-and-community/building-regulation

Building Research Establishment www.bregroup.com

Chartered Institute of Building Chartered Institute of Building www.ciob.org

Chartered Institute of Housing www.cih.org

Chartered Institute of Legal Executives www.cilex.org.uk

Chartered Institution of Civil Engineering Surveyors https://cices.org

Institute of Residential Property Management www.irpm.org.uk

Institute of Workplace and Facilities Management https://iwfm.org.uk

Institution of Civil Engineers www.ice.org.uk

Institution of Structural Engineers www.istructe.org

International Project Management Association https://ipma.world

Isurv www.isurv.com

Joint Contracts Tribunal www.jctltd.co.uk

Leasehold Advisory Service (LEASE) www.lease-advice.org

Ministry of Housing, Communities & Local Government www.gov.uk/government/publications/tenant-fees-act-2019-guidance

National Residential Landlords Association www.nrla.org.uk

National Trading Standards Estate and Letting Agency Team www.nationaltradingstandards.uk/work-areas/estate-agency-team/

Powys County Council National Trading Standards Estate Agency Team https://en.powys.gov.uk/article/3986/National-Trading-Standards-Estate-Agency-Team

Project Management Institute www.pmi.org

The Property Ombudsman www.tpos.co.uk

The Property Redress Scheme www.theprs.co.uk

Propertymark www.propertymark.co.uk/membership.html

Rent Smart Wales www.rentsmart.gov.wales/en/home/

Residential Property Surveyors Association www.rpsa.org.uk/membership.php

RICS Home Surveys Licences www.rics.org/uk/products/home-surveys-licences/

RICS Valuer Registration Scheme www.rics.org/uk/upholding-professional-standards/regulation/valuer-registration/

Royal Institute of British Architects www.architecture.com

Royal Institution of Chartered Surveyors www.rics.org/uk/

Royal Town Planning Institute www.rtpi.org.uk

Sava https://sava.co.uk

THE BASICS OF REAL ESTATE LAW

UNDERSTANDING LAND LAW

Why is it so important to understand real estate law? Whilst surveyors do not necessarily need the depth and detail of knowledge required by a lawyer, they do still need to understand the legal context in which they, and their clients, are operating. Surveyors must be able to recognise potential legal issues at an early stage; they may need to explain legal concepts to clients, and they may need to brief solicitors. They also need to know when to seek legal advice. Let us look at some examples in which a real estate practitioner may need to understand and apply the law:

- Liaising with solicitors during a sale and purchase;
- Checking boundaries in title deeds and at the Land Registry if there is a dispute;
- Identifying a neighbour's right of way across a site proposed for purchase;
- Recognising that a covenant may prevent site development.

Legal problems can be a deal-breaker in a property transaction, and they can make property management challenging. Solicitors do not usually visit the properties they are dealing with, so the surveyor or agent may be the 'eyes on the ground', able to flag up potential issues that need further investigation before they become a major concern – and expense – for the client.

Understanding legal basics can therefore help a surveyor to provide a good service to their client; it is part of being an expert, a

DOI: 10.1201/9781003155256-7

professional, and – importantly – it can help the practitioner to avoid the many legal pitfalls that can trap the uninformed.

THE LAW

In this chapter, we will look at some legal basics, that provide a framework for areas of study and for practice, to develop your knowledge and understanding of real estate as a profession. Land-lord and tenant law and some specific property rights are addressed in more detail in separate chapters.

A useful starting point is to consider the law itself. What do we mean by the law and what do we mean when we talk about something being legal? There are three types of law that real estate practitioners need to be aware of:

- Common law;
- Equity;
- Legislation.

We will look at each one in turn.

COMMON LAW

In England and Wales common law is the law that has evolved over centuries, based on the decisions of the courts. These decisions may set legal precedents, which means that they create rules and principles that become law. Criminal courts are beyond the scope of this book, although there are crimes concerning real estate, for example in relation to health and safety, and money laundering. For our purposes it is the civil courts that we are concerned with when studying land law. When we use the terms 'legal' and 'in law' we are referring to the common law.

Courts are organised in a hierarchy that enables appeals to be made to a higher court if the judge's decision is not accepted by a party to a dispute. The general rule is that the lower courts, for example the County Court, must follow the decisions made by the courts further up in the hierarchy – the High Court, the Court of Appeal, and the Supreme Court. Each is required to follow the decisions of the courts above it. Historically, the House of Lords was the highest court, but the creation of the Supreme Court in 2009 heralded a clearer separation of Parliament and the judiciary.

EQUITY

Equity originated in the Courts of Chancery and has also evolved over centuries. The role of equity is to alleviate the harshness that can characterise the common law. Equity is therefore founded on values of fairness and justice and it can be recognised by its maxims, or principles. Examples of these equitable maxims are: 'equity regards as done, that which ought to be done', and 'he who comes to equity comes with clean hands'. Equity will therefore have regard to the conduct of the parties when considering what is fair and just. We will see some examples of equity in practice when we look at aspects of land law in more detail later on.

Equity also offers remedies, which may be more appropriate than common law remedies, in some disputes. For example, a court may award damages in common law – financial compensation for a breach of a right – whereas equity might grant an injunction to prevent the breach occurring. An important distinction is that a claimant who successfully proves the breach in court will be entitled to common law remedies such as damages. This contrasts with equitable remedies such as an injunction (a court order that either prohibits someone from doing something or requires them do so something specific), which is discretionary. This means that the court can decide whether to grant the remedy to the claimant and the conduct of the claimant may influence the court's decision.

We have seen that equity is based on principles of fairness. Equity can step in to prevent injustice by offering an equitable interest to someone who intended to create a legal (i.e. a common law) interest, but who failed to do so because they did not follow the procedure required by common law. Equity also recognises certain rights in land – such as restrictive covenants – that only have limited application at common law.

Originally common law and equity were dealt with by different courts, but these functions were combined into one court system in the 1870s. A court can now decide any issue, regardless of whether it relates to common law or to equity. However, although the actual courts have merged, common law and equity remain separate types of law. If the common law and equity conflict, equity prevails, which means that it takes priority over common law.

Legislation is created by Parliament in the form of statutes, or Acts of Parliament. These can influence both common law and equity. For example, the Law of Property Act 1925 tells us which rights and interests in land can be legal and, consequently, which rights and interests can only be equitable.

It is the role of judges to interpret and apply legislation to the legal disputes that reach the courts.

The decisions of the courts create case law and you will see the importance of the decisions of the courts in all areas of the law. A useful tip concerns case law: when speaking about a court case, legal professionals do not say 'versus', they say 'and'. To take an example of a case referred to below, we write '*Buckland v Butterfield*', but we say: '*Buckland and Butterfield*'. It is usual to refer to the year in which the court made its decision, or in which the case appeared in the official law reports, and to provide the full case citation in an academic assignment or in a professional report. This ensures that the reference is to the correct decision as a dispute may progress through a succession of courts right up to the Supreme Court over several years, with each court making a different decision.

WHAT IS LAND?

When we talk about real estate, and land, what do we actually mean? This point is considered in Chapter 2, and it is useful to consider it further here. We may be referring to a piece of land – an actual part of the earth's surface – or to a building on that land. We may mean a part of a building which does not itself directly touch that land, for example a flat or an office in a high-rise. Most people will be familiar with the idea that land and buildings form real estate. But what about something less tangible – rights of way, for example?

Land is defined by Section 205(1)(ix) of the Law of Property Act 1925 as including:

- The land itself and things which are part of it, for example trees growing on the land;

- Buildings on the land;
- Minerals beneath the land;
- Rights relating to the land.

Ownership extends to the airspace above the land, and the ground beneath it. Clearly, this definition is broad. However, case law – *Bernstein of Leigh (Baron) v Skyviews & General Ltd 1978* – tells us that there are limits to it; the airspace above the land is only owned to the height necessary for the ordinary enjoyment of the land. Therefore, an object protruding from a neighbouring property into the airspace above your garden may be a trespass, but an aeroplane flying overhead at high altitude would not be trespassing over your property.

Similarly, ownership extends below the ground, so, for example a neighbour could not extend their basement beneath your property; to do so would be a trespass. However, there are some exceptions – the Infrastructure Act 2015 allows deep-level access beneath the property of another (defined as at least 300 metres) to exploit oil or geothermal energy.

FIXTURES AND CHATTELS

When dealing with real estate we need to know what is included. We have mentioned buildings on the land, trees growing on it, the airspace above it, and the earth beneath the land. But what about the things placed on it or attached to it? These can be divided into:

- Fixtures – items which become attached to the land and form part of it;
- Chattels – the personal belongings of the owner.

This is an important topic for the real estate professional, as the extent of a property that is being bought and sold, leased, managed, valued, or surveyed needs to be identified in order to avoid disputes. Solicitors will ask sellers to complete Fixtures and Contents Forms during the conveyancing process to ensure all the parties understand what is included in, and excluded from, the transaction. However, as we have said, solicitors do not typically visit the properties they are dealing with. It is often the surveyor, agent, or property manager who is the 'eyes on the ground' and able to identify any items that could cause a dispute to arise.

The basic position is that a fixture is part of the land, so a buyer would expect to find that item at the property when they complete their purchase. A chattel is a personal belonging that the seller would expect to take with them when they sell.

This is a useful example of the practical application of case law. When considering whether an item is a fixture or a chattel, *Buckland v Butterfield 1820* demonstrates the basic principle that an item attached to the land, becomes part of the land. In this example, a conservatory built on to the property formed part of the property and was a fixture.

However, the position is not always clear. When considering whether something is a fixture or a chattel, a key case is *Holland v Hodgson 1872*. This case gives us an important two-stage test to apply in order to decide whether an item is a fixture or a chattel:

1   The degree of annexation – how firmly attached is the item? Will the item or the property be damaged by removal of the item?
2   The purpose of annexation – why has the item been attached? What was the intention behind the annexation? Does the annexation improve the property itself or is it purely to enjoy the item?

Both the *Holland v Hodgson* tests need to be applied, but the second test – the purpose of annexation – is the most important. A further possibility is that the item forms part of the overall design of the property, becoming an integral feature, and therefore a fixture rather than a chattel. This can relate to architecture, interior design, or landscaping. Case law provides us with examples:

- *D'Eyncourt v Gregory 1866* tells us that free-standing statues, chandeliers, and a clock were fixtures where they were part of the overall design of a stately home;
- In *La Salle Recreations v Canadian Camdex Investments Ltd 1969*, carpets were part of the style of design of a hotel and as a result were held to be fixtures.

Botham v TSB Bank PLC 1996 gives us more useful examples –
kitchen units and sink were fixtures, whereas kitchen appliances,
light fittings, carpets, and curtains were chattels. In *Leigh v Taylor
1902*, a tenant tacked tapestries to a wall to hold them in place (quite
a high degree of annexation). However, the purpose of annexation
was to enable the tenant to enjoy the tapestries. It had not been
the tenant's intention that the tapestries would become part of the
property, for the landlord to keep once the tenancy ended so in this
case the tapestries were chattels.

OWNERSHIP OF LAND

In England and Wales all land is owned by the Crown (see Chapter 2). This means that a citizen who owns real estate is not actually
the ultimate owner; rather the Crown, as an institution, is the
owner. If, for example, someone dies without heirs, and without
leaving a will, any real estate that they own reverts to the Crown.

Historically, this system of land ownership goes back hundreds
of years. Over time our system of tenure (tenure means 'to hold')
developed into two legal estates recognised by Section 1 of the Law
of Property Act 1925 as capable of being legal (i.e. recognised by
the common law). These are:

- Fee simple absolute in possession (known as a freehold);
- Term of years absolute (known as a leasehold).

When we acquire real estate, we actually acquire one of these two
estates in land. The difference between the two is that freehold
ownership lasts indefinitely, whereas a leasehold is limited in time,
so a leasehold estate ends when the lease expires or is terminated.
Leasehold is largely unique to the UK (with the exception of Scotland), with other countries having different forms of ownership,
such as the condominium structure in the United States. However,
in Hong Kong leasehold is the only form of tenure available.

The Commonhold and Leasehold Reform Act 2002 created
commonhold as a way of owning property. Commonhold is a new
type of freehold (and so is a legal estate) and was intended to offer
an alternative to leaseholds for residential flats. However, commonhold has not been popular; developers and their solicitors have

continued to create new leasehold flats, perhaps because this is a familiar and well-established tenure, and converting existing leaseholds into commonhold is not a simple process. Consequently, at the time of writing there are very few commonholds in existence.

Clearly, ownership of land is not always straightforward. We have seen that there are different estates in land. We have also seen that the actual definition of land is not always clear. If land is in the sole ownership of one person, the position is usually relatively clear: that person will be the owner, although that ownership may be subject to other interests in the property, such as a mortgage. The situation becomes more complicated if another person has contributed in some way but is not named as an owner, or if property is owned by more than one person at the same time (concurrent ownership).

Common law and equity recognise different forms of land ownership and different rights relating to land, so the distinction between common law and equity is important here. The person named as the purchaser on the deed transferring ownership of land (up to a maximum of four owners), or the person registered as the proprietor at HM Land Registry will be the legal owner of a property. However, there may be other 'owners'; trusts and equitable interests are an important aspect of the law in this respect, and we will consider these next.

TRUSTS OF LAND

A trust is an arrangement in which the legal and equitable interests in land are separated. Trustees own the legal estate in the land, but the equitable (or 'beneficial') interest is held on trust for one or more beneficiaries. An interest under a trust is an equitable interest under Section 1(3) of the Law of Property Act 1925. This means that the legal ownership may be different to the rights to occupy the land or to receive any income from it. Trusts may be created expressly or implied by law.

EXPRESS TRUSTS

An express trust is one that has been created intentionally. This can be by a deed of trust, but it can simply be in writing, signed by the person creating the trust (Section 53(1)(b) of the Law of Property

Act 1925). Alternatively, a trust can be expressly created in a will. For example, a parent may leave the family home in his or her will, to trustees to hold on trust for the children.

IMPLIED TRUSTS

Trusts are not always created expressly. As we have said, trusts may be implied by law; equity may step in to create a beneficial interest in land for the benefit of someone who does not hold the legal interest, based on the conduct of the people involved.

Resulting trusts

A resulting trust is an example of an implied trust and may arise if one party contributes towards the purchase of a property but is not named as the registered proprietor at the Land Registry, or is not named on the deed transferring ownership of the property. The equitable interest of the beneficiary under the trust will be in proportion to the contribution made to the purchase price. Therefore, the presumption is that the legal owner will hold the equitable interest on trust for all those who contributed to the purchase. This presumption does not apply if the intention was to make a gift, as may be the case, for example in 'bank of mum and dad' situations, in which parents help their children to buy a home. However, it may apply, for example in commercial transactions in which the intention would not be to make a gift.

Common intention constructive trusts

There is another type of implied trust, called a common intention constructive trust. This is more flexible than a resulting trust, as the share of the beneficiary is not necessarily directly connected with or in proportion to a financial contribution. For this reason, its application can often be seen within the contexts of family and personal relationships; the legal owner of the home may hold a share of the property on trust for their non-owner spouse or partner.

We have seen that equity evolved from ideas of fairness and justice. It is characterised by principles, also known as maxims. One such maxim is that equity treats as done that which ought to be done. So, if the intention was that a property would be shared, equity will step in to create that shared interest, even if that is not the position at common law.

A constructive trust may arise if the intention that the property would be shared was expressly stated and the person without the legal interest relied on that express statement to their detriment, that is that person changed their circumstances based on the belief that they had a share in the property. If the intention to share the property was express, the detriment requirement will have a low threshold. For example, carrying out landscaping work, providing childcare, and paying household expenses, as in the case of *Eves v Eves 1975*, were sufficient to imply a common intention constructive trust.

If there has been no express statement that the property was to be shared, the court may imply the common intention. Again, the person claiming the share of the property must have acted to their detriment in reliance on the common intention that the property would be shared. The threshold is higher where there is no express common intention. For example, a direct contribution to the purchase price, or a direct contribution to mortgage repayments may enable the court to infer the common intention necessary for a constructive trust to arise.

Common intention may be implied in other circumstances. For example, paying for renovations, or contributing to household expenses to enable a partner to pay the mortgage – as in *Le Foe v le Foe 2001* – may be sufficient to create a constructive trust. An important consideration here is whether the person claiming the share of the equitable interest in the property has acted as an owner would be expected to act.

PROPRIETARY ESTOPPEL

Equity can grant ownership of real estate on the basis of proprietary estoppel, which is best demonstrated by the key case of *Thorner v Major 2009*. David Thorner worked for his relative, Peter Thorner, on Peter Thorner's farm. He did so for 30 years, without pay, on the expectation that he would inherit the farm. When Peter Thorner died without leaving a will the farm was inherited by other relatives. David Thorner claimed proprietary estoppel, as he had relied upon the assurance that he would inherit the farm and the House of Lords – then the UK's highest court – held that the farm did pass to David.

Proprietary estoppel may therefore apply if it would be unconscionable for a person to revoke an assurance that another person had relied on to their detriment. The use of 'unconscionable' is another example of equity seeking to do what is just and fair, by reference to morally unacceptable behaviour; a property owner may be prevented – estopped – from denying that someone else might be entitled to the property.

CO-OWNERSHIP

The scenarios discussed arise if ownership has not been clearly addressed by the parties. However, co-ownership – ownership by more than one person – is a day-to-day occurrence when people buy property together, whether as a couple or, for example, friends clubbing together to buy a property. When people buy land together, ownership should be clearly agreed, the legal owners should be registered as such at the Land Registry and the equitable interests should also be clearly understood by all the co-owners. So, assuming ownership has been clearly agreed and correctly registered at the Land Registry, what laws apply to co-ownership?

In all co-ownership situations a trust of land arises under the Trusts of Land and Appointment of Trustees Act 1996. This is a statutory trust because it has been created by an Act of Parliament. The trust separates the legal and equitable interests. This means that the legal owners – the trustees – hold the equitable interest on trust for the beneficiaries.

The legal owners and the beneficiaries may well be the same people. For example, if a couple buy a property together, they will both be registered at the Land Registry as the legal owners and will be trustees under the trust of land that arises under the 1996 Act. They will also both have equitable interests as beneficiaries under the trust of land. As trustees, they will therefore hold the beneficial interest on trust for themselves as the beneficiaries.

The concept of the curtain of the trust is important here: only the legal owners – the trustees – will be registered as the proprietors at the Land Registry. The equitable interests under the trust will not be apparent, because they are hidden behind the curtain of the trust and are not shown on the Register. In the example of our couple buying a property together, their legal ownership will be apparent from inspection of the Register. However, their equitable interest will not be apparent so it will not be possible to establish whether they in fact hold the equitable interest for someone else – their children perhaps – nor will the proportions in which they own their shares be apparent. It may be the case that they have equal shares. Alternatively, they may have decided that they have unequal shares, perhaps because they did not contribute to the purchase price equally. This information will not be apparent from inspection of the Register.

We then need to consider how these legal and equitable interests will be held under the trusts of land. There are two ways that co-owners can hold land – as joint tenants or as tenants in common. We will consider the characteristics of each shortly, but first of all it is important to understand the following key points:

- 'Tenancy' and 'tenant' in this context refer to the relationship between the owners of the legal and equitable interests (as joint tenants or tenants in common); it is not referring to the relationship between a landlord and a tenant;
- The legal interest – that is the interest of the trustees – can only be held as joint tenants;
- The equitable interest of the beneficiaries can be held as joint tenants or as tenants in common;
- Under Section 34(2) of the Law of Property Act 1925 there can only be four legal owners, who will be the first named on the deed transferring the property to the owners when they bought it. There can be any number of beneficiaries entitled to the equitable interest. If, for example, six friends clubbed together to buy a house, the first four named in the transfer of the house would be the legal owners. These four would be named as the owners at the Land Registry and they would hold the property as trustees, on trust for all six friends. There would be four trustees holding the legal estate and six beneficiaries entitled to the equitable interest in the house.

CHARACTERISTICS OF A JOINT TENANCY

If co-owners hold property as joint tenants, they share their interest in the property, so no one has a distinct share. There may be up to four legal joint tenants (the legal interest can *only* be held as joint tenants), and any number of equitable joint tenants, but the law will see them as one entity. In order for there to be a joint tenancy, the four unities must apply; see *AG Securities v Vaughan 1988* for a useful discussion of this. The four unities can be remembered as PITT:

- **Possession** – the joint tenants all have the right to possess the whole property;
- **Interest** – they have the same interest in the property (e.g. freehold or leasehold);
- **Title** – their interest was acquired under the same document;
- **Time** – their interest was acquired at the same time.

Survivorship is another very important characteristic of a joint tenancy. This means that if one joint tenant dies, their interest in the property passes automatically to the surviving joint tenant(s). Consequently, a joint tenant cannot leave their interest in a property to someone else in their will and it cannot pass to someone else under the intestacy rules if they have not left a will. The final surviving joint tenant will acquire the whole interest and become a sole owner, so the trust of land will come to an end as there will no longer be co-ownership.

Joint tenancies are frequently used by couples who intend their partner to automatically acquire their share in their home. It follows that joint tenancies are not suitable for owners who want to leave their interest to someone else under their will. Joint tenancies are also unsuitable if the owners wish to retain distinct shares, for example because they made unequal contributions to the purchase price and they wish that to be reflected in the ownership of the property.

CHARACTERISTICS OF A TENANCY IN COMMON

A tenancy in common can only exist in equity because the legal estate can only be held as joint tenants. A key characteristic is that survivorship does not apply to a tenancy in common; hence a tenant in common can leave their interest under their will to whomsoever they choose.

The four unities – PITT – do not apply in full to a tenancy in common, which requires only unity of possession, that is each tenant in common is entitled to occupy the whole. Otherwise, tenants in common can acquire their interests at different times, and under different documents. Under a tenancy in common, it is presumed that the parties hold equal but distinct shares, but it is possible for this to be varied so that tenants in common may hold the property in unequal shares, for example because they made different contributions to the purchase price. A tenancy in common would be appropriate in our example of friends clubbing together to buy a house, as they would usually expect to have distinct shares that reflect their contributions, which they can sell, or leave in their wills.

SEVERANCE OF A JOINT TENANCY

An equitable joint tenancy can be converted into a tenancy in common by a process called severance. This applies only to the beneficial (equitable) interest, because the legal interest can only be held as joint tenants under Section 36(2) of the Law of Property Act 1925.

Joint tenancies can be severed in several ways:

- By notice in writing under Section 36(2) of the Law of Property Act 1925 – this can be unilateral, so the agreement of the joint tenants is not necessary here;
- By mutual agreement – contrasting with unilateral action as mentioned in the first point earlier;
- By conduct during a joint tenant's lifetime, for example one joint tenant sells their interest, so destroying the unities of title and time;
- Other circumstances, for example if a joint tenant is declared bankrupt, the joint tenancy will be severed. Survivorship will not apply, so protecting the other owners, whose shares will be separate from the share owned by the bankrupt person. Under a tenancy in common, share(s) will not automatically pass to the bankrupt person should the other owner(s) die.

CONVERTING A TENANCY IN COMMON INTO A JOINT TENANCY

A tenancy in common can be converted into a joint tenancy if the co-owners wish to do so. The correct procedure must be followed, including creating or updating the deed of trust and an application will be needed to the Land Registry. There is more information on land registration later on in this chapter.

PROTECTING THE BENEFICIAL INTERESTS OF TENANTS IN COMMON

As we have seen, it is only the legal owners who are registered as the proprietors at the Land Registry, whereas the beneficial (equitable) interests are held behind the 'curtain' of the trust. If the beneficial interest is held as joint tenants, survivorship will apply, in which case a buyer can pay the purchase money to a sole surviving legal owner. If the beneficial interest is held as tenants in common, the beneficiaries will want their share of the sale proceeds as they will each have distinct shares in the property. How can the beneficial interest of tenants in common be protected in the event of a sale of the property? We will consider land registration in more detail later, but as regards tenants in common, a Restriction can be placed on the register, worded as follows:

> *No disposition by a sole proprietor of the registered estate (except a trust corporation) under which capital money arises is to be registered unless authorised by an order of the court.*

This indicates that there is a trust of land, and although it does not give any details it does alert a buyer to the existence of beneficial (equitable) interests in the property.

We then have to consider what a buyer would do with this information. This leads us to the concept of overreaching, which is an important aspect of the sale and purchase of real estate. Overreaching occurs if purchase money is paid to the trustees, being at least two in number, in which case the beneficial interests are overreached. If there is only one trustee, a second trustee must be appointed. The buyer, having paid at least two trustees, will acquire the property free from the beneficial interests. The interests of the beneficiaries will be converted from interests in the property itself, to interests in the sale proceeds, which they will be able to claim from the trustees (subject to the terms of the trust).

LAND REGISTRATION

We have mentioned land registration: systems of land registration are common, for example Australia has land registration systems for each State and Territory, as do the USA (again in relation to each State), Hong Kong and many European Union nations. In the UK there are separate registers for England and Wales (together), Scotland, and Northern Ireland.

This section focuses on land registration in England and Wales, where HM Land Registry is the database of land ownership and interests, which evidences (and in fact creates) ownership of land. Unregistered land does still exist, but it has been compulsory to register land in England and Wales in certain circumstances since 1990, and compulsory registration existed in some local areas before this date.

The register is intended to mirror the actual ownership of the land and the rights and restrictions that affect it, although there are some interests known as overriding interests that affect land but are not shown on the register. These are explained in more detail later on in this chapter.

Land registration provides a form of state guarantee regarding the accuracy of the information on the register, and it makes conveyancing – the transfer of land ownership from one person to another – easier and more transparent. Information held at the Land Registry is available to the public for a small fee and as it is guaranteed, the state will compensate for any losses incurred if the Land Registry has made an error on the Register.

THE REGISTER

The register is divided into four sections:

- **Property Register** – this describes the property (which will have its own unique title number) together with any rights that benefit it, such as an easement;

- **Proprietorship Register** – this displays the name(s) of the legal owner(s), who are known as the Registered Proprietors. This is a key point to remember – if there are co-owners of the property, the ownership shown is that of the trustees under the statutory trust of land, not of the beneficiaries who have an equitable interest. This is known as the curtain of the trust – the details of the trust and the names of the beneficiaries are not included on the Register, as they are 'behind the curtain of the trust';
- **Charges Register** – this shows any matters affecting the property, for example mortgages secured on the property, and restrictive covenants that burden it;
- **Title Plan** – a plan of the property, showing its boundaries. The plan may also show the position of easements and other interests affecting the property. With unregistered property it is necessary to check the plans attached to title deeds. These plans are commonly stated to be 'for identification purposes only'. Similarly, the Land Registry plan shows the general, rather than the exact, position of boundaries. Hence, it is important to compare the title plan with boundaries on site to identify any discrepancies.

REGISTRATION

The key piece of legislation is the Land Registration Act 2002 (LRA). Section 1(1) of the LRA states that transactions relating to land must be registered. It is helpful to look at land that is already registered, and unregistered land, separately when we consider this in more detail.

Registered land

If land is already registered, a change will need to be made to the Register if there has been a 'registrable disposition'. The main registrable dispositions to be aware of are:

- Transfers of the land to a new owner, who must be registered as the Proprietor;
- Creation of a new lease, if the new lease is for a term exceeding seven years;

- Creation of mortgages;
- Creation of easements.

Unregistered land

Section 1(2) of the LRA states that some transactions relating to unregistered land trigger first registration, so the land changes from being unregistered, to becoming registered. The main types of transactions that trigger first registration of unregistered land are:

- Transfers of a freehold, for example by a sale or gift;
- Creation of a new lease, if the new lease is for a term exceeding seven years;
- Assignment of an existing lease (i.e. a transfer of an existing lease from one landlord or tenant to a new landlord or tenant) if the lease has more than seven years unexpired;
- Creation of a mortgage.

PROTECTING INTERESTS IN LAND

Some interests in land will be protected by a Restriction or Notice on the Register, for example mortgages, restrictive covenants, and trusts. A Restriction restricts the Registered Proprietor's ability to deal freely with the land. For example, a lender may place a Restriction on the Register requiring the lender's consent to a sale. As we have seen, if there is a trust of land, in which the beneficiaries hold the equitable interest as tenants in common, a Restriction on the Register will prevent a sale by a sole owner. This protects the interests of the beneficial tenants in common. A Notice protects other interests such as a legal lease that is for a term of seven years or less, or an option to purchase the land.

OVERRIDING INTERESTS

Overriding interests are interests that are not shown on the Register; under the LRA they still bind a purchaser of the land. This means that a buyer could buy the property subject to someone else's right to occupy the land.

Examples of overriding interests are:

- A beneficiary under a trust who also occupies the property;
- A tenant with a lease that does not require registration, because the term of the lease (i.e. its duration) does not exceed seven years;
- An implied legal easement

(see Chapter 9)

If registered land is affected by an overriding interest it may be possible to overreach that interest if the overriding interest is equitable, as is provided for in Section 2 of the Law of Property Act 1925. The effect of overreaching is that the equitable interest transfers from the property itself and instead becomes an interest in the sale proceeds (see earlier).

FAILURE TO REGISTER

A failure to register a transaction within the required time period has serious implications, as a legal interest will not be properly transferred or created. Instead, equity steps in to create an equitable interest until the situation has been rectified. For example, if the transaction was the grant of a new lease of over seven years, the tenant would not acquire a legal lease; rather there would be a contract to grant a lease, which is an equitable interest. The parties would need to comply with the contract by creating the new lease, which would then be registered in order to become a legal lease.

This is an important point: a buyer does not become the legal owner of a property until they are registered as the proprietor at the Land Registry. Full transfer of ownership does not take place on completion of the sale even though the buyer will be able to collect the keys and take possession – move in – on completion.

CLASSES OF TITLE

Registered land is classed according to its status:

- **Absolute** – Most properties are registered with Absolute title, which is the best class of title;

- **Good Leasehold** – This class of title may be applied to a lease if the right of the landlord to grant the lease has not been verified (usually where the landlord's title is unregistered);
- **Possessory** – This would apply if there are no title deeds to evidence ownership, so ownership is established by possession of the land, or if ownership is being claimed via adverse possession. Possessory titles are rare;
- **Qualified** – These are very rare but might apply if there is a specific defect in the title, in which case the defect will be stated in the Register.

It is possible to upgrade titles by application to the Land Registry. For example, Possessory title can be upgraded to Absolute title once the Possessory title has been registered for 12 years. Alternatively, lost documents that resulted in a Possessory or Qualified title may be found, enabling the title to be upgraded to Absolute.

UNREGISTERED LAND

It is useful to consider unregistered land further, as this still exists, and real estate professionals are likely to come across it in practice.

Land remains unregistered because there has been no registrable disposition of it to trigger first registration. Therefore, land that has not changed ownership or has not been leased (for a term exceeding seven years), or mortgaged since compulsory registration was introduced will remain unregistered, unless it has been registered voluntarily (unregistered land can be registered voluntarily at any time by application to the Land Registry).

There is no central record of the ownership of unregistered land, which is evidenced by individual title deeds rather than by registration. Title deeds are not publicly available, so unregistered land lacks the transparency of registered land and this can make transfers more time-consuming and complicated.

Interests such as restrictive covenants that affect unregistered land can be protected by entry on the Land Charges Register. This is a department of the Land Registry; as a Land Charge, the interest will be registered even though the land itself is not registered.

FAILED LEGAL ESTATES AND INTERESTS

We mention earlier that a failure to register a registrable disposition can result in an equitable, rather than legal, estate or interest being acquired. Formalities are key to ensuring that ownership in, and rights over, real estate are recognised by the common law. In addition to registration, the general position under Section 52 of the Law of Property Act 1925 is that a legal estate or interest must be created or transferred by deed. Section 1 of the Law of Property (Miscellaneous Provisions) Act 1989 tells us that a deed must be:

- Stated to be a deed, for example it will say 'this deed' on the front page;
- Executed as a deed, which means that it is signed and witnessed, or, in the case of a company, it is signed by the correct authorised signatories;
- Delivered, which happens when the date is inserted into the deed. The date of a deed is therefore left blank until the parties are ready for it to be delivered.

Failure to comply with these formalities may result in the creation of an equitable (rather than legal) estate or interest, provided the requirements of Section 2 of the Law of Property (Miscellaneous Provisions) Act 1989 have been met:

- The transaction must be in writing;
- The document must include all the terms of the agreement between the parties, or it must refer to another document, which includes all the agreed terms;
- All parties to the transaction must sign the document (or identical copies of the document).

There are some exceptions to this. For example, some legal interests can be implied by conduct, rather than expressly created in writing. Under Section 54 of the Law of Property Act 1925, leases not exceeding three years duration generally do not need to be created by deed and they can even be created by an oral agreement.

ADVERSE POSSESSION

Adverse possession is a means of acquiring ownership of land by what most people would understand as 'squatters' rights'. When we think of ownership, we often think of it as 'absolute' and it can be difficult to accept that a person can simply take away very valuable property belonging to another person. This can be easier to understand if we think back to the beginning of this chapter, when we considered how land is owned. If you recall, ultimately all land in the UK is owned by the Crown – by the Monarchy as an institution. Estates in land, with either freehold or leasehold tenure, are then held by the people we think of as the owners of the land. If the holder of an estate in land does not adequately look after that land, they risk losing it to someone else who has assumed the role of an owner, and who apparently takes better care of the land. This is called adverse possession and it is an important point for real estate practitioners who, as we have said, must be aware of any third parties using or occupying land, in order to avoid rights or ownership being acquired inadvertently.

As the name implies, adverse possession depends on the possession of land for an unbroken period of time. There are two aspects: factual possession and intention to possess. Factual possession will depend on the circumstances, but in essence, the squatter must possess the land in the way that an owner would. In addition, the squatter must intend to possess the land, to the exclusion of anyone else including the registered proprietor. This could be evidenced by, for example, fencing around the land, where there is also factual possession if the land in question is in actual use.

The period of time required to claim adverse possession differs, depending on whether or not the land is registered with the Land Registry. If land is unregistered, a person claiming ownership of land by adverse possession must have been in possession of it for at least 12 years. If the land is registered, ownership can be claimed after ten years of possession.

However, in the case of registered land, if a claim is made for adverse possession, the Land Registry will notify the registered proprietor of the land, who can:

- Not respond, in which case the claimant will be registered as the proprietor;

- Consent to the claim, in which case the claimant will become the new registered proprietor;
- Object to the claim, in which case the parties will be invited to negotiate. They may, for example, agree that the claimant may remain on the property under a licence granted by the registered proprietor. If they are unable to settle the matter, the dispute will be referred to the First-tier Tribunal (Property Chamber) to make a decision;
- Serve a counter notice in which case the claim will be dismissed unless one of the these circumstances applies:

  - That the registered proprietor should be prevented ('estopped') from repossessing the land because it would be unconscionable for them to do so. Here, equity steps in to protect a squatter where it would be unfair for the registered proprietor to reclaim the land;
  - That the claimant should in the circumstances be registered as the owner for some other reason, for example, they have become entitled to the property under a will;
  - The claim relates to a disputed boundary and for the ten-year period the claimant had reasonably believed that they owned the land;

- If one of these three reasons applies the squatter will become the new owner, even if the registered proprietor objects.

A registered proprietor who opposes a claim for adverse possession must evict the squatter within two years. Failing to do so will enable the squatter to be registered as the new proprietor of the land.

Although adverse possession can result in an owner losing the entirety of their land, it can apply to small areas of land such as unclear boundaries between properties. For this reason, it is important to check plans at the Land Registry or in the title deeds, against the property actually on-site; discrepancies could lead to boundary disputes and claims for adverse possession.

AND FINALLY – SOME ADVICE ON TACKLING LEGAL PROBLEMS

Landlord and tenant law and rights to land owned by other people are considered in separate chapters; when you read these, do refer back to the information in this chapter as it is also relevant to these topics. The concepts outlined in this chapter demonstrate the complexity of land law and the, sometimes intricate, relationship between legal principles; even apparently simple definitions such as 'land' and 'ownership' can be complicated. When approaching a legal problem it is important to do so methodically. Identify the relevant facts and the area of law and apply the legal principles and legal authority to those facts to reach your reasoned conclusion to address the problem. Legal assignments often have scope for argument; there may not be a right or wrong answer; rather you may need to analyse each element of the situation you are presented with, using your judgement to indicate a likely outcome should the matter reach the courts. In practice, you would instruct a legal professional to deal with problems for you, but it is helpful to have already researched the issue and to have a basic understanding of it. This makes it easier, and cheaper, to obtain the advice you need.

FURTHER INFORMATION

Card, R, Murdoch, J, and Murdoch, S (2011) *Real Estate Management Law* 7th Edition Oxford: Oxford University Press

Davys, M (2009) *Land Law* 11th Edition London: Red Globe Press

THE LANDLORD AND TENANT RELATIONSHIP

WHY DO WE NEED TO UNDERSTAND THIS TOPIC?

Understanding the landlord and tenant relationship, coupled with knowledge of landlord and tenant law and practice, is important both personally (if, e.g. you rent under an Assured Shorthold Tenancy or you have bought a long leasehold flat) and professionally. Perhaps you undertake landlord- and tenant-related work for clients, or you operate from leasehold business premises. Students may be set scenario-based assignments to demonstrate their understanding of this area of law and practice. Examples of the application of this topic include:

- Advising landlords on rights to recover maintenance and management costs from tenants;
- Advising on compliance with break clause conditions when ending a lease;
- Carrying out a valuation for the owner of a flat who wants to extend their lease;
- Negotiating terms of a new lease on a new property.

The ability to communicate and negotiate is important when dealing with many landlord and tenant matters, as the relationship often involves the need to negotiate the best terms for the client. We have been involved in many lease negotiations and it is sometimes necessary to be creative to reach a mutually satisfactory conclusion. This is reflected in some of the RICS mandatory competencies, such as communication and negotiation, and client care. We recommend

DOI: 10.1201/9781003155256-8

that you also refer to guidance set out in the RICS Code for leasing business premises 1st edition 2020. The landlord and tenant relationship can be adversarial, and we have been involved in dispute-resolution proceedings in courts and tribunals. The Code aims to protect tenants who may not fully understand the transaction and to encourage fairness and collaboration between those representing the parties.

However, to practise effectively, it is necessary to underpin these skills with technical knowledge. We will begin by considering the nature of a lease.

WHAT IS A LEASE?

A term of years absolute – a lease – is one of the legal estates in land permitted by Section 1 of the Law of Property Act 1925 (the other legal estate being a freehold). The phrase 'term of years absolute' means that a leasehold estate in land has a specified, limited duration, so it contrasts with a freehold, which lasts indefinitely. Leases can be for any period, including months, rather than years; we have dealt with leases from 6 months to 999 years. This period is called the 'term'.

The definition 'term of years absolute' can be misleading. It is possible for a lease to be for a fixed – absolute – period, as we have said. However, it is also possible for a lease to be periodic. This means that it is for a period – for example, a week, a month, or a year – that repeatedly and automatically renews until action is taken to end it. This is common in residential tenancies, which are often weekly, monthly, or yearly.

A lease can only be granted out of a freehold estate, or out of another leasehold estate. If a lease is created out of another leasehold estate, it is known as a sub-lease. This means that a single property may be subject to several different legal estates, with each owner registered as the proprietor, in England and Wales, at HM Land Registry if the term of the lease exceeds seven years. This may also affect the status of the people involved. For example, the owner of a freehold block of flats (the landlord) grants a 125-year lease of a flat to a tenant, who then rents the flat to a sub-tenant for 12 months. The tenant of the 125-year lease is also the landlord in relation to the 12-month tenancy.

This raises another interesting point. A person who acquires a lease will be registered as the owner, in England and Wales, at HM Land Registry if the lease exceeds seven years. They will consider themselves to be the owner of the property and they will, in fact, own a legal estate in the property. However, technically they will be a tenant, as the legal relationship under the lease will be landlord and tenant. Terminology can also be confusing if you are unfamiliar with leases, and some terms are used interchangeably. So, leases and tenancies are one and the same, as are landlord/lessor, and tenant/lessee/leaseholder.

CHARACTERISTICS OF A LEASE

A lease is unusual in that it is both an estate in land that is recognised by the law, and it is a contract between the landlord and tenant, that sets out the agreement between them. Consequently, contract law and land law may interact to affect this arrangement.

From a landlord and tenant law perspective, case law – *Street v Mountford 1985* – gives us the criteria to apply to determine whether an arrangement creates a lease. It also tells us that it is the actual characteristics of the arrangement, rather than the label attached to the arrangement, that determines whether a lease has been created:

1) **Exclusive possession** – The tenant must have the right to possess the property to the exclusion of all others, including the landlord.
2) **Certainty of term** – The duration of the lease must be certain. This means that the landlord and tenant must know when the term will end. This can be on the expiry of a fixed term of years. Alternatively, if the term is periodic, it will run as, for example a weekly or monthly tenancy, in which case the landlord and tenant will know when it could end by giving notice.

If an arrangement does not confer exclusive possession and certainty of term, it is not a lease. It may, however, be a licence. Licences are personal rights to occupy a property, rather than legal estates in land. For example, a lodger, who cannot exclude a homeowner from the property but may be able to exclusively occupy a bedroom, is likely to have a licence rather than a lease. Other arrangements, such as informal agreements between family and friends, and employment that requires staff to live in, will not usually create a lease. In Chapter 7 we consider the difference between the common law, which recognises only legal estates and interests, and equity. We outline the criteria required to create a legal estate and we explain that failure to comply with these criteria may instead create an equitable interest. These criteria apply in addition to the requirement for exclusive possession and certainty of term. Therefore, a legal lease must confer exclusive possession and certainty of term, be created by deed and registered at HM Land Registry (in England and Wales), unless it falls within certain exceptions.

RENT

Most people would consider the payment of rent to be an essential characteristic of a lease. However, *Ashburn Anstalt v Arnold 1989* decided that payment of rent is not an essential characteristic of a lease, although it is still a common feature of many leases. In some cases (typically long residential leases) the rent will be a peppercorn – in effect a zero rent – so no money is due.

Rent will usually be payable in advance on specified dates, typically on the quarter days: 25 March, 24 June, 29 September, and 25 December. The lease will usually state that payment must be made without any deduction or set-off. This means that the tenant cannot withhold any rent, even if the landlord has failed to comply with their obligations under the lease.

Rent reviews are important as they help maintain the investment value for the landlord. They are also a significant area of practice for surveyors, who frequently become involved in the valuation and negotiation of the new rent. Reviews may take place periodically throughout the term of a lease. It is important to check the lease carefully to see whether the landlord has the authority to review the rent, when the rent may be reviewed, and the procedure to be followed. It is also essential to check whether 'time is of the essence' as if this is stated in the lease, failure to comply with the timetable outlined will result in a failure to review the rent. Section 13 of the Housing Act 1988 enables the landlord of Assured and Assured

Shorthold Tenancies to increase the rent in certain circumstances by giving notice to the tenant. These tenants have the right to challenge the rent at the First-tier Tribunal (Property Chamber).

When we first entered the industry, standard commercial leases tended to be 25 years with five-yearly upward only rent reviews, or even 21 years leases with seven-yearly upward only rent reviews. Over the past few years there has been a trend towards shorter leases reflecting the increased desire for flexibility amongst occupiers. There has also been some pressure to make rent reviews upward and downward in the UK (i.e. the rent can increase or decrease on review). In Ireland and Australia upward only rent reviews have now been banned. In the UK many tenants are taking short five-year leases without reviews, taking their chances at lease renewal.

In commercial leases, some landlords will agree rent-free periods as an incentive to tenants. The rent-free period helps the landlord to attract a tenant to a vacant property. It can particularly help tenants if there is a period at the start of the lease in which the tenant cannot trade but is incurring significant costs because they are preparing the premises for their use. This is commonly seen in new shopping centres where tenants take units in a 'shell condition', that is without internal fittings and without a shop front and install their own.

Rents may also be set rather creatively, to help attract tenants. For example, stepped rents are usually set at a lower than market rent when the lease starts, with increases over the term of the lease. A turnover rent is a proportion of the turnover of the tenant's business. This can help to reduce the burden on a struggling tenant. However, we are aware of a shop let at a turnover rent, which experienced a negative turnover. The volume of online purchases returned to the shop meant that the value of refunds was greater than the value of the items sold by the shop. In this case, the shop's negative turnover resulted in the landlord receiving no rent, demonstrating the need to carefully draft lease clauses to reflect all eventualities.

DEMISE

The demise, or the demised premises, is the property leased to the tenant, normally described in detail in the lease and shown outlined on the plan that accompanies it. This may sound simple, but it can be very intricate, and a badly drafted lease can cause considerable problems. The demise may be an entire building or site. Alternatively, it may be very restricted, including only the internal non-structural components. It is important that the demise is clearly defined in the lease, to ensure that the extent of the leased premises is clear. It is also important because repairing covenants usually refer to the demise, so an error can result in, for example, disputes over responsibility for repairs.

The parts of the property that are excluded from the lease are usually called the reserved property.

REVERSION

The 'reversion', in legal terms, is the landlord's interest in the property once the lease has ended and the property reverts to the landlord.

LEASEHOLD COVENANTS

A covenant is a promise in a deed or lease. The covenants in a lease set out the obligations and responsibilities of the landlord and tenant. A lease is a contract, so the covenants reflect the agreement made between the parties. It is important to read the lease carefully when addressing an assignment or when dealing with landlord and tenant matters in practice. However, it is also very important to remember that legislation and case law may affect the covenants in a lease, so the contents of the lease, and the law, must be considered together.

Covenants may be:

- Expressly stated in the lease;
- Implied into the lease by the law;
- Qualified – requiring landlord's consent to an action by the tenant;
- Fully qualified – where landlord's consent is required, consent is not to be unreasonably withheld;
- Absolute prohibitions – where the lease will ban the tenant from carrying out certain actions.

If the landlord or tenant breaches a covenant, they are failing to comply with a contractual obligation and legal action could be taken by the other party to enforce the terms of the lease. Usually, a lease will contain more covenants by the tenant than the landlord. The tenant is in actual occupation of the premises and the landlord will wish to exercise some control over that occupation, to protect their investment. However, tenant covenants which overly restrict the tenant's use of, and rights to alter or dispose of, the premises may be reflected in the rent and marketability of the property.

Typical lease covenants are outlined as follows.

QUIET ENJOYMENT

This is an important covenant, which the law implies into a lease if it is not expressly stated. Quiet enjoyment means that the landlord covenants to allow the tenant to possess and enjoy the property undisturbed and uninterrupted. Examples of a breach of a quiet enjoyment covenant would include a landlord entering the property without giving proper notice, obstructing the tenant's access to the property, or attempting to evict the tenant without following the proper legal process. Landlords and agents need to be mindful of the quiet enjoyment covenant when dealing with tenants, to avoid an unintentional breach.

ALIENATION

Alienation clauses relate to the tenant's right to deal with their leasehold estate in land. It includes:

- Assignment – the transfer of the tenant's interest under the lease to a third-party assignee, who becomes the tenant in place of the outgoing tenant;
- Subletting (also sometimes called underletting) – the granting of a new lease by the tenant to a third party, who becomes a subtenant. If a tenant sublets their premises, they remain a tenant in relation to their landlord, but they also become a landlord in relation to the sub-tenant;
- Mortgaging – granting an interest in the property as security for a loan. You can read more on mortgages in Chapter 9.

Although the landlord and tenant may negotiate the alienation provisions in the lease, it is common for landlord's consent to be required to alienation of the whole of the premises, with alienation of part of the premises being prohibited.

The Landlord and Tenant Act 1927 intervenes in alienation. Section 19(1)(a) of this Act stipulates that if the lease requires the landlord's consent to alienation, consent cannot be unreasonably withheld. Section 19(1A) of the Act has limited application (to assignments of new – post 1 January 1996 – commercial leases only) but it is nevertheless important. This sub-section enables the landlord and tenant to agree in the lease conditions that will apply to any consent to assignment or circumstances in which consent can be refused. Under Section 19(1A) these conditions and circumstances will be automatically reasonable.

If the landlord consents to alienation, this will usually be done in a licence to assign or a licence to sublet.

ALTERATIONS

Typically, a lease will distinguish between structural alterations and non-structural alterations, prohibiting structural alterations and requiring landlord's consent to internal non-structural alterations. If consent is given, it will usually be in a licence for alterations. However, this is a matter for negotiation between the landlord and tenant before the lease starts, subject to Section 19(2) of the Landlord and Tenant Act 1927. This provides that if the landlord's consent is required, consent cannot be unreasonably withheld if the proposed alterations are an improvement to the property. The case of *FW Woolworth & Co v Lambert 1937* tells us that an improvement is judged from the tenant's perspective. In practice, the tenant is likely to consider the alteration to be an improvement (why would the tenant want to do the work if it is not to their benefit?), so the landlord cannot unreasonably withhold consent. Tenant's improvements will be excluded from valuations for future rent reviews if they are formally recorded as such.

INSURANCE

It is common for landlords of residential properties to covenant to insure the property (but not the tenant's contents) against specific risks, known as insured risks. Insured risks might include, for example, flooding, fire, explosion, malicious damage, terrorism, and damage from water leaks. The landlord might recover the insurance premium from the tenant either via a service charge or by a separate insurance rent. In commercial leases the tenants may be directly responsible for insuring the property if the lease is a lease of the whole. If the building consists of leases of parts of the premises to several different tenants, the landlord will insure the whole building and be reimbursed via each tenant's insurance rent payment. It would not be practical or possible for each tenant just to insure their own demised premises. Insurance needs to be considered alongside repairing covenants, as we see later.

REPAIRS

The repairing covenants in a lease are often complex and various arrangements may apply, depending on the negotiations between the parties, the type of lease, and the law. Some typical arrangements include:

- FRI leases – the tenant is responsible for repairing and insuring the premises. Where a commercial building is leased to more than one tenant each tenant will only have direct repairing responsibility for its own demised premises. However, it will reimburse the landlord for the cost of repairing the structure and retained parts of the building via the service charge and for the cost of insuring the building via the insurance rent. Such a lease will be an FRI or 'clear' lease in effect as rent received by the landlord will thus be pure profit;
- Internal repairing and insuring (IRI) leases – the tenant takes on a less onerous obligation to repair and insure the interior only;
- Internal repairing leases – the tenant's only obligation is to repair the interior; all other costs and responsibilities are borne by the landlord. These are rare but are found, for example in Grade I listed buildings where insurance would be very costly;
- Indirect repairing obligations – the tenant does not have a direct repairing obligation but indirectly contributes towards the cost of repairs carried out by the landlord by paying a service charge.

These leases are often described as 'effective full repairing and insuring'. In long residential leases, the tenant will typically be responsible for maintaining the interior non-structural demise and pay a service charge towards the cost of the external and structural repairs;

- Statutory repairing obligations – in residential tenancies of less than seven years, Section 11 of the Landlord and Tenant Act 1985 imposes repairing obligations on the landlord, who must repair the structure, exterior and installations, such as pipes, wiring, and heating systems. The landlord also has other legal obligations, relating to the condition and testing of gas and electrical installations. However, tenants must act in a 'tenant-like manner'. This phrase comes from the case of *Warren v Keen 1954* and means that the tenant must take care of the property, for example by unblocking sinks and replacing light bulbs, and the tenant must not damage the property.

In commercial properties, a schedule of condition may be prepared before the start of the lease, recording the condition of the premises at that point in time. Both parties should sign and date this to record their acceptance that it is a fair representation of the existing condition. Failure to repair may result in a schedule of dilapidations being prepared on behalf of the landlord specifying the repairs that the tenant must carry out or pay for at the end of the lease. Depending on the wording of the repairing covenant, the negotiations between the landlord and the tenant, and the future use of the property, the tenant may not be required to put the property in a better state of repair than is recorded in the schedule of condition. Legal advisers need to ensure that repairing covenants are drafted correctly, to reflect the intentions of the parties.

Repairing obligations can be a source of dispute between landlords and tenants, so it is useful to briefly consider remedies for breach of a repairing obligation. These will usually be in the form of damages (money paid as compensation). However, the amount of the damages awarded to a landlord for breach of a tenant's repairing covenant may be limited. Section 18(1) of the Landlord and Tenant Act 1927 caps damages to the amount by which the value of the reversion is diminished by the breach. This may be less than the actual cost of the repairs.

The correct procedure must be followed under Section 1 of the Leasehold Property (Repairs) Act 1938 in certain circumstances. The detail of these Acts is outside the scope of this chapter, but it is useful to be aware of an alternative remedy available to the landlord, called a Jervis v Harris clause. This allows the landlord to enter the property, carry out the repairs and charge the cost to the tenant. This is a remedy we have used in practice, and it can be quick and effective compared to a claim for damages or forfeiture of the lease.

When considering repairing covenants in a lease, it is important to check the demise. Repairing covenants typically refer to the demise, so the tenant must repair the demised premises and the landlord must repair the remainder (usually called the reserved property). This can be a complicated process in practice, involving several reviews of the lease, but reading and interpreting leases is an important skill for students and real estate professionals.

We have mentioned that it is usual for leases to state that the property must be insured against specified risks. Insured risks and repairing covenants work together to refine the repairing obligation, so a tenant who may otherwise be responsible for repairs to a property may not be required to carry out those repairs if the damage has been caused by an insured risk. For example, a tenant may covenant to carry out repairs to the demised premises, but if damage is caused by a burst water pipe, and the lease says that this is an insured risk, the tenant does not have to carry out the repair. This applies regardless of whether the landlord has taken out insurance against that specific risk.

The meaning of 'repair' needs to be considered carefully by both landlords and tenants. Subtle variations in wording can create significant differences in the obligation. This is a matter for legal advisers when drafting the lease. However, surveyors should consider using a schedule of condition to record the condition of the property at the start of the tenancy and a schedule of dilapidations to establish any works the tenant needs to carry out at the end of the tenancy if the tenant has failed to adequately repair.

SERVICE CHARGES

Service charges are a variable charge payable under a lease in relation to maintenance, repairs, services, management, and insurance costs (alternatively, insurance may be demanded separately as insurance rent). These will vary between accounting years to reflect the costs incurred during that period. Residential service charges are subject to several legal rights conferred on leaseholders to protect them from unreasonable costs and to involve them in decisions on expenditure. You will find more information on service charges in Chapter 13.

USER

Leases typically contain covenants by the tenant regarding the permitted use of the premises (the user covenant). These enable the landlord to retain some control over the asset, whilst allowing the tenant to reside in, or run their business from, the premises. The user clause in a commercial lease will often refer to planning Use Classes; you will find more information on these in Chapter 3. In a residential lease it is common for the use to be restricted to a single private dwelling. In this case, use for short-term holiday lets can breach the user covenant, as evidenced by the case of *Nemcova v Fairfield Rents Ltd 2016*.

A user clause may permit change of use with the landlord's consent (a qualified covenant) and it may also state that consent is not to be unreasonably withheld (a fully qualified covenant). A very restrictive user covenant may affect the tenant's ability to adapt and diversify the use of the premises. It may also make it more difficult to assign the lease or to sublet the premises, as the market for the premises will be reduced. However, a restrictive user covenant may be reflected in a lower rent and therefore a lower capital value for the landlord. Conversely, the tenant may need to pay a higher rent if the user covenant is widely drafted, as this additional flexibility will be of greater value to the tenant.

ENFORCING LEASEHOLD COVENANTS

Leases can last for many years – it is common, for example for long residential leases to have a term of 999 years. It follows then that a lease may be bought and sold many times during its term. The covenants in the lease need to be capable of being enforced between the original landlord and tenant, both of whom signed the contract – the lease – so they have a direct contractual relationship. However, the covenants may also need to be enforceable between subsequent owners of both the landlord and the tenant's estates in the land. This is a complex area, and it is not the purpose of this chapter to go into detail as there are specialist texts available. However, we outline some basic principles to help your understanding.

There are two rules that apply, depending on whether the lease was dated before 1 January 1996, when the Landlord and Tenant (Covenants) Act 1995 came into force. It is important to be aware of each set of rules, as there are many current leases that were created before 1996, under the old rules, as well as new leases, created on or after 1 January 1996.

THE OLD RULES – PRE-1996

The signatures of the original landlord and tenant on the lease bind them to that lease – they have privity of contract (a contractual relationship). They promise to ensure compliance with the covenants for the full term, even if it lasts for many years and even after they have sold their interest. This is an onerous position for the original parties to be in, as when they sell, they lose control but retain liability.

A lease is both a contract and an estate in land and this brings us to the concept of privity of estate: the relationship between the current landlord and the current tenant. Privity of estate can enable covenants to be enforced against subsequent landlords and tenants in certain circumstances. However, while privity of estate may allow a covenant to be enforced against subsequent landlords and tenants, the original parties remain liable for breaches of covenant as they have privity of contract. Therefore, a subsequent landlord or tenant may have the choice of enforcing the covenant against either the original party or the current party.

THE NEW RULES – 1996 ONWARDS

If the lease is dated on, or after, 1 January 1996 new rules will apply, under the Landlord and Tenant (Covenants) Act 1995. The new rules abolish the continuing liability of the original landlord and tenant and so help alleviate the unfairness associated with privity of contract. An original tenant, who has assigned (transferred) their interest as tenant, will be automatically released from the contract under Section 5 of the Act. This means that an outgoing tenant will not be liable for breaches of covenant by a new tenant, who automatically becomes responsible for complying with the tenants' covenants in the lease, because of Section 3 of the Act.

There is, however, a limited way in which an original tenant's liability might continue under Section 16 of the Act. A lease may require the tenant to obtain the landlord's consent to assignment if the tenant wishes to sell or dispose of the lease – this consent may be subject to the tenant entering into an Authorised Guarantee Agreement (AGA), if it is reasonable to do so or if it is expressly stated in the lease. An AGA is a guarantee by an outgoing tenant that the new tenant (the assignee) will comply with the lease covenants. If the assignee breaches any lease covenant the outgoing tenant will be liable under the AGA. However, this liability only relates to a breach by the assignee, it does not apply to any subsequent tenants, so it is still preferable to the old rules from an original tenant's perspective. During the term of a lease there may be many tenants; each tenant can be required to enter into an AGA, providing a guarantee in respect of the next tenant until that (new) tenant assigns the lease to the next tenant.

So far, we have applied the new rules to the tenant, but what happens if the landlord wishes to dispose of the reversion? The situation is quite different here, as the landlord is not automatically released from the covenants under the lease. Instead, the landlord must apply to the tenant for a release, or to the court if the tenant does not provide this release. Alternatively, the lease itself can state that the landlord is released from covenants on assignment. Under Section 3 of the Act, the new landlord (the assignee) will become automatically liable for compliance with the landlord's obligations in the lease.

HOW DOES A LEASE END?

A lease is a finite estate in land, which means that when the term – the duration – of the lease ends, the lease expires. This is called effluxion of time – the 'natural' coming to an end of the lease at the expiry of the term.

However, leases may end before the expiry of the term, due to the action of one or both parties, or due to the effect of certain events upon the lease. Ways of ending leases are outlined as follows.

BREAK CLAUSES

The lease may include a clause enabling either party, or both, to give notice ending the lease during its term. This is called a break clause and it may contain conditions, which must be complied with if the break is to be effective; payment of rent, compliance with repairing and other covenants, vacant possession, and notice periods being typical examples of break conditions. These can be difficult to comply with, as evidenced by the amount of case law, which is outside the scope of this chapter, but you will find details of further information at the end of this chapter.

Break clauses can be extremely useful if either party wishes to retain some flexibility. They offer tenants an alternative to subletting or assignment of the lease if the tenant wishes to vacate the premises before the lease has expired. The landlord may also offer break clauses as an incentive to attract tenants.

DISCLAIMER

A lease can be disclaimed by a trustee in bankruptcy (if the tenant is an individual) or by the liquidator (if the tenant is a company) under the Insolvency Act 1986. This may be necessary if the lease is a liability rather than an asset because it cannot easily be sold or because it involves a liability to pay money, such as rent.

FORFEITURE

Forfeiture is the re-entering – repossession – of the premises by the landlord because the tenant is in breach of a covenant in the lease, for example to repair or to pay rent. It is usual for a lease to contain a forfeiture clause, entitling the landlord to claim forfeiture but under Section 146 of the Law of Property Act 1925, unless the breach is the non-payment of rent, the landlord must first serve a notice on the tenant with information on the breach and how forfeiture can be avoided (e.g. by remedying the breach).

Forfeiture clearly has serious consequences for a tenant, but the tenant may be able to apply to court for relief from forfeiture. The broad principle is that the court may exercise its discretion to award relief, in which case the landlord will not be able to forfeit the lease. However, it is likely that the tenant will have to remedy the breach where it is possible to do so. This is a complex area, particularly in relation to residential leases. The detail is beyond our scope, but you can find further reading at the end of this chapter.

Forfeiture is the ending of the lease and, therefore, of the landlord and tenant relationship. If the tenant is in breach, but the landlord's actions indicate the intention to continue the lease, the landlord is said to have waived the right to claim forfeiture for that breach. For example, demanding rent from a tenant who is in breach of a covenant in the lease will be construed as an intention that the lease is to continue; the right of the landlord to forfeit the lease is therefore likely to have been waived. Waiver is a critical matter for landlords and their professional advisers as the right to claim forfeiture is easily compromised. It is important to have procedures in place to prevent an unintentional waiver, for example a close relationship between the accounts team and the management surveyor or a file, or stop, note to prevent rent being demanded if the tenant is in breach of covenant and the landlord is considering forfeiture.

During the Covid-19 pandemic, the government intervened in the commercial landlord and tenant relationship by preventing forfeiture for non-payment of rent, via Section 82 of the Coronavirus Act 2020.

FRUSTRATION

Frustration is a contractual concept, reflecting the lease as a contract between the landlord and the tenant. *National Carriers Ltd v Panalpina (Northern) Ltd 1981* stated that frustration could apply to a lease in principle. A lease may be frustrated if circumstances change after the lease has been entered into, meaning that it is no longer possible for the lease to continue or it is illegal for it to do so. The change in circumstances must relate to the fundamental nature of the agreement. For example, if an office building is destroyed by fire, it will no longer exist, rendering its use impossible. The purpose behind the creation of the leases will have been frustrated – it can no longer be achieved. Therefore, the parties' obligations under the leases may end. Frustration is extremely rare in practice.

MERGER

Merger is the merging together of two estates in land through common ownership that extinguishes the lesser interest. For example, if a leaseholder acquires the freehold of their property the lease will end, and the former leaseholder will become the freehold owner.

We mention enfranchisement as: the collective acquisition of the freehold of a block of flats by a majority of the leaseholders of those flats. In this instance, merger would not occur, as the acquisition of the freehold would usually be via, for example, a company set up by the leaseholders for this purpose. The leaseholders remain as such, but they will have shares in the company, which becomes the landlord.

NOTICE

A periodic tenancy can be terminated by notice given by one party to the other. The basic principle is that the minimum notice must be equivalent to one tenancy period. For example, if the tenancy runs from month to month, at least one month's notice must be given, expiring on the last day of the month. A yearly tenancy requires at least six months' notice to terminate. The tenancy agreement may stipulate the notice period to be given, but statute also intervenes, particularly in relation to residential tenancies. A minimum of four weeks' written notice is required to end a residential tenancy under the Protection from Eviction Act 1977 and in the case of an Assured Shorthold Tenancy, the landlord must give two months' notice to terminate the tenancy under Section 21 of the Housing Act 1988. However, during the Covid-19 pandemic the Coronavirus Act 2020 extended this notice period to six months, subject to some exceptions. In addition, the government imposed a stay on possession proceedings, preventing the eviction of tenants from their homes.

REPUDIATION

A lease may be terminated by repudiation if one party commits a breach (fails to meet their obligations under the lease) to such an extent as to make it clear that they reject the lease, and this rejection is accepted by the other party to the lease. Repudiation is a contractual concept, reflecting the status of a lease as a contract. It relates to the 'essence' of this contract, so the breach must be significant, enabling the injured party to bring the contract to an end. Repudiation is available to both the landlord and the tenant. However, if a tenant is in breach of the lease, the landlord may have the option of forfeiture as a means of ending the lease (see separate section). Forfeiture is not available to the tenant, so repudiation offers the tenant a means of ending a lease if the landlord is in breach. For example, a landlord's failure to maintain premises could be a repudiatory breach, enabling the tenant to accept the repudiation, end the lease, and seek alternative accommodation. Although repudiation seems to be accepted as applicable to leases, there is some uncertainty on this point, as a lease is an estate in land as well as a contract. As with frustration (see earlier), repudiation is rare.

SURRENDER

Surrender is the voluntary 'giving up' of the premises by the tenant, which is accepted by the landlord. Surrender must therefore be a mutual process; it cannot be unilateral, and it has the effect of terminating the lease.

A lease may be surrendered in one of two ways:

- Express surrender, by deed under Section 52(1) of the Law of Property Act 1925;
- Surrender by operation of law, arising from the conduct of both parties. The actions of the parties need to be unequivocal. Typically, the tenant will vacate the premises and return the keys to the landlord, who will accept the return of the keys and retake possession of the property.

A payment may be made in return for the surrender, either from the landlord to the tenant (a 'reverse premium') or from the tenant to the landlord, depending on the circumstances and market conditions at the time.

SECURITY OF TENURE

A lease is a finite estate in land and can be a wasting asset, as its value reduces as it nears its expiry date. This is not usually an issue for a very long lease – 999 years for example – but it can be a problem for shorter leases. Expiry of a lease can leave a residential tenant homeless, and a business without the premises from which they operate. For this reason, legislation has introduced security of tenure to protect a tenant who might otherwise be severely disadvantaged.

BUSINESS LEASES

Section 24 of the Landlord and Tenant Act 1954 entitles a qualifying tenant to remain in the premises on expiry of the lease and to request a new lease from the landlord, on similar terms to the existing. Sections 25 and 26 of the Act provide a time-bound process of service of notices and counter notices by landlord and tenant, depending on whether it is the landlord or the tenant who starts the process. The notice will state whether the landlord is prepared to grant a new lease and on what terms, or whether the tenant wants to take a new lease and on what terms.

Security of tenure in business leases can be limited. Firstly, it is possible for the landlord and tenant to agree at the start of the lease that the tenant will 'contract out' of the Act, which means that the tenant gives up the right to security of tenure. It is also possible for the landlord to claim specific grounds under Section 30 of the Act for regaining possession of the premises, even if the tenant does have security of tenure. Examples of these grounds include the landlord's intention to use the premises for its own use (provided they have been the landlord for at least five years), or to redevelop the premises.

RESIDENTIAL LEASES

In the 20th century, the Rent Acts conferred security of tenure and rent controls on residential tenancies. However, although there are still Rent Act-protected tenancies in existence, the situation changed with the Housing Act 1988. This Act created two new types of tenancies: Assured Tenancies and Assured Shorthold Tenancies. When the fixed term of these tenancies expires, they continue as periodic tenancies, and a court order is needed before a tenant can be evicted. However, there is a key difference between these two types of tenancy: a landlord of an Assured Tenancy can only regain possession by proving a ground for possession under the Act (e.g. rent arrears), whereas a landlord of an Assured Shorthold Tenancy has the option of serving a notice under Section 21 of the Act terminating the tenancy, without needing to prove a ground for possession. Therefore, Assured tenants have a greater degree of security of tenure than Assured Shorthold Tenants. Assured Shorthold Tenancies have become extremely popular in the private-rented sector and are a factor behind the boom in buy-to-let investment that occurred from the mid-1990s. However, you will see from Chapter 14 that there are moves to review landlords' rights to regain possession and it is possible that Section 21 notices may be abolished.

Further legislation in the form of the Protection from Eviction Act 1977 protects residential occupiers (subject to some exceptions) from harassment and unlawful eviction.

So far, we have considered short-term tenancies. Security of tenure differs in the case of long residential leases, which exceed 21 years, and which are let at a low rent. For tenancies entered into on or after 1 April 1990, a low rent means £1,000 or less per year in Greater London or £250 or less per year elsewhere. If the lease was entered into before this date, the rent must be less than two-thirds of the rateable value of the property on 31 March 1990. The detail of these complex provisions is outside the scope of this chapter, but the general principle is that Schedule 10 of the Local Government and Housing Act 1989 provides security of tenure in the case of a long residential lease. The lease will automatically continue on the same terms under Schedule 10 until the landlord serves notice on the tenant either stating that the landlord is seeking possession of the property on one of the authorised grounds (e.g. rent arrears) or the landlord proposes to grant the tenant an assured monthly periodic tenancy. The tenant does not need to move out unless the court orders possession. If an Assured Tenancy is granted, the tenant will no longer be an owner. However, the tenant will be able to remain in the property but will usually have to pay a market rent.

A tenant of a long residential lease also has rights to extend the lease or to buy the freehold (enfranchise), which are outlined in the next section. This means that, in reality, tenants are more likely to extend their leases than to allow them to expire and to then rely on the 1989 Act.

LONG RESIDENTIAL LEASES AND LEASEHOLDER RIGHTS

The law confers certain rights on tenants with long residential leases granted for a term of more than 21 years. It is important that real estate professionals working in this area are aware of these rights and their implications. In the broader context, awareness of the rights of long leaseholders and the protection of their interests has gained increasing social and political significance in recent years. This is discussed further in Chapter 14. It is not the purpose of this chapter to explain the procedures that apply and the criteria for qualification (both the buildings and the leaseholders must qualify to exercise these rights) but you will find detailed information on the Leasehold Advisory Service (LEASE) website listed at the end of this chapter. Although the legislation prescribes the procedures to follow, landlords and tenants may negotiate if they wish, without the need to follow the formal processes. This is an important area for surveyors; valuers may value properties for lease extension and enfranchisement purposes and estate agents may find that sales are impacted by the need to extend a lease to increase the value and marketability of a property.

ENFRANCHISEMENT

Leaseholders can join to exercise their legal right to buy the freehold of their block of flats under the Leasehold Reform, Housing & Urban Development Act 1993 (LRHUDA). This is a form of compulsory purchase; if the leaseholders collectively decide to enfranchise, provided the qualification requirements are met and the leaseholders follow the correct procedure, they will be entitled to buy the freehold regardless of whether the landlord wishes to sell. Ownership of the freehold estate gives the leaseholders more control over the management of their block as, in effect, they become their own landlords.

Both the property and the leaseholders must qualify for the right to be exercised by a majority, via a 'Nominee Purchaser' (an individual, or a company in which each participating leaseholder has a share).

Valuers will calculate the value under Schedule 6 of the Act, which will compensate the landlord for loss of: ground rents; the reversion; the opportunity to redevelop the property or an adjoining property. Marriage value may also be payable if the leases have 80 years or less left unexpired. Marriage value is the increase in the value of the combined leasehold and freehold interests after enfranchisement. Finally, as well as paying their own costs, leaseholders must pay the landlord's reasonable costs of enfranchisement.

THE RIGHT TO EXTEND THE LEASE OF A FLAT

LRHUDA may allow the owner of a long lease of a flat to buy an additional term of 90 years on top of the existing unexpired term. For example, if a lease has 40 years unexpired, the leaseholder can acquire a new lease for 130 years. The benefit to the leaseholder is the security achieved by the additional term and the added value; as the lease approaches its expiry date, its value will decrease, and it will become difficult to sell or mortgage.

The new, extended, lease will be the same as the old lease, but ground rent will only be a notional 'peppercorn', so the leaseholder will not have to pay ground rent even if they had to do so under the old lease. The landlord will need to be compensated for their loss. Under Schedule 13 of the Act this covers: loss of ground rent; the 90-year delay in the reversion (when the property reverts to the landlord at the end of the lease); marriage value (see the section on enfranchisement earlier); and loss of redevelopment opportunities. As with enfranchisement, the leaseholder will need to pay their own and the landlord's reasonable costs.

It is important to remember that the right to a lease extension for a flat is an individual right, whereas the right to enfranchise in relation to a block of flats is a collective right. The parties may negotiate a new lease informally between them if they wish, but there is also a procedure to follow under the Act if necessary. This is outside the scope of this chapter, but you will find more information on the LEASE website provided at the end of this chapter.

The government proposes to change this to a right to a 990-year extension. However, at the time of writing this has not yet taken effect (see Chapter 14).

THE RIGHT TO ENFRANCHISE OR EXTEND THE LEASE OF A HOUSE

The Leasehold Reform Act 1967 grants a right to the long leaseholder of a house to obtain the freehold or to extend the lease once, for 50 years from the expiry of the existing lease. Again, there are government proposals to change this to a 990-year extension, but this has not yet been implemented at the time of writing (see Chapter 14).

THE RIGHT OF FIRST REFUSAL

A landlord who wishes to dispose of a property containing flats must first offer that property to the leaseholders of the flats, on the same terms and at the same price as the landlord is proposing to dispose of the property to a third party. This is a called the Right of First Refusal. A majority of the leaseholders may exercise the right in response to the landlord's decision to dispose of the property, but they cannot initiate the process. If the leaseholders do not accept the offer, the landlord may sell the property to someone else during the subsequent 12-month period, on the same terms, and at the same, or a higher price. If the leaseholders do not accept the offer, and the landlord decides to sell at a lower price or on different terms, the landlord must again offer the property to the leaseholders.

It is a criminal offence for the landlord to fail to comply. The leaseholders can buy the property from the landlord's purchaser, at the same price and on the same terms, if the landlord has not first offered the property to them.

PROFESSIONAL GUIDANCE

There is extensive published guidance on landlord and tenant matters, some of which has government approval. Commercial sector guidance includes the RICS Code for leasing business premises 1st edition 2020. In the residential sector, the RICS Service charge residential management code 3rd edition 2016, the Private Rented Sector Code of Practice 2015 and the ARHM Private retirement housing code of practice England 2016 are examples. The landlord and tenant relationship is complex and interlinked with other key topics so this guidance is important and we recommend that you familiarise yourself with it. One aspect of the landlord and tenant relationship is the existence of dual (or multiple) contemporaneous estates in a single property – that of the landlord and tenant and possibly one or more subtenants. In the next chapter we consider other rights and interests that may exist in relation to real estate.

FURTHER INFORMATION

ARHM (2016) *Private Retirement Housing Code of Practice: England* London: Association of Retirement Housing Managers Available from: www.arhm. org/publication-category/code-of-practice/

Card, R, Murdoch, J, and Murdoch, S (2011) *Real Estate Management Law* 7th Edition Oxford: Oxford University Press

Davys, M (2009) *Land Law* 11th Edition London: Red Globe Press

Garner, S and Frith, A (2017) *A Practical Approach to Landlord and Tenant* 8th Edition Oxford: Oxford University Press

RICS (2015) *Private Rented Sector Code of Practice* 1st Edition London: Royal Institution of Chartered Surveyors Available from: www.rics.org/uk/upholding-professional-standards/sector-standards/real-estate/private-rented-sector-code-1st-edition/

RICS (2016) *Service Charge Residential Management Code and Advice to Landlords, Leaseholders and Agents* 3rd Edition London: Royal Institution of Chartered Surveyors Available from: www.rics.org/uk/upholding-professional-standards/sector-standards/real-estate/service-charge-residential-management-code/

RICS (2020) *Code for Leasing Business Premises* 1st Edition London: Royal Institution of Chartered Surveyors Available from: www.rics.org/uk/upholding-professional-standards/sector-standards/real-estate/code-for-leasing-business-premises-1st-edition/

Scarrett, D and Wilcox, J (2018) *Property Asset Management* 4th Edition Abingdon, Oxon: Routledge

WEBSITES

Association of Residential Managing Agents https://arma.org.uk
Association of Retirement Housing Managers www.arhm.org
Institute of Residential Property Management www.irpm.org.uk
Leasehold Advisory Service (LEASE) www.lease-advice.org

INTERESTS IN REAL ESTATE

INTERESTS IN REAL ESTATE

In Chapter 7 we considered real estate and its ownership. However, it is possible to have rights in relation to real estate without directly owning it. These may be legal (recognised by the common law), or they may only exist in equity (equitable interests). The concepts of common law and equity are discussed further in Chapter 7, but in general, legal interests are more robust than equitable interests, as they bind future owners of the land and are easier to enforce in court.

There is also a distinction between personal rights and proprietary rights. Personal rights are between the parties to an agreement. Proprietary rights attach to the property. Personal rights are weaker than proprietary rights; they do not generally bind future owners of the property and they are enforced against the person who granted the right, rather than against the property itself. For example, a hotel guest has a personal right, created by a contract, to occupy a room and use the facilities. If the hotel cancels the booking, the guest can ask for a refund, but they cannot insist upon occupying the room they had booked. This contrasts with the proprietary right enjoyed by a tenant who has acquired exclusive possession of the rented premises.

The main interests in land recognised by Section 1(2) of the Law of Property Act 1925 as capable of being legal interests are:

- Easements
- Profits a prendre

DOI: 10.1201/9781003155256-9

- Mortgages
- Rentcharges
- Rights of entry

Section 1(3) of this Act then tells us that all other interests in land are equitable interests. The principal equitable interests covered in this chapter are restrictive covenants and estate contracts. Others – interests under trusts, proprietary estoppel rights and failed legal interests – are covered in Chapter 7.

We will consider each interest in turn.

EASEMENTS

Easements are a type of right benefitting one property over another property that is owned by someone else. Easements are common – and very useful – in practice and may range from the obvious and apparent, for example, a right to walk along a path or drive down a driveway belonging to someone else; or less visible, such as a right for drainage pipes to pass below the surface of neighbouring land.

Easements can protect, and enhance, the use of a building, perhaps conferring a right to receive sufficient light through a window or a mutual easement of support between terraced or semi-detached houses. We dealt with a case involving demolition of a fire damaged building in a terrace. The demolition resulted in flooding in the neighbouring basement during heavy rain, as the neighbour was no longer protected by the demolished premises. The situation was resolved by re-building the fire-damaged property, but the case illustrates the importance of this type of right and the interdependence of some buildings.

An easement attaches to the land itself so that it can be enjoyed by any owner of the land. To be legal, usually the easement will be expressly created in a deed (Section 52 of the Law of Property Act 1925), although as we will see later, legal easements can be created in other ways.

The concepts of dominant and servient land need to be understood when considering easements. The dominant land is the land which enjoys the benefit of the easement. The servient land is the land which is burdened by the easement. You may encounter the term 'tenement' in relation to easements. This is another word for land; hence it is common to refer to the dominant tenement and the servient tenement.

It is important that the real estate professional understands easements. This is because easements can affect the use, value, and marketability of both the dominant and servient tenements. They can also be acquired through long usage, as we discuss later. Therefore, property owners and managers must be alert to third parties entering onto the property as it is possible that habitual use can be upgraded to a legal right. Furthermore, the owner of the servient tenement must allow the owner of the dominant tenement to use the easement. So, for example, if the easement is a right of access, the access route must not be obstructed; to do so could result in legal action being taken by the dominant owner against the servient owner. We came across a situation where, in the process of finalising a major redevelopment, we discovered an easement to allow a means of escape in case of fire from an office building. This nearly prevented the major redevelopment of the site and required major negotiations and payments to resolve the issue.

HOW ARE EASEMENTS CREATED?

Easements can be granted – created by the owner of one piece of land for the benefit of another piece of land. Alternatively, they can be reserved, when a landowner retains rights when selling off a piece of land. Easements can be expressly created. However, they can also be implied, which means that an easement may be created unintentionally.

EXPRESS EASEMENTS

Express easements are created intentionally, so checking documentation and inspecting the register of title at HM Land Registry will reveal their existence. Express easements must be created by deed to be legal. If they are not created by deed, they may be equitable if they comply with Section 2 of the Law of Property (Miscellaneous Provisions) Act 1989. This requires the easement to be in writing, containing all the agreed terms, and signed by all the parties.

IMPLIED EASEMENTS

The situation is more complex in the case of implied easements. To imply an easement, the court will apply certain tests to the circumstances, to decide whether an easement can be inferred.

The first consideration is whether the right that is being claimed is capable of being an easement. To do this, we must apply the four tests in *Re Ellenborough Park 1955*:

1   Is there dominant and servient land?
2   Does the right accommodate the dominant land? To decide this test, consider whether the right benefits the land itself. For example, could it benefit any owner of the land, rather than one specific owner?
3   Are the owners of the dominant land and the servient land different?
4   Is the right itself capable of being an easement? Consider whether:

   •   The person granting the easement is legally capable of doing so (e.g. are they the landowner?);
   •   The easement is sufficiently clear and identifiable;
   •   The interest is a type recognised by the courts as an easement (e.g. a right of way would be recognised as a type of easement).

It should be noted that this is not referring to public footpaths or bridle paths, such as would be seen on an Ordnance Survey map, but to the private rights enjoyed by the owner of a specific property over someone else's property.

If the *Re Ellenborough Park* criteria are satisfied, and the use is therefore capable of being an easement, the next step is to consider how the easement may have been implied. There are various ways that a court may infer that an easement has been created:

The rule in Wheeldon v Burrows 1879

Wheeldon v Burrows applies to the grant of an easement typically when part of a property is sold, creating two properties in separate ownership. On the sale of part, types of use previously enjoyed by the owner of the whole property may become easements benefitting the new owner of part.

For example, the owner of Property A uses their driveway to reach their paddock (which adjoins their house), from the road. If the paddock is sold to a new owner, creating a separate Property B, an easement along the driveway of Property A to reach the paddock (Property B) may arise. The new owner of Property B would therefore have the right to use the driveway to reach their property, which now benefits from an easement. The use of their own driveway by the owner of Property A to reach their paddock before the sale is a quasi-easement and it may become an actual easement once Property A has been separated into two properties under different ownership. In our example, Property B is the new dominant tenement and Property A is the servient tenement.

For a quasi-easement to be converted into an easement, under *Wheeldon v Burrows*, the use of the quasi-easement must have been continuous and apparent, and it must have been in use at the time of the sale of part. For example, an identifiable path that is in regular use would be continuous and apparent. The use must also be necessary for the reasonable enjoyment of the property claiming the benefit of the easement. In our example, if the owner of Property A has been regularly using the driveway (which is clearly identifiable and is therefore apparent), to reach the paddock, and is doing so up to the point of the sale, the paddock (Property B) will benefit from the conversion of the quasi-easement into an easement provided it is necessary for the reasonable use of Property B.

Section 62 of the Law of Property Act 1925

Easements can also be implied under Section 62 of the Law of Property Act 1925, when land has been sold. Section 62 provides that when land is transferred from one owner to an other new owner (such as on a sale) the transfer will be deemed to include all easements and rights that relate to the land. For Section 62 to apply there must have been a deed transferring ownership or creating a lease of the property. The dominant and servient land must also be occupied by different people, although under *P&S Platt Ltd v Crouch 2004*, this may not be necessary if the use of the right has been continuous and apparent at the time the land is transferred to the new owner or the new lease is created.

The effects of Section 62 and of *Wheeldon v Burrows* can be wide-reaching. For this reason, it is common for both Section 62 and *Wheeldon v Burrows* to be excluded when buying and selling real estate. This means that the buyer and seller expressly state that the transfer does not include any rights that might otherwise be implied for the benefit of the new owner.

Prescription

The law also enables easements to be implied by Prescription, or long usage. There are three ways of acquiring an easement by Prescription. For one or more of these methods to create an easement:

- The use of the right being claimed must have been continuous;
- It must relate to a claim by one freehold owner against another freehold owner;
- It must have been used as of right.

Continuous use means that the use must be regular. Use as of right means that the person claiming the easement must consider themselves to be entitled to it, rather than because their use was secret, or involved force, or because they had permission from the freeholder to use the land.

We mentioned that there are three ways of acquiring an easement by Prescription. These are:

- **Common Law**. Use of the right needs to be from time immemorial, which means since 1189. However, it is highly unlikely that a person claiming an easement by this method could prove use since 1189. Instead, if the use can be proven for 20 years this will suffice as evidence of use since time immemorial, unless there is evidence that there had not actually been use since time immemorial;
- **Lost modern grant**. This is based on the idea that the document granting an easement has been lost. If it can be evidenced that use of the easement took place for a period of 20 years at some time in the past, the doctrine of lost modern grant may

presume the easement to have been created. If there is evidence that the easement could not actually have been granted, a claim under lost modern grant may fail;

- **Prescription Act 1832**. Again, this allows an easement to be claimed though long usage, in this case for 20 or 40 years. This Act is perhaps less likely to be encountered in practice and the detail is outside our scope here, but you can find further sources of information at the end of this chapter.

PROFITS A PRENDRE

Profits a prendre are rights to take a something from someone else's land, for example, to graze animals (taking the vegetation from the land), to catch fish, or to collect firewood. Profits a prendre are generally similar to easements, as 'appurtenant profits' benefit dominant land. However, a 'profit in gross' differs from appurtenant profits, in that it is not attached to dominant land. This means that it is not necessary for the person who enjoys the right to own benefitting land. A profit can be 'several', which means that it is enjoyed solely by the person benefitting from it to the exclusion of others, including the owner of the land. Alternatively, a profit can be used in common with other people.

MORTGAGES

A mortgage – also known as a charge – is an interest in a property granted by a borrower (the mortgagor) to a lender (the mortgagee) as security in return for a loan. The general principle is that if the borrower defaults, the lender can repossess and sell the property to recover their money. There are some key points to understand:

- It is common to confuse the mortgagor and mortgagee and to refer to a buyer obtaining a mortgage. The mortgage is the interest granted in the property in return for the loan, so strictly, a buyer does not obtain a mortgage, they obtain a loan. In return for the loan, the borrower gives the lender an interest in the property; hence the borrower – the donor of the interest – is called the mortgagor. The lender receives the interest in the mortgaged property. As recipient (donee) they are called the mortgagee;

- Historically, ownership of property was transferred to the mortgagee and the mortgagor was able to buy the property back once the loan had been repaid;

- The equity of redemption is the mortgagor's right to recover the mortgaged property (to redeem) once the money owed to the mortgagee has been repaid;

- The legal redemption date of a mortgage is the theoretical date (usually six months from the date of the mortgage) after which the mortgagee can exercise their rights if the mortgagor has defaulted. It is also the date after which the mortgagor can redeem the mortgage;

- In contrast to the historic position, the mortgagor does now retain ownership of the legal estate, but the equitable right to redeem is still relevant. The mortgagor always has an equitable right to repay the loan, ending the mortgagee's interest in the property;

- A mortgagee needs to take reasonable steps to ensure that a borrower is aware of the implications of the mortgage if:

  - There is a non-commercial relationship between the borrowers (e.g. spouses) and
  - There is a risk that the trust between the borrowers has been abused by one of them.

There is considerable case law on misrepresentation and undue influence in these circumstances; *Royal Bank of Scotland PLC v Etridge (No2) 2002* provides useful further guidance, and you will find the reference in the Table of Cases.

If the mortgagor defaults in their payments, the mortgagee has powers to protect their position.

The main powers enable the mortgagee to:

- Take possession, usually to gain vacant possession of the property to sell it. If the property is residential, the court can delay possession for a reasonable time to enable repayment;

- Sell the property at its market value at the time of the sale. This is important in practice, although it is subject to certain conditions under Sections 101 and 103 of the Law of Property Act 1925. The buyer acquires the property free from the mortgagor's rights. The proceeds of sale must be used to pay off the debt, with any balance left due to the mortgagor;

- Appoint a receiver to actively manage a mortgaged commercial property. For example, the receiver may collect the rent if the property has been leased to tenants.

Loan security valuation is a significant area of work for many valuers. Consequently, it is a competency for APC candidates and RICS Valuation – Global Standards (the Red Book) and the UK Supplement both contain guidance. Mortgage fraud is a risk in this area of work, and we have encountered cases in practice. Firstly, a husband forged his wife's signature on a mortgage deed and secondly, a mortgage was secured on the borrower's neighbour's flat. Another example of mortgage fraud is a buy-to-let purchaser trying to obtain a homeowner's loan, at a lower rate of interest.

RENTCHARGES

A rentcharge is a periodic sum payable to a third party (known as the rent owner) by the owner of a freehold property. Rentcharges should not be confused with the ground rent or market rent payable under a lease or tenancy.

The Rentcharges Act 1977 has abolished the creation of new rentcharges, with limited exceptions. The main exception is estate rentcharges, which are created to cover the cost of maintenance, repairs, insurance, or the provision of services benefitting freehold land. This is sometimes seen in housing estates with shared roads or other facilities.

It is possible to redeem (buy out) a rentcharge. Rentcharges are also due to be extinguished by Section 3 of the Act from 2037 or on the expiry of 60 years from the date the rentcharge first became payable, whichever is later.

RIGHTS OF ENTRY

Rights of entry are a way of enforcing compliance with an obligation by taking possession of the property to which the obligation applies. The right applies principally in the landlord and tenant relationship and is also known as forfeiture. You will find more information on this in Chapter 8.

Rights of entry can also be attached to rentcharges, considered earlier, as a means of enforcing the payment of the rentcharge.

FREEHOLD COVENANTS

A covenant is a promise in a deed or a lease. The person who made the promise is called the covenantor. The person who benefits from the promise is known as the covenantee. In this section we will look at the basics of covenants that apply to freehold land. We do not go into detail as there are specialist texts available. Covenants in leases are considered separately in Chapter 8. Freehold covenants are an important topic in real estate law modules, and they are also frequently encountered in practice.

Freehold covenants are equitable interests in land. Covenants can be positive or restrictive (restrictive covenants are sometimes called negative covenants). A positive covenant requires some action or expenditure on the part of the person who has made the promise. For example, a covenant to erect and maintain a boundary fence would be a positive covenant, because it requires a positive action – it is not possible to comply with the covenant by taking no action. Restrictive covenants prevent the owner of a property from doing something on that property, so it is possible to comply with a restrictive covenant without doing anything – in particular without spending money. For example, a covenant not to build on a piece of land is a restrictive covenant; compliance simply requires the owner to refrain from building. One of our houses, for example, has a restrictive covenant stating that we cannot erect any buildings within 17ft of the front boundary of the plot.

The concepts of benefit and burden apply to covenants. One property (the dominant tenement) will benefit from the promise, the other (the servient tenement) will be burdened by it. So, if, for example the owner of a house sells a paddock next to the house and imposes a restrictive covenant to prevent building on that paddock, the owner of the house will benefit from the covenant (by preventing unwanted development) whereas the new owner of the paddock will be burdened by the prohibition and will be obliged to comply with it.

Covenants become more complicated when properties are bought and sold and the original covenantor and/or covenantee no longer owns the property. The situation here is complex and we must distinguish between the benefit and the burden when deciding whether a covenant runs with the land.

PASSING ON THE BURDEN OF A COVENANT

The burden of complying with a restrictive covenant does not pass to a new owner under the common law. However, equity might enable it to pass to the new owner if certain conditions are met. These conditions are set out in *Tulk v Moxhay 1848*:

- The covenant must be restrictive, so *Tulk v Moxhay* does not apply to positive covenants;
- The covenant must accommodate the land that it benefits. For example, the benefitting and burdened land must be sufficiently close to each other for the covenant to benefit the dominant land and the person claiming the benefit of the covenant must have an interest in the dominant land;
- The original covenantor and covenantee must have intended the burden of compliance to pass on to future owners of the servient land. This intention is now implied by Section 79 of the Law of Property Act 1925;
- The buyer of the burdened land must be aware of the covenant. This is known as having notice of it. Registration of the covenant at HM Land Registry (if the land is registered) or on the Land Charges Register (if the land is unregistered) constitutes notice of the covenant. Therefore, if the buyer is not actually aware of the covenant, but it has been registered, the buyer will be treated as being aware of it.

It follows that the burden of a positive (as opposed to a restrictive) covenant cannot pass to future owners, so it can only be enforced against the original covenantor. This creates a problem for the original covenantor, who has promised to comply with the covenant and must continue to do so even if he or she has sold the property and no longer has control of it. In practice, this problem can be addressed by asking the buyer to provide an indemnity to the seller so that if the buyer breaches the covenant the buyer will repay the original covenantor any losses if the original covenantor is sued for breach of covenant. If the servient land changes ownership more than once, an indemnity chain will be created, with each successive buyer providing an indemnity to their seller. However, this is not ideal, and the original covenantor still risks being sued if a subsequent owner breaches the covenant.

The case of *Halsall v Brizell 1957* provides another means of addressing this problem. *Halsall v Brizell* decided that if someone benefits from a right, they cannot then avoid the responsibilities that might attach to that right. For example, if a right is granted subject to an obligation to contribute towards the cost of providing or maintaining that right, the benefit of the right cannot be enjoyed without the corresponding contribution towards the cost. This might occur when a shared access road to an estate is used; use of the road may make the cost of maintaining it recoverable from the covenantor.

PASSING ON THE BENEFIT OF A COVENANT

A person buying property that benefits from a covenant is likely to want to acquire that benefit. Equity enables the benefit of positive and restrictive covenants to pass to a buyer in certain circumstances:

- Annexation of the covenant to the land: This is the most common – and therefore the most important – means of passing the benefit of a covenant. If a covenant expressly states that it should be for the benefit of a specific piece of land, it will attach to that piece of land and effectively become part of it. If not expressly stated, Section 78(1) of the Law of Property Act 1925 may annex the benefit of a covenant to a piece of land, again potentially allowing future owners to benefit from the covenant;
- It is possible for a seller to assign (transfer) the benefit of a covenant to a buyer, enabling the buyer to enforce the covenant if necessary;

- Development schemes on a housing estate, where the developer, and future owners of houses on the estate, will want to have some control over other owners, to retain the character, uniformity, and density of the scheme.

The benefit of a covenant can also pass to a buyer under common law either expressly (in writing under Section 136 of the Law of Property Act 1925) or it can be implied if:

- The covenant 'touches and concerns' the land, meaning that it must benefit the dominant land;
- The original covenantor and covenantee intended the benefit to pass on to future owners of the dominant land. This intention can be expressly stated in the covenant itself, or it can be implied by Section 78(1) of the Law of Property Act 1925;
- The owner of the dominant land must have held a legal estate in the land when the covenant was originally created. The buyer of the dominant land must also acquire a legal estate in the dominant land to claim the benefit of the covenant.

ENFORCING COVENANTS

The rules on passing the benefit and burden of a covenant outlined earlier may enable a covenant to be enforced. However, covenants are complex, and it is useful to summarise key points:

- To enforce a covenant the covenantee must have the benefit, and the covenantor must have the burden, of the covenant, hence the need to consider the position of subsequent owners;
- The original covenantor (who has promised to comply with the covenant) remains contractually liable for compliance with the covenant, even after a sale of the property;
- The benefit and burden go hand in hand. This means that if a covenantee wants to enforce a covenant relying on equitable rules, the covenantor must have the burden of complying in equity. Similarly, if a covenantee is seeking to rely on enforcement in common law, the covenantor must have a common law obligation to comply with the covenant;

- The original covenantee can enforce the covenant against the original covenantor as a contractual agreement between them;
- If the original covenantee sells the benefitting land, subsequent owners may be able to enforce the covenant against the original covenantor, if the subsequent owners have acquired the benefit of the covenant under the rules outlined earlier. In this situation, the common law rules on the transmission of benefit will be preferred as any remedy will be available as of right (equitable remedies are always only granted at the court's discretion);
- If the original covenantor has sold the burdened land, the subsequent owners of the burdened land will not have to comply with the burden of the covenant if it is a positive covenant. This is because neither common law nor equity permits the burden of a positive covenant to pass to subsequent owners. However, subsequent owners may be personally contractually liable under a chain of indemnity covenants (see earlier);
- If the original covenantor has sold the burdened land, equity may require the subsequent owners to comply with the burden of the covenant if it is restrictive, under the conditions in *Tulk v Moxhay 1848*;
- It follows that even if the owner of the land has the benefit of a covenant, if the current owner of the burdened land does not have to comply with the burden, limited real benefit may be acquired. Although the original covenantor can be sued, the covenantor is no longer in control of the land so enforcement may be difficult.

The equitable rules applicable to restrictive covenants are the most important in practice. This is because the burden of compliance with a restrictive covenant can pass to subsequent owners of the burdened land and may be enforceable in equity. Equity offers injunctions as a remedy to stop a breach of covenant occurring, although the courts can order the covenantor to pay damages instead. If the original covenantor is being sued for breach of covenant, but no longer owns the property, an injunction will be unsuitable as the covenantor will not have control over the property. In this case, damages will be the more appropriate award.

DISCHARGING OR MODIFYING COVENANTS

Covenants can have a serious impact on the use, value, and market-ability of real estate. Therefore, there may be situations in which the owner of the burdened, servient, land may want to remove or alter the covenant. This can be done in several ways.

Section 84 of the Law of Property Act 1925 provides the owner of the burdened land with four grounds for discharging (releasing) or modifying a covenant:

- The covenant is obsolete, for example due to changes in the property or the neighbourhood;
- The covenant restricts a reasonable use of the land, provided the covenantee will not suffer a significant financial or other loss. Even if the covenantee will suffer a significant loss, the covenant may still be discharged or modified if it is in the public interest to do so, provided the covenantee can be compensated for their loss;
- The covenantor and covenantee agree to discharge or modify the covenant;
- Discharging or modifying the covenant will not cause injury to the covenantee.

It is common to take out restrictive covenant insurance to protect against claims for breach of covenant. The cost and availability of cover will depend on the covenants breached and the risk of the enforcement action being taken.

Covenants are a complex area. In practice, the RICS expects surveyors to recognise the limits of their expertise. Specialist legal advice is therefore likely to be required, particularly regarding enforcement of covenants. However, an understanding of the basics will assist the real estate professional and covenants commonly form a significant element of the land law module on real estate degrees.

ESTATE CONTRACTS

Estate contracts are equitable interests which are commonly encountered in practice. You may, for example, be familiar with the phrases 'subject to contract' and 'exchange of contracts' – these refer to an agreement to transfer or create an estate or interest in land. This is a type of estate contract. They are part of the conveyancing process, discussed further in Chapter 10. The contract does not actually transfer legal ownership of the property, as this does not occur until the transaction has been completed and registered at HM Land Registry, if it is registrable. However, the contract does create an equitable interest in the property, provided it complies with certain formalities. Section 2 of the Law of Property (Miscellaneous Provisions) Act 1989 states that contracts for the sale or other disposition of an interest in land, in England and Wales, must:

- Be in writing;
- Include all the terms agreed between the parties, either in the document or by reference to another document;
- Be signed by or on behalf of the parties.

It is possible for each party to sign a separate but identical copy of the agreement and to then exchange copies – hence we refer to the exchange of contracts stage of a transaction. This contract stage is not always necessary, but it is frequently used to create a binding obligation on the parties to complete the transaction at a future date once further formalities have concluded.

The estate contract means that the buyer has an interest in the property before becoming the legal owner. It is therefore necessary to consider the risk of damage to the property before completion of the transaction. The contract may stipulate that the property is at the risk of the buyer, or it may state that the seller retains this risk. It is common for the buyer to insure the property, from exchange of contracts to protect their equitable interest. Alternatively, the contract may stipulate that the seller is to continue to insure the property up until completion. We encountered an example of a large traditional brick barn, which collapsed after the buyers had exchanged contracts, but before they had become the barn's legal owners. The collapse destroyed the barn and its contents, which were included in the sale. The buyers were able to negotiate a reduction in the purchase price, but the case illustrates the importance of clear agreement regarding risk and insurance in case things do go wrong.

A contract can be conditional, which means that it is subject to a specified event (such as obtaining planning permission) occurring.

OPTIONS

An option agreement is another type of estate contract which grants a prospective buyer the option to acquire a property if they wish to do so. The difference between an option and a contract to buy land is that the option does not commit the prospective buyer to proceed with the purchase. The option will usually involve payment of a fee to the property's owner, and it will also last for a specified duration. The property's owner must sell the property to the option holder if the option is exercised within this time period.

An option may be used by, for example, a developer awaiting planning permission or perhaps testing the local market with a small development before acquiring further land for expansion.

OVERAGE

An overage agreement is a contractual agreement between a buyer and a seller that a further payment will be made to the seller on a specific event occurring after the sale has completed. For example, a plot of land with development potential may be sold without planning permission. The value of the plot will increase if planning permission is subsequently granted, so the seller will be entitled to a further payment, usually based on a percentage of the increase in value. As a contractual agreement, an overage is not an interest in land as such. However, it is useful to include it here, as it is common in practice, enabling a former landowner to claim payment for land possibly several years after disposal.

Overage agreements can benefit both parties. The seller gains the sale and additional payment if the buyer can increase the value of the property. The buyer purchases the property at a lower price and in effect spreads the cost of the acquisition, mitigating the financial risk of (for example) planning permission being refused.

WAYLEAVES

A wayleave is a third party right over land similar to an easement. It is an agreement between a landowner and a telecoms or utility supplier to place equipment such as poles, pylons, and cables across the land, usually for a small fee. Unsurprisingly, these agreements are very common in view of the miles of wires and cabling needed to supply services to users. Wayleaves also provide a right of access for maintenance of the equipment.

LICENCES

A licence is a personal permission or agreement which can usually only be enforced against the parties to the licence. Once again, this is a complex area and there is much case law on this topic, which is outside the scope of this chapter. However, the basic position is that a licence does not bind future owners of the property and it does not confer an interest in the property itself. Examples of licences include:

- Occupiers who do not enjoy the exclusive possession and certainty of term necessary to create a lease (see Chapter 8);
- Lodgers;
- Hotel guests (see our example earlier);
- Customers in a shop.

The licence prevents the licensee to whom it grants permission, from being a mere trespasser on the property.

CHANCEL REPAIR LIABILITY

This is an ancient obligation of some property owners to contribute towards the cost of repairs to their parish church. Legal advisers will check whether a property is subject to a chancel repair liability during the conveyancing process and it is usual to take out insurance to cover a claim. Although relatively unusual, many buyers would be unaware of this liability, and we do have experience of managing a large country house, which was subject to a chancel repair liability.

STATUTORY RIGHTS

Legislation confers specific short-term rights in relation to property owned by others, to facilitate the repair and maintenance of property. The Party Wall etc. Act 1996 is one frequently encountered in practice. This provides procedures and a dispute resolution process to follow if work is needed on a shared wall or structure.

The Access to Neighbouring Land Act 1992 enables an owner who needs to carry out repairs to their property to apply to court for access to neighbouring land to carry out those repairs. For example, if a building is constructed right to the boundary, it may be possible to maintain parts of that building only by entering onto the neighbouring land. The Act provides a means of gaining the required access. In practice, it can be easier to arrange access informally with neighbours rather than resort to the law.

PUBLIC RIGHTS

The rights and interests outlined earlier are rights enjoyed by an individual in relation to property owned by another person. They differ from rights enjoyed by the public. For example, an easement is a private right, enjoyed by the owner of a specific property, whereas anyone can use a public footpath or bridle path, regardless of where they live.

Common land can be used by the public for certain activities – walking, for example – although other activities such as horse riding may be prohibited. It will usually be possible to roam across common land, without need to stay on designated paths. Town and village greens can also be used by the public although again, some activities may be prohibited. In some cases, residents of specific areas may have the right to graze livestock on common land. Freemen of the City of London have the ancient right to drive a flock of sheep across the Thames to market without paying tax.

REGISTRATION OF INTERESTS IN REAL ESTATE

Some interests in real estate are overriding interests. This means that they are not shown on the register of title at HM Land Registry, but they can still bind a purchaser. Overriding interests are outlined further in Chapter 7. Other interests should be protected by registration, and some (most commonly, easements and mortgages) will not become legal interests until they are registered. It is therefore common to see a range of interests on a title register, for example:

- The Property Register may include details of easements benefitting the property;
- The Proprietorship Register may include a Restriction requiring a mortgagee's consent to any transactions;

- The Charges Register will list mortgages and restrictive covenants affecting the property;
- Other interests, such as estate contracts, may be protected by a Notice on the Charges Register.

LOOKING AHEAD . . .

The rights and interests outlined in this chapter are complex historic rights, which have evolved over many years to encompass common law, equity, detailed case law, and legislation. This can make them a confusing area of study, and a challenging topic for both students and practitioners. The Law Commission has recommended the reform and simplification of covenants, easements, and profits a prendre and in 2017 the government indicated its intention to implement these reforms.[1] However, at the time of writing in 2021 this has not occurred. Therefore, these remain key aspects of the study and practice of real estate in their present form. We recommend that you also refer to Chapters 7 and 8 as they cover related topics. The next chapter, which covers real estate transactions, will also help to put some of the rights and interests in real estate into context.

NOTE

1 Law Commission (undated) *Easements, Covenants and Profits a Prendre* Online. Available from: www.lawcom.gov.uk/project/easements-covenants-and-profits-a-prendre/

FURTHER INFORMATION

Card, R, Murdoch, J, and Murdoch, S (2011) *Real Estate Management Law* 7th Edition Oxford: Oxford University Press

Davys, M (2009) *Land Law* 11th Edition London: Red Globe Press

WEBSITES

Gov.UK www.gov.uk/common-land-village-greens
Gov.UK www.gov.uk/guidance/party-wall-etc-act-1996-guidance
Gov.UK www.gov.uk/guidance/rentcharges

REAL ESTATE TRANSACTIONS

WHAT ARE REAL ESTATE TRANSACTIONS?

As we have seen in the law chapters, there are a wide variety of real estate transactions in terms of size, scope, and purpose, but they all involve some form of transfer of ownership of real estate, or rights relating to real estate. It is clear from Chapters 7, 8, and 9, that transferring ownership is a complex process and requires the involvement of legal professionals. There is however a stage before the transfer of ownership, that also usually requires professional input, and this is the process of introducing the two parties to the transaction. To put buyer and seller, or landlord and tenant, in contact with each other requires the exposure of the real estate to the market. This is usually carried out by a real estate agent, whatever type of real estate, or transaction, is involved. Although it is possible to transact without the involvement of an agent, it can be risky as the best price might not be achieved, negotiations can become protracted, and the parties are likely to lack specialist knowledge.

WHAT IS A REAL ESTATE AGENT?

As outlined in Chapter 6, a real estate agent is an individual who arranges the purchase, sale, or rent of any type of real estate. The agent will be instructed by a client, or principal, to act on their behalf. This relationship will, in virtually all real estate cases, be a contractual one. This means that the agent will be paid to carry out certain duties on behalf of the principal. As it is a contractual relationship, failure to carry out the agreed duties will be a

DOI: 10.1201/9781003155256-10

breach of contract. All agents are required to demonstrate a certain level of skill and expertise. The RICS provides detailed mandatory requirements[1] that all chartered surveyors must comply with concerning issues such as ethics and professionalism, the duty of care of an agent, dealing with conflicts of interest, and working under clear and fair Terms of Engagement. The RICS has also developed specific mandatory requirements for residential real estate agents[2] and for commercial real estate agents.[3] These professional statements together set out the specific responsibilities of the agent with a view to ensuring, and demonstrating, that they are working to the highest professional and ethical standards. They encourage the fairness and transparency that is expected in all real estate transactions both in the UK and worldwide.

WHY USE A REAL ESTATE AGENT?

Using an agent has some key benefits:

- They are specialists in their field and will be aware of the regulations and laws concerning property transactions that must be complied with;
- They should have good market knowledge of values, potential buyers or tenants, and competing real estate interests;
- They will recommend appropriate marketing plans and materials targeted to prospective buyers and tenants;
- They will arrange EPCs and check documents with lawyers and local authorities;
- They will book, and carry out, all inspections with clients, prospective purchasers, or tenants, and other agents;
- They will negotiate detailed terms before instructing the legal team;
- They will normally be members of a professional organisation or trade association and be qualified or licensed to practise.

Overall, use of an agent should save the client time, and provide reassurance that the optimal transaction terms have been agreed. An agent will have the necessary knowledge and expertise to ensure that the real estate has been suitably exposed to the market and the terms agreed reflect current market conditions.

WHAT ARE THE DUTIES OF A REAL ESTATE AGENT?

Prior to taking an agency instruction, for sale, purchase, or letting, some pre-instruction steps must be completed before any work is carried out. These include:

- Compliance with all relevant legislation which includes:
  - Unfair Contract Terms Act 1977
  - Estate Agents Act 1979
  - Supply of Goods and Services Act 1982
  - Estate Agents (Provision of Information) Regulations 1991
  - Cancellation of Contracts made in a Consumer's Home or Place of Work etc. Regulations 2008
  - Consumer Protection from Unfair Trading Regulations 2008
  - Business Protection from Misleading Marketing Regulations 2008
  - Bribery Act 2010
  - Money Laundering, Terrorist Financing and Transfer of Funds (Information on the Payer) Regulations 2017
- Confirmation of client identity and safeguarding against money laundering;
- Carrying out conflict of interest checks;
- Completing written Terms of Engagement including details of all fees and expenses, and the complaints-handling procedure;
- Agreeing how clients' money is to be handled;
- Ensuring that there are robust GDPR arrangements in place.

An agent has a duty of care to their client which involves performing their duties with skill, care, and diligence in a professional and ethical way. Before taking on a new client, the agent will need to carry out identity checks which might include:

- For individuals – asking for details of passports and bank accounts; and
- For organisations – memorandum and articles of association, and company accounts.

Agents should also ask for proof of sources of funds to guard against money laundering. This might take the form of bank statements or solicitors' confirmation. The next step is to deal with any conflicts of interest. The RICS[4] defines a conflict of interest as:

> *anything that impedes your ability to focus on the best interests of the client.*

Assessing whether there is a conflict is entirely down to the judgement of the agent. Conflicts of interest commonly occur when an agent might have acted for one party and is then instructed by another. With the merger and acquisition activity in real estate consultancies, it has become more common to find an agent acting for both parties. We attended a meeting once, as the client, to find that the prospective tenant was represented by an agent from the same consultancy. Any obvious conflict such as this should be notified to the client in writing. The client can then decide how they would like to deal with any potential conflicts which could include, for example, the erection of information barriers. Information barriers are an administrative process that prevents different parties in the same organisation accessing each other's information. The client may provide 'informed consent' to the conflict whereby they decide that, despite the risk of an adverse impact, due to the conflict of interest, they still want to proceed with the same agent. In the case mentioned earlier, our agent was based in London and the tenant's retained agent was based in the US, although they were from the same real estate consultancy. We therefore agreed to accept the use of information barriers, providing informed consent, so that neither party had to lose their retained agent. If we had been unhappy with the conflict, then one agent would have had to withdraw from their contract.

The written Terms of Engagement will include details of the work to be carried out by the agent, any fees, charges, or commissions payable, details of the complaints handling procedure and arrangements to be made in respect of clients' money, such as which party benefits from the interest and the process and timing for accessing the money. The Terms of Engagement should also supply information on the processes in place to ensure client confidentiality and compliance with the GDPR provisions. It is important to provide as much detail as possible in the Terms of Engagement to avoid any confusion, or later argument, about what work should be done. The other element that must be included in the written Terms of Engagement is the basis of agency and there are a variety of these that can be offered, and agreed between the parties, including sole agency, sole selling rights, joint sole agency, multiple agency, sub-agency, and an introductory fee arrangement. A brief overview of each is provided. It is vital that the basis of agency is clearly explained to the client and the specific definitions provided in the RICS documentation[5] should be used.

SOLE AGENCY

Sole agency is where one agent is appointed to market a property and the agent will only be entitled to a fee if it either introduces, or negotiates with, the purchaser or tenant. Sole agency is normally agreed for a limited time period to give the client the opportunity to change agents if the first agent fails to perform satisfactorily.

If the basis of the agency is stated to be sole agency, then the agreement must include the wording:

> *You will be liable to pay remuneration to us, in addition to any other costs or charges agreed, if at any time unconditional contracts for the sale of the property are exchanged (or, in Scotland, unconditional missives for the sale of the property are concluded):*
>
> - *With a purchaser introduced by us during the period of our sole agency, or with whom we had negotiations about the property during that period, or*
> - *With a purchaser introduced by another agent during that period.*[6]

As can be seen from this wording, even if another agent introduces the successful purchaser or tenant, the sole agent is entitled to a fee. This can be problematic when the sole agency agreement is terminated and the eventual purchaser, or tenant, is one that was originally introduced by the first agent. It is important to keep precise and detailed records of all interest in the premises as it may be necessary to prove the introduction to obtain a fee.

SOLE SELLING RIGHTS

Under sole selling rights, the agent appointed will be entitled to their fee and any costs, during the period of the contract, whoever the property is sold to. This could mean that even if the client sold, or let, their property to a friend, a fee would still payable. Sole selling rights give the agent greater protection in terms of getting their fees paid but can be viewed as onerous by the client. If the agreement states that sole selling rights are the agency basis then the contract must include the following wording:

> You will be liable to pay remuneration to us, in addition to any other costs or charges agreed, in each of the following circumstances:
>
> - if unconditional contracts for the sale of the property are exchanged (or, in Scotland, unconditional missives for the sale of the property are concluded) in the period during which we have sole selling rights, even if the purchaser was not found by us but by another agent or by any other person, including yourself and
> - if unconditional contracts for the sale of the property are exchanged (or, in Scotland, unconditional missives for the sale of the property are concluded) after the expiry of the period during which we have sole selling rights, but to a purchaser who was introduced to you during that period or with whom we had negotiations about the property during that period.[7]

Agents can be appointed not only as sole agents with sole selling rights but also as joint sole agents with, or without, sole selling rights.

JOINT SOLE AGENCY

In a joint sole agency contract, two, or more, agents will be appointed and agree to share the fees regardless of who finds the ultimate buyer or lessee. Usually, the fee will be split equally but it can be negotiated to be different percentages depending on the amount of work carried out. We were once appointed as local agents jointly with a London agent on a small industrial estate. We carried out all viewings and negotiations and the London agent advertised the estate. In hindsight, to reflect the different amounts of work carried out by each agent, we should probably have tried to negotiate a higher percentage of the fee but there was the danger that the London agent would then have approached one of our competitors. Fees, payable by the client, for joint sole agency, tend to be higher than for sole agency but it can be necessary in situations, such as that outlined, where the London agent would not have wanted to have to travel for two hours to do viewings and the most likely tenants were local businesses that, as local agents, we already knew.

JOINT OR MULTIPLE AGENCY

In this situation, the client appoints as many agents as they feel are necessary to market their property but the only agent to earn a fee is the one who finds the successful purchaser or tenant. This can be advantageous to the client as it is cheaper than joint sole agency, ensures that the property is fully exposed to the market, and can generate some competition between agents to be the one to agree the sale or lease. It can, however, result in confusion when different agents have different applicants. Over-exposure of the property can make the client look desperate, and some agents might not agree to work on a multiple agency basis due to the possibility of carrying out a lot of work for no fee.

SUB-AGENCY

An agent may wish to appoint a sub-agent to assist in their work, but this must be authorised by the client. The sub-agent will not have a direct relationship with the client, and the main agent may be responsible for both their actions and payment of their fees.

INTRODUCTORY FEE ARRANGEMENT

Where there is no agency instruction, that is an agent has not been retained by the client but they are aware of the premises and have interest from a potential purchaser or tenant, they may approach the client with a request for an introductory fee arrangement. In this case, the client may agree to pay the agent a fee, if it is a purchaser or tenant that their own agent has not found. The fee will be by agreement but ensures that the agent who brought the property to the purchaser or tenant gets some recognition for the work they might have put in. Any existing arrangement with the client and their retained agent will still need to be honoured. Another example of where an introductory fee might be used is where the property owner has no plans to dispose of the property, but the agent is aware of a potential purchaser or tenant, who has not retained them, and makes contact to see if they can arrange a deal.

All these forms of agency have been described in relation to the disposal of property interests, but they can also be put in place for the acquisition of property where an agent might be retained to find suitable property for a client. This has become increasingly common in the residential property market, both in the UK and worldwide, for high net-worth individuals that do not have the time to source their own properties. Businesses may also decide to use, and pay, acquisition agents with the time and expertise to prepare short-lists of properties that suit their requirements and negotiate suitable terms based on their market knowledge.

As we discussed in Chapter 5, many organisations require real estate as a resource to enable them to carry out their core business. Others, as discussed in Chapter 4, use real estate as an asset to generate income and capital gains. For either purpose, the real estate needs to be acquired.

ACQUISITIONS

Before acquiring real estate, those carrying out the acquisition need to identify the core purpose of the acquisition. Is it for investment, development or occupation, or a combination of reasons? Having established the core purpose, or purposes, of the acquisition the next step is to start trying to define the type of real estate required. The key factors to be considered for investment, development, and occupation for a business are suggested later. There would be slightly different factors in relation to occupation of a residential property but, as you all live somewhere, it is assumed that you are familiar with the factors you, or the person you live with, considered prior to acquiring your current accommodation.

INVESTMENT

If the core purpose is investment, the decision will include considering factors such as:

- Price;
- Value – and the potential to add value;

- Attitude to risk and reward;
- Location – up and coming or on the decline;
- Demand and supply;
- Availability and cost of finance;
- Condition – any works required and, if so, the likely cost and timeframe for these works;
- Type – new build or existing;
- Government policy;
- Taxation implications;
- Interest rates;
- Responsibility for, and costs of, maintenance and repair;
- If let, lease terms and tenant covenant strength;
- Main reason for investment, that is capital gain, regular secure income stream, or both;
- Complexity of management.

DEVELOPMENT

If the core purpose is development, the decision will include considering factors such as:

- Location;
- Infrastructure;
- Previous use of the site or property including any potential issues with contamination;
- Legal title including any easements and restrictive covenants;
- Government policy;
- Planning policies;
- Price;
- Potential value;
- Feasibility, viability and sensitivity analyses;
- Time period;
- Financing availability;
- Taxation implications;
- Phase in the economic cycle;
- Supply and demand of different asset classes, both existing and in the future;
- The developer's attitude to risk.

OCCUPATION FOR THE PURPOSE OF A BUSINESS

If the core purpose is occupation for a business, the decision will obviously vary depending on whether it is offices, retail, industrial, leisure, or another use. Regardless of which type of real estate it is, some of the key factors likely to be considered are likely to include:

- Location – proximity to infrastructure, customers, and staff. Whether it all needs to be in one place or in multiple locations;
- Type – modern or traditional;
- Tenure, that is freehold or leasehold – which is likely to be best value for money;
- If leasehold, main terms including, amongst others, length of term, renewal rights, break clauses, rent reviews, rights to assign or sublet, repairing obligations, service charges, permitted use;
- Size – sufficient size for now or with built in expansion or contraction to allow flexibility;
- Supply and demand of the specific type of real estate required as this will impact on availability and therefore price;
- How long it is likely to be held for – the difficulty of answering this question led to the emergence of the serviced office sector;
- Availability of appropriate staff;
- Financing of the acquisition;
- Any taxation implications;
- Any aspects of the business that could be outsourced to reduce space requirements;
- Running costs to include service charges, rates, etc.;
- Sustainability factors;
- Any adaptation needed to make it optimal;
- Access to technology;
- Adjacent businesses;
- Hybrid or homeworking to reduce space requirements.

Once the type of real estate to be acquired has been defined, the next stage is to decide whether this can be done personally or whether a real estate advisor is required. For most sizeable transactions, an acquisition surveyor, or agent, will be appointed. The scope of work, or Terms of Engagement, will depend on the client's requirements. It may be that the client identifies the building and then hands it over to the agent to negotiate terms, or the agent may be tasked with the whole process including searching for, and creating a short list of, appropriate premises. Either approach requires a clear understanding of the scope of the instruction. A search or acquisition agent will provide expert advice and can save the purchaser or lessee time and money. They may also be able to access properties before they come to the market.

One key aspect that needs to be considered when acquiring real estate, as mentioned earlier, is the holding period, that is how long the premises are likely to be required for and how easy it will be to dispose of them when the time comes.

DISPOSALS

The approach to disposing of premises will be different depending mainly on whether it is a freehold or a leasehold disposal. Freehold and leasehold interests were discussed in detail in Chapters 7 and 8. The agent will then progress through a series of steps, many of which will be broadly similar for an acquisition. These steps include checking legal documentation, carrying out inspection and measurement, obtaining comparable evidence, deciding on the recommended method of disposal, carrying out appropriate marketing, negotiating, agreeing heads of terms, instructing solicitors, and completing the transaction. Each of these steps will be considered in turn.

THE STAGES OF A REAL ESTATE TRANSACTION

CHECKING LEGAL DOCUMENTATION

Disposing of freehold premises, once the pre-instructions steps have been completed, including completion of Terms of Engagement, usually starts with obtaining a copy of the legal title to ensure that the client is able to dispose of their interest and to check for any restrictive covenants and other rights and interests in the property.

For leasehold disposals, the agent will need to obtain a copy of the lease to check, initially, what the alienation clause permits. If, for example, assignment and subletting are not permitted, under any circumstances, the only option would be to agree a surrender to the freeholder. This would inevitably require the payment of a premium.

Legal documentation will provide details on the extent of the property together with any rights or benefits such as car parking spaces. One of our colleagues once inspected a property that involved a three-hour journey but, unfortunately, they had not accessed the lease plan before they went so ended up measuring and inspecting only a part of the demised premises; a time-consuming, and therefore expensive, mistake.

The agent should also check that there is an up-to-date EPC in place prior to commencement of marketing. If there is not, then the agent will often arrange for one to be prepared as part of their duties.

INSPECTION AND MEASUREMENT

Whether disposing of, or acquiring, real estate it is essential that a thorough inspection is carried out. The inspection, and measurement, will provide the basis of any future agreement for disposal. The agent will need to take photographs, and notes, that are sufficient to use as a basis for providing a price for the interest and to prepare a brochure or marketing particulars. Inspection and measurement are core APC competencies for many RICS pathways.

Precise measurement of real estate is necessary as it forms the basis of the market value and enables comparison with alternatives. The approach to measurement of real estate has been evolving over the past few years. IPMS are in the process of being developed for all asset classes and we are currently using two different systems. The first edition of the Code of Measuring Practice was issued in 1979. Since then, there have been a further five editions and the sixth edition, published in May 2015, is currently in use.[8] This edition is, for the first time, globally applicable, and although only a guidance note, rather than a professional statement, it is perceived as best practice and a good reason for departing from it would be needed should any claims for negligence be made. The RICS Code of Measuring Practice, 6th Edition, applies to all classes of building other than offices and residential. These asset classes are now covered by RICS Property Measurement, 2nd Edition[9] and this is a professional statement, rather than a guidance note, which means that it is mandatory for RICS members and regulated firms. Eventually, all asset classes will come under RICS

Property Measurement. IPMS Industrial was published in 2018, and IPMS retail in 2019 and both are likely to be included in the 3rd Edition of RICS Property Measurement. One of the key differences is terminology. The Code of Measuring Practice refers to Gross External Area (GEA), Gross Internal Area (GIA), and Net Internal Area (NIA) whereas the IPMS refer to IPMS 1, 2, and 3. There are also slight differences in these measurements, and it is common for agents to provide both areas on sales and letting particulars, just as they continue to provide sizes in both square feet and square metres.

When inspecting a property for the purposes of a real estate transaction, the agent needs to look not only at the subject premises, in detail, but also beyond. In addition to measuring, an agent will also check the method of construction, the state of repair, the use, and any ancillary demised areas such as car parking and bin stores. Agents also need to consider the surrounding area, including infrastructure, and adjacent uses as all of these can have impact on the value of the premises. When inspecting, they should also note down any advertising boards as these may provide useful comparable evidence when arriving at their valuations.

MARKET EVIDENCE

A discussion of the use of comparable evidence to arrive at market value is provided in Chapters 11 and 12. However, valuations that are prepared as part of an agency instruction for the purposes of acquisition or disposal do not need to follow all the standards within the Red Book. Why is this? As discussed in Chapter 11, a Red Book valuation can only ever be an estimate rather than an exact figure and it reflects the time of the valuation and other relevant aspects. A valuation for an agency instruction will also be an estimate but it usually factors in a negotiating margin. This has led to criticism, particularly in the residential market, where certain agencies have a reputation for 'over-valuing' to obtain the instruction then, when the property fails to generate any interest, dropping the price. The key point here is that market value can be very different to the price paid so the agent's market knowledge and expertise will be used to decide on a price that is appropriate to generate the required level of interest and find a purchaser or tenant.

One of us lives in a house adjacent to a graveyard. When this was valued for sale by agents the difference in values was over 50% between the lowest and the highest. One agent felt that the graveyard was a negative factor that would put off purchasers not wanting to live next door to human remains and therefore reduced their valuation. Another agent felt that it was a positive factor, due to the protection from development, and the mature trees adjoining the garden, and increased their valuation. This subjectivity is one reason for factoring in a negotiating margin. It is difficult to predict who the potential purchasers are and what they might be prepared to pay.

In the commercial sector, prior to the pandemic, mobile phone shops and coffee shops were renowned for offering rental levels above market value. This was due to the need for a greater market presence than that of their competitors making them able to justify paying higher than market rent. Another example from the commercial sector, that we dealt with, was an office building with a book value of just over £5 million. Our intention was to let the building on a short-term lease and then carry out an extensive refurbishment to increase its value. One of the prospective tenants was a serviced office operator who wanted to purchase the freehold. We were not interested in disposing of the freehold as we had an approved asset management plan for the building, and we did not need the capital receipt to support our strategy. We did, however, invite the interested party to submit a bid just to see what they thought the building was worth. When it came in at £7 million we revisited our strategy. How was it possible for a building with a Red Book valuation of just over £5 million to generate a bid of £7 million? Had our valuers got it wrong or was the purchaser's valuation flawed? The difference between the two figures came down to the different purposes of, and approach to, the valuation. Our Red Book valuation was based on an investment valuation using the rental income we could generate for a short-term lease and a yield reflecting this. The prospective purchaser's valuation was based on their business model of refurbishing to provide serviced office suites and charging a service fee to occupiers. If we had decided to sell the building prior to receiving this interest, the agents would have been unlikely to be aware of the specific pricing details of this potential use and might well have priced based on the Red Book valuation assumptions. This would have resulted in a far lower price for us.

Whether arriving at market value or a value for sale or letting, the same basic approach is employed. The agent will need to look at comparable evidence from the local area.

COMPARABLE EVIDENCE

The RICS provides specific advice on the analysis of comparable evidence[10] in the form of an information paper. An information paper provides practice-based information and research and is intended to therefore provide general guidance only on how to analyse evidence. One of our students asked for a session on how to analyse comparable evidence as they wanted us to provide specific percentages for deduction or addition that they could apply in all cases across all evidence. Unfortunately, it is not that simple. The analysis of evidence relies heavily on the agent's, or valuer's, personal knowledge and experience. There are three stages to using comparable evidence to compile valuations: identifying appropriate comparable evidence; analysing the evidence; and applying the evidence.

Identifying appropriate comparable evidence

It might appear that the first stage is straightforward, particularly with the wealth of technology at our disposal to find, and collate, evidence. When purchasing a new running watch, for example, it was very easy for us to research on the Internet and secure the 'best' price, which, incidentally, was not the cheapest price. The watch being sold was identical from every outlet, but the cheapest outlet was based overseas and had several negative reviews. Therefore, the watch at the 'best' price was ordered taking account of the reputation of the seller. The purchasing or letting process is much more challenging in real estate. Finding a comparison for certain types of real estate can be tricky. In developing countries, for example it may be difficult to find enough suitable evidence of similar properties. It can also be difficult in a stagnant market, such as during the global pandemic, and, in the UK, when Brexit negotiations were ongoing, as the volume of transactions was significantly reduced. It can also be difficult in a rapidly changing market, either rising or falling, where evidence quickly becomes dated.

In some cases, when comparing, for example apartments in a block, it is easy to compare one apartment of the same size and very similar location with another, particularly when there is an active market. It is, however, more difficult to find comparisons for unique properties. One of our first instructions was the sale of an abattoir located surprisingly close to the town centre. It was a challenge to value for sale as the most lucrative, alternative use was difficult to establish. It would have been far more difficult to value for say accounts purposes. It is obviously more challenging to find evidence for unique properties and this is where the approach to the analysis of evidence becomes particularly important.

The more 'different' a property is from its comparables, the more adjustments need to be made. As discussed in Chapter 2, the property market is an imperfect one and one of its characteristics is that all real estate interests are unique. Appropriate adjustments therefore need to be made to reflect differences between the comparable evidence and the subject premises. Ideal comparable evidence would offer:

- A large number of recent transactions;
- Almost identical properties;
- Open-market, rather than off-market, transactions.

It would also:

- Be capable of verification, for example by the parties involved, other agents, the land registry or similar;
- Have no special circumstances surrounding the transaction.

Judging the earlier example, of apartments in a block, by these criteria, they are probably the type of property interest that comes closest to offering ideal comparable evidence. Other real estate comparable evidence, due to the unique nature of property and the relatively limited number of transactions, needs to be adjusted, with a view to providing justification and support to the valuation put forward.

There are various aspects that can be compared when analysing properties and the main ones include: location; building size, age, construction, specification, layout, efficiency and flexibility of use; basis of tenure and, if leasehold, the provisions of the lease; and, the date, and type, of transaction. Comparison may be based on rental levels or yields or both, and comparison forms a part of all methods of valuation (see Chapter 12).

Comparable evidence can be drawn from market transactions, indices, and automated valuation models. The best comparable evidence is that of an open market letting, or sale, at market value with which the agent was personally involved. There is then what is known as a 'hierarchy of evidence' ranked from the most reliable, to the least. In terms of market transactions, this hierarchy is based on the level of confidence in the accuracy of the data. Clearly, when personally involved, the agent can be very confident of the reliability and validity of the data although it may still be interpreted differently. However, when considering publicly available data such as online databases, or press reports, caution is needed as the level of detail is unlikely to be sufficient and the evidence may be historic. The agent can use these sources as introductory ones to the transaction, but then needs to thoroughly research the deal to find out if there are any other matters that impact on the headline values reported. The date of the transaction is an important aspect of comparable evidence. Ideally it will be as recent as possible but where it is possible to track trends in prices, historic evidence can be useful. In the residential market, where there are numerous transactions, agents may cross-check their opinion of value by applying house price growth to the figure the house most recently sold for. The real estate market can, however, move very rapidly, either upward or downward, and agents need to be aware of which way the market is moving, and how quickly, to assist with the precision of their appraisals.

Analysing the evidence

Once comparables have been collated, the evidence needs to be analysed and adjusted to arrive at a market appraisal. As explained in Chapter 11, providing advice on value for sale or letting is not a Red Book valuation but a similar approach to the analysis of evidence is used. It is important to collect as much information as possible on each comparable and keep notes on how the value of the subject premises was arrived at. This will involve making specific adjustments to the evidence to reflect each difference, and then arriving at a figure that reflects these differences. For example, take two office suites of the same size, in the same building, where one is held on a FRI lease, and one is held on an IRI lease. Obviously, the tenant holding the IRI lease would be willing to pay more than the tenant under the FRI lease as they would have no additional expenses for repairs and maintenance. This could be estimated at being worth say an extra 5% in rent. If the subject premises were held on an FRI lease, then the IRI evidence would need to be adjusted downwards by say 5%. One of our students said that they understood the percentage adjustments but wanted to know what percentages to apply. This is another situation where the knowledge and judgement of the agent are required. In the example of the offices, if the office suite was in a Grade I listed building that required a lot of repair and maintenance then the adjustment might be as high as 10% or more, but if within a brand new modern building then a lower percentage could be applied.

Percentage adjustments are commonly used for commercial properties. Residential properties tend to be adjusted using actual capital or rental figures. For example, a garage could be worth an additional £10,000 on a house price or an extra £100 a month for rental, depending on the area. Adjustments for repairs and maintenance are one of the easier ones to make as they can be more easily quantified by relating them to likely repair costs. It becomes more difficult when adjusting for location, or size (known as a quantum adjustment), as the agent needs to try to quantify what could be considered a subjective adjustment; one agent may believe a location is much better, and another may believe it is only a little better. The process of adjustment is based on market knowledge and experience.

Applying the evidence

It is common to use a matrix as a framework for analysis that can easily be understood by all. Figure 10.1 provides an indicative example of a simple matrix in relation to a new logistics and distribution unit listing elements of comparison against property address. Although there are various approaches, in this case we have adjusted each comparable to arrive at a rent per square metre (psm) to be applied to the subject premises. It is assumed that the subject premises are to be let on a 20-year FRI lease, subject to five yearly upward only rent reviews with no break clauses. The level of asking rent will depend on market conditions at the time. This example assumes that the market is strong; therefore the rent selected, based on the analysis of comparable evidence, is pitched at a level slightly higher than the evidence to allow for a negotiating margin. The size of these adjustments, in percentage terms, would be based on the agent's knowledge of the area and the market. It is assumed that, in this example, all evidence is dated within the past few months, but, if this were not the case, additional adjustments would need to be made to reflect the timing of the most recent event at which the rent was reviewed. There would also be a greater number of adjustments than shown, to cover additional aspects such as incentives, condition, specification, and rent review basis.

The RICS provides guidance[11] on the elements of comparison likely to apply to all sectors of real estate to be included in the matrix, and the type of evidence to use for the various specific real estate sectors. For example, the elements of comparison relating to agricultural land

	Unit A Modern Park	Unit C Modern Park	Unit 2 Old Park	Subject premises New Park
Rent	230160	488150	837000	
Area IPMS	38360 much smaller -5%	88820 smaller -2.5%	124000 no adjustment	126280
Rent psm	10	9	7	
Specification	Similar, no adjustment	Similar, no adjustment	Not as good, +5%	
Repairing obligation	IRI – 5%	FRI, no adjustment	FRI, no adjustment	
Location	Similar, no adjustment	Similar, no adjustment	Not as good, +5%	
Lease term	6-month tenancy -10%	10-year lease with five-year tenant only break clause -5%	20-year lease, no adjustment	
Car parking	Similar, no adjustment	Similar, no adjustment	Poor +5%	
Total percentage adjustment to rent	-20%	-7.5%	+15%	
Adjusted rent psm	8	8.33	8.05	Say 8.50 psm
Suggested rent for subject premises				1,073,380

Figure 10.1 Example of a comparable evidence matrix for a logistics and distribution unit

might include factors such as soil type and access to water and drainage whereas for development sites key elements of comparison are likely to include permitted use and density, infrastructure, and access.

In the example of the comparable evidence matrix in Figure 10.1, it was assumed that the property was a new logistics and distribution unit that was to be let on a new lease. The agent would advise on the terms of the lease to be offered, not only the rent to quote but also the main Heads of Terms to include, amongst others lease length, rent review frequency and basis, and repairing obligations. For a freehold disposal, price is the main consideration but there may also be special conditions or timing considerations. In the UK there are three main methods of disposal.

METHODS OF DISPOSAL

These three methods are auction, tender – both formal and informal – and private treaty. Although these methods mainly relate to sales, there could be situations where a lease is offered on an informal tender basis – such as where there is a lot of interest in a unit – so the agent decides to go to best bids. This is unusual, as the lease terms are likely to be subject to negotiation, so it is difficult to accept the highest rental offer unless the lease terms are non-negotiable. This has been done in a newly constructed shopping centre, for example, where the lease was a standard one and interest levels were very high.

Auction

An auction is a method of sale that has a specific, fixed, time scale for exchange and completion. An auction can be of just one property or of multiple properties, each one known as a 'lot'. The auctioneer will invite bids, and will usually specify a guide price, and interested parties will make their bid in the sale room; the highest bid will secure the property. In some cases, the vendor will have put a reserve price on the property and, if it fails to meet this price, the property will not be sold. Otherwise, the property will sell to the highest bidder and as the gavel (the auctioneer's hammer) falls, the successful bidder is required to sign a contract and pay a deposit, with exchange on the property taking place immediately. Completion will usually take place 28 days later.

For both parties, an auction provides some certainty as, if the successful bidder fails to complete, they will be in breach of contract and will lose their deposit and possibly have legal action taken against them. From the seller's point of view, auctions tend to get considerable publicity and they can set a reserve, but the price achieved depends on who is in the auction room on the day. An auction may not reach as high a price as could have been achieved by private treaty. Auctions are also a relatively expensive method of sale, due to the costs of promoting and holding the auction, which will be payable whether the property reaches its reserve or not. If a property fails to sell at auction, it may be perceived as 'tainted', so any subsequent offers are likely to be lower. Auctions are a public method of sale so are sometimes popular with organisations, such as the public sector, who want to demonstrate transparency and openness. From the buyer's point of view, although they have certainty that they have secured the property, they need to carry out all necessary research before they bid which may include surveys and arranging finance. There will be no opportunity to negotiate terms, timings or, for example, make a bid conditional on obtaining planning consent. Auctions are therefore used for properties where the seller wants to sell quickly, often because the property is in a poor state of repair or because it is difficult to value precisely. We sold a buy-to-let flat at auction following treatment for dry rot, as there was concern that other parts of the building could be affected. The decision was taken to sell quickly, in view of the cost and disruption of further remedial work; auction achieved the dual objectives of speed and certainty.

Tender

A tender is like an auction, but it is blind. It involves the preparation of tender documentation which is issued to prospective purchasers. Best bids will be put forward but, in this case, none of the parties know what their competitors are offering. Tenders can be formal where sealed bids, often with a deposit, will be submitted, by a specified date and exchange of contracts will take place immediately the offer is accepted in a similar way to auctions. With a tender, however, the seller can choose which bid to select which may not necessarily be the highest. Informal tenders also have a specified date and ask for sealed bids but there is no legal contract created, as there is with a formal tender. The purchaser has time to carry out further negotiations and inspections prior to exchanging contracts. The advantage of tenders over auctions are that they are private so not everyone knows the price agreed and they can be made subject to conditions such as obtaining planning consent. Tenders can however result in the purchaser paying considerably more than the next highest bidder and, again, they can be an expensive method of sale due to the costs of putting the tender pack together.

Private treaty

Private treaty is the most common method of sale in England and Wales and simply involves marketing the property to find suitable purchasers. A price, or guide price, will be set and negotiations will take place. Sometimes sales will take place 'off market' where a direct approach is made. This method gives sufficient time to carry out surveys and investigations but there is no specific timescale within which the sale needs to be completed. There is also no certainty that the sale will complete until exchange takes place. This can result in 'gazumping' where after terms have been agreed another purchaser offers a higher price, or 'gazundering' where, after terms have been agreed and the deal is about to exchange the purchaser drops their price. By this time both parties have spent money on legal fees and surveys therefore they are reluctant to withdraw. In some cases, parties will sign a 'lock out agreement' which means that for an agreed period they will deal exclusively with the purchaser they have agreed terms with. Private treaty costs tend to be lower than those of auction or tender but in an active market, where there are multiple prospective purchasers making bids, the agent may decide to go to an informal tender, after initial marketing, by asking all parties to submit their best and final bids.

These methods are usually in relation to sales only although in a very active letting market, informal tenders may be used to invite best bids for leases. Informal tenders may be suitable for the sale of long residential leases, as the buyer will pay a premium to purchase the lease, in a similar way to buying a freehold property. Auctions would not be used for new leases due to the need to negotiate detailed terms however they are frequently used for existing residential long leases with only a short term remaining. Whichever method of sale is selected, the next stage is to market the property and the approach is broadly the same for a lease as for a freehold.

MARKETING

When we first started in the industry, we tended to agree with our clients a marketing campaign and budget. This generally included preparing particulars for the property, putting a board on it, advertising it in the Estates Gazette – if a relatively high-value property, or a site likely to be attractive to national buyers – or in the local press if a lower value property. We would also check our list of those seeking property. We then reviewed the sources, and levels, of interest to try to establish which were the most successful methods. Today, we not only use similar methods but also have the benefit of the Internet and social media and sizeable properties may have their own website or, as a minimum, digital particulars that will then be placed on a suitable web platform. Social media is also widely used by agents to promote their instructions. In both cases, there is also the option to start with 'soft marketing' whereby the agent approaches specific targeted parties before the full marketing campaign starts, giving selected prospective purchasers a chance to get in early before full marketing. This could benefit both parties by a quick deal being agreed, reducing void costs, and making savings on marketing costs. A successful marketing campaign will expose the property widely and result in at least one interested party, ideally more, as competition may increase the offer that completes on the deal. During the marketing period, it is essential that the agent keeps their client well-informed of progress. Unless the market is very strong, it is highly unlikely that a prospective purchaser, or tenant, will offer the full terms required by the client and this is where the agent's skills of negotiation are required.

NEGOTIATION

In this phase the agent needs to try to arrive at a deal that suits both parties, known in business as a 'win/win'. Even when the price has been agreed, they then need to discuss other aspects such as timing and what is included and excluded from the sale. For a leasehold transaction, there may be negotiations around letting incentives. These commonly include rent-free periods, stepped rents, rent caps, capital contributions, and service charge caps. The level of incentives offered will depend on the state of the market. If the market is considered to be 'hardening', that is demand is high, and supply is low, then the level of incentives will be lower. If, however, the market is 'softening', and supply exceeds demand, then increased incentives will be needed to secure the deal. The basis of negotiation is to try to arrive at an outcome that both parties are happy with. This requires planning, good communication, and a will, on both sides to achieve a deal. Negotiation and communication are both core APC competencies for some pathways. Once all the details have been agreed these then need to be formally recorded.

HEADS OF TERMS

Heads of Terms are a document prepared by the agent that set out the formal agreement reached by the parties. For a sale, this will include details such as the address of the property, the price agreed, how this is to be paid, and when, the names and addresses of parties to the sale and their solicitors, an indicative exchange and completion date, plus any other conditions to be applied. For a piece of land that might be developed later, for example, the Heads of Terms might include an overage clause. An overage clause allows the seller to benefit from any substantial uplift in value following the grant of planning permission. There may also be a requirement for rights of way or access, or restrictive covenants. Heads of Terms are not legally binding and are normally stated to be subject to contract. The more detail provided by the agent in the Heads of Terms, the fewer disagreements there are likely to be during the process.

For commercial leasehold properties, in England and Wales, there are now recommended heads of terms contained within the Code for Leasing Business Premises.[12] In addition to the names and addresses of the parties, the address of the premises, and the rent, there are details of the key lease provisions including aspects such as lease length, alienation rights, break rights, rent review provisions, repairing obligations, and use. The objective of this document was to improve the fairness of negotiations, particularly for parties that are not professionally advised. They should also make the drafting of leases more straightforward, and timely. Some of these elements will have a major impact on value such as break clauses and repairing obligations; therefore these areas will often lead to spirited negotiation to ensure that the rent reflects the terms agreed.

INSTRUCTING PROFESSIONALS

The agreed Heads of Terms will be forwarded by the agent to solicitors to draft leases or contracts. The agent might also need to liaise with other professionals such as draughtsmen to prepare plans of the premises; or building surveyors, to prepare schedules of condition for leasehold premises; or financiers or mortgage brokers to clarify financial arrangements. The agent will remain responsible for driving the transaction to completion and this requires constant communication with all parties.

EXCHANGING CONTRACTS

Usually in a conveyancing transaction, legal advisers will prepare contracts, which commit the parties to the transaction but allow for completion later, when final legal formalities have been carried out. The buyer and seller will each sign an identical copy of the contract, which is then exchanged between them. Contracts are discussed in more detail in Chapter 9.

COMPLETING THE TRANSACTION

Following exchange of contracts, legal advisers will prepare the deed (usually a Form TR1), transferring the property to the buyer. If the transaction involves the creation of a new lease, both sides will need to approve the detailed draft clauses and covenants. The parties will then sign the deed or lease. Completion takes place when the deed or lease is dated, and the purchase price (if any) has been paid. On completion the agent will need to ensure that keys are released, any building management documentation is handed over, and that, if it is a lease completion, arrangements are made to collect rent going forward whether the agent is doing the management themselves or handing over to another firm. Details of the transaction should then be recorded in the database for use with future instructions.

REGISTRATION OF THE TRANSACTION

Following completion, the transaction may need to be registered at HM Land Registry, to finalise the transfer of ownership or the creation of the tenant's new leasehold estate. Land registration is discussed further in Chapter 7.

LEASEHOLD TRANSACTIONS

This chapter has concentrated on disposals and acquisitions as some of the most common property transactions but there are also specific transactions relating to leasehold interests. These include lease renewals, rent reviews, assignments, sub-lettings, surrenders, and sale and leasebacks. Some of these are covered in brief in Chapter 8. The process of negotiating many of these transactions requires the same approach to the use of comparable evidence, negotiation, and formal recording of the agreement as outlined earlier in this chapter.

Lease renewals

The transaction for a commercial lease renewal will depend on whether the lease is inside or outside the security provisions of the Landlord and Tenant Act 1954. If outside the Act, then on lease expiry the tenant will need to negotiate a new lease with the landlord with no rights to remain therefore they have a weaker negotiation position than if their lease is inside the Act which gives them some protection. There is a series of notices to be served on a lease within the Act and strict timescales as set out in Chapter 8. Once terms have been negotiated and agreed solicitors can be instructed to draw up a new lease. Failure to agree terms will result in a referral to court which is a lengthy and costly process. To try to overcome delays and costs, the RICS and the Law Society jointly set up Professional Arbitration on Court Terms (PACT) which is a method of alternative dispute resolution whereby both parties agree that determination of renewal lease terms will be decided by an independent third party. This saves both cost and time but with the reducing number of long leases being granted there are fewer cases that require settlement by a third party.

Rent reviews

This is another property transaction which will involve collation and analysis of evidence, negotiation, service of notice, and formal recording of the agreement. If the two parties fail to reach agreement, on a revised level of rent, the rent review clause will normally provide for referral to a third party which can be an expert, arbitrator or, occasionally, a mediator. It is particularly important to have clear records of collation and analysis of evidence for third-party decisions. Although an expert can use their own knowledge of the specific market, an arbitrator's decision is based purely on the reports and evidence provided to them; therefore, they must be clear.

Assignments and sub-lettings

Most leases allow for some form of assignment or sub-letting. It may be of the whole, or part, of the premises and will usually require the landlord's consent which is not to be unreasonably withheld. Most assignment clauses require an AGA as defined in the Landlord and Tenant (Covenants) Act 1995. An AGA is an undertaking by the outgoing tenant, to the landlord, that guarantees the incoming tenant's obligations under the lease such as payment of rent, service charges, and carrying out repairs. If the incoming tenant (assignee) fails to comply with their obligations, then the outgoing tenant (assignor) will have to do so. Although no discussion of evidence of value should be needed for an assignment, an assignee may often have additional requirements that are brought into the request for an assignment such as a change of use or alterations; therefore some negotiation may take place. It is important, however, to be aware of the expectation of dealing with a request for assignment expeditiously to avoid legal action.

Surrenders

It is also possible, by agreement between the parties, to surrender a lease that is no longer required, but this will often require payment of a premium by the departing tenant to compensate the landlord.

In some cases, such as development situations, the landlord may be prepared to pay a premium to the tenant for a surrender to save time and achieve certainty of possession. The premium will be based on the loss to the parties of the lease not running to the end of the term. It is also possible for a surrender and regrant to be agreed whereby an existing lease is surrendered in exchange for a new lease that might provide greater security, more contemporary terms, or other benefits to both parties.

Sale and leaseback

As discussed in Chapter 5, real estate is used as a resource for some organisations. It can be however a resource that accounts for a large part of the organisation's assets, and some organisations have identified that their occupational real estate can be utilised to provide finance for use elsewhere in the business. Some major national retailers that held freehold units have sold the freehold and taken leases on the premises (see Chapter 5). This releases capital and can improve their balance sheets. For the purchasers, they benefit from a well-established tenant with a good covenant. A good, or strong, covenant means that the tenant appears to be financially secure and creditworthy therefore likely to pay their rent.

This chapter has provided an overview of the most common real estate transactions carried out in all sectors, both freehold and leasehold. It does not cover the full complexity of real estate transactions but aims to highlight key considerations. It also demonstrates the importance of those involved in property transactions combining knowledge of relevant guidance, legislation, and regulations, with the softer skills of communication and negotiation, to successfully complete a wide range of transactions. In the next two chapters, we will consider valuation concepts and methods to gain a better understanding of how formal valuations, rather than those market appraisals used for property transactions, are prepared.

NOTES

1 RICS (2016) *Real Estate Agency and Brokerage RICS Professional Statement, Global* 3rd Edition August Online. Available from: www.rics.org/uk/

upholding-professional-standards/sector-standards/real-estate/real-estate-agency-and-brokerage/

2 RICS (2017) *UK Residential Real Estate Agency RICS Professional Statement, UK* 6th Edition September Online. Available from: www.rics.org/uk/upholding-professional-standards/sector-standards/real-estate/uk-residential-real-estate-agency/

3 RICS (2016) *UK Commercial Real Estate Agency RICS Professional Standards and Guidance* 1st Edition October Online. Available from: www.rics.org/globalassets/rics-website/media/upholding-professional-standards/sector-standards/real-estate/uk-commercial-real-estate-agency-1st-edition-rics.pdf

4 See note 1

5 See note 3

6 See note 3

7 See note 3

8 RICS (2015) *Code of Measuring Practice Guidance Note, Global* 6th Edition May Online. Available from: www.rics.org/globalassets/rics-website/media/upholding-professional-standards/sector-standards/valuation/code-of-measuring-practice-6th-edition-rics.pdf

9 RICS (2018) *RICS Property Measurement* 2nd Edition Online. Available from: www.rics.org/globalassets/rics-website/media/upholding-professional-standards/sector-standards/real-estate/rics-property-measurement/rics-property-measurement-2nd-edition-rics/

10 RICS (2012) *Comparable Evidence in Property Valuation* 1st Edition Information Paper Online. Available from: www.rics.org/globalassets/rics-website/media/upholding-professional-standards/sector-standards/valuation/comparable-evidence-in-property-valuation-1st-edition-rics.pdf

11 See note 6

12 RICS (2020) *Code for Leasing Business Premises* 1st Edition February Online. Available from: www.rics.org/globalassets/rics-website/media/upholding-professional-standards/sector-standards/real-estate/code-for-leasing_ps-version_feb-2020.pdf

FURTHER READING

Card, R, Murdoch, J, and Murdoch, S (2011) *Real Estate Management Law* 7th Edition Oxford: Oxford University Press

National Trading Standards Estate Agency Team (2019) *Protecting Consumers Safeguarding Businesses* Online. Available from: https://en.powys.gov.uk/article/4854/Advice-for-Estate-Agents

RICS (2017) *Conflicts of Interest* 1st edition March Online. Available from: https://www.rics.org/globalassets/rics-website/media/upholding-professional-standards/standards-of-conduct/conflicts-of-interest/conflicts_of_interest_global_1st-edition_dec_2017_revisions_pgguidance_2017_rw.pdf

REAL ESTATE VALUATION CONCEPTS

WHAT IS VALUE?

Value encapsulates the benefits a good, service, or asset provides to its existing, or potential, owner. Although value is often calculated in monetary terms, it could also be assessed in functional, social, or psychological terms. This value forms the basis of the exchange between parties and reflects what the parties agree the item is worth.

Although often used interchangeably, there is a subtle distinction between value and worth. For example, when purchasing a house, its value will be estimated by the estate agent; however its worth, to the buyer personally, may be considerably more than the value attributed to it. When one of us purchased our existing home, it was a few doors down from our current house, and close to friends, schools, and transport. Moving was relatively straightforward as the two properties were so close to each other and we were even to take our telephone number with us. This made the house more valuable to us than to other potential purchasers. This difference between value – in the open market to all potential buyers – and worth – value to a specific investor – is clarified within the RICS Valuation – Global Standards, widely known as the Red Book.

WHAT IS VALUE IN RELATION TO REAL ESTATE?

As outlined in Chapter 2, real estate is a significant store of value and it is essential to be able to assess this value to facilitate the functioning of the real estate market. The RICS has refined definitions of value over the years, in tandem with the International Valuation Standards Council (IVSC),[1] to try to achieve a consistency in

DOI: 10.1201/9781003155256-11

approach to valuations. This became increasingly important, as the market became a global one, to enable owners and investors to be able to compare properties, in different geographical regions, on the same basis. There are different definitions of value but less than there used to be. One of the most often used is the value of an asset for exchange which is known as its market value.

The RICS Red Book uses the International Valuation Standards (IVS)[2] definition of **market value** as:

> *The estimated amount for which an asset or liability should exchange on the valuation date between a willing buyer and a willing seller in an arm's length transaction, after proper marketing and where the parties had each acted knowledgeably, prudently and without compulsion.*[3]

Analysis of this definition demonstrates that market value can only ever be an *estimate* rather than an exact figure and that it must be related to a *specific date*. This is particularly important during times of rapid change when a valuation can become out of date very quickly. *A willing buyer and a willing seller* mean that forced sale, or less commonly forced purchase, value is excluded from the definition. For example, where a property must be sold to repay debts this is likely to be a forced sale, by an unwilling seller, that is likely to result in a figure lower than market value being achieved. Many open-ended property funds, that is those with unlimited shares that managers are required to redeem on request, had to suspend trading during 2020/21. This is because the Covid-19 global pandemic resulted in large numbers of investors wanting to withdraw their money, but this would mean funds would have to sell properties very quickly to meet redemptions. Not only is it very difficult to sell property during a pandemic, but a flood of properties onto the market would further depress values. There was also a difficulty in valuing properties accurately during the Covid-19 pandemic due to the uncertainty. The RICS Red Book provides guidance on valuation uncertainty declarations to assist valuers asked to assess market value under unusual market conditions. More recently the RICS has published specific advice on dealing with valuation uncertainty during the Covid-19 pandemic.[4] Finally, it is important to note that market value can be defined slightly differently for other purposes, such as for inheritance or capital gains tax purposes, where specific, modified, definitions are provided.[5]

Market value is distinguished from **worth**, or investment value, which is defined, by the IVS, and adopted in the Red Book as:

The value of an asset to the owner or a prospective owner for individual investment or operational objectives.[6]

The distinction between the two is that market value refers to the value of an asset that is exposed to the open market where all buyers and sellers can compete for the interest. Worth, however, reflects the value to a specific party for a specific purpose. For example, an office building may have a market value of £5 million but if the adjoining occupier is looking to expand, they may be prepared to pay the above market value as it is worth an additional sum to them to avoid the relocation costs involved in moving to another site. Such a purchaser would be defined as a *special purchaser,* that is an individual or organisation that has strategic reasons for paying in excess of the market value of an asset.

WHAT IS THE RED BOOK?

The first edition of RICS the Red Book was published in 1976 and it has undergone thorough, and increasingly regular, revisions since then. The 1970s property crash in the UK caused increasing concern regarding valuations due to some high-profile negligence cases such as *Singer and Friedlander v John D Wood 1977*. In this case, the plaintiffs, who were merchant bankers, claimed £600,000 plus interest for an alleged breach of the duty of care, owed to them by the defendant, in carrying out a valuation of Manor Farm in Eastcombe, Gloucestershire. Manor Farm was 140 acres of land proposed for residential development. Lyon Homes Limited had agreed to purchase the land in December 1971 for £620,000. A year later the defendants valued 131 acres of the land at £2,000,000 and the owners, Lyon Homes Limited, borrowed money from a variety of sources including the merchant bank owned by the plaintiffs. The Lyon Group collapsed leaving the plaintiffs suffering a £600,000 loss. The plaintiffs were awarded a settlement figure of £491,250 plus interest. The judge did however accept that there was a permissible 'margin of error', or bracket, that a competent, careful, and experienced valuer would arrive at and that this was generally 10% on either side of the valuation figure or up to 15% in exceptional circumstances.

High-profile cases such as this undermined confidence in valuers and the RICS responded to this by initiating research into valuation methods and developing guidance notes on practices and procedures in the valuation process. This standardisation of the approach to valuations for loan purposes was intended to assist valuers in achieving the level of accuracy required.

The RICS continued to commission research, such as the Mallinson Report 1994[7] and the Carsberg Report 2002,[8] in pursuit of increased valuation accuracy and continues to update the Red Book on a regular basis. The Red Book, entitled 'Valuation – Global standards' contains mandatory rules and guidance for RICS members and Registered Valuers to follow when they are undertaking valuations. The RICS continues to develop valuation practices and, at the time of writing have commissioned an Independent Review into the Valuation of Property Assets for Investment Purposes due to report with recommendations by the end of 2021. The review is to examine how valuations of property assets for investment purposes are conducted. It will make recommendations with a view to ensuring that valuation practices continue to be fit for purpose. Evidence is to be obtained on methodology, risk analysis, independence, objectivity, and measuring confidence.

The Red Book is regularly updated to ensure that it covers all necessary areas as the market evolves. It incorporates IVSC's International Valuation Standards. The Red Book also provides a mandatory performance framework and reflects the growing importance of professional technical and performance standards that require the delivery of high-quality valuation advice to meet client requirements. The focus is on transparency, consistency, and the avoidance of conflicts of interest. It continues to evolve and is regularly updated to reflect changes in expectations concerning matters such as sustainability and, more recently, how to deal with the Covid-19 pandemic. Some of the standards set out are mandatory, and must be followed; other standards are advisory, providing guidance only. Unless specifically stated otherwise, all Professional Standards and Valuation Technical and Performance Standards (VPSs) are mandatory for written valuations. Valuation Practice Guidance – Applications (VPGAs) are advisory only and concern the practical application of the standards to a specific context. This might include valuation for a specific purpose or valuation in relation to a particular asset type.

WHAT IS THE PURPOSE OF VALUATION?

A valuation most commonly provides an estimate of market value for an asset, although other bases of value may be specified. A robust, consistent, credible, and transparent system of valuation is needed to support the Real Estate market and to comply with government and regulatory requirements. Stocks and shares are traded and priced on a continuous basis, reacting to changes in the external environment, whenever stock markets are open. The real estate market, however, is slower moving and less transparent but still requires consistent and supportable valuations to function effectively.

There has been considerable debate over the years as to whether valuation is an art or a science. The decision in *Singer and Friedlander Ltd v John D Wood and Co 1977*, outlined earlier, suggested that, as valuation is an art rather than a science, it is acceptable to have a bracket within which the valuation falls. It can, however, be argued that valuation is a combination of art and science. The science involves the application of the correct measurement approach, selection of the appropriate methodology, and collation of relevant comparable evidence. The art involves interpretation of the facts by the individual valuer using their skills and experience and then presenting the valuation in an appropriate form.

WHY MIGHT VALUATIONS BE REQUIRED?

It is essential that the valuer understands the purpose of the valuation that they are undertaking to ensure that an appropriate valuation approach is taken. A valuation may be required for a variety of reasons including:

- Purchase or sale transactions
- Acquisitions, mergers, and sales of businesses
- Rental values and fair rents
- Financial reporting
- Tax assessments – rating, council, capital gains, and inheritance tax

- Secured lending – mortgages and loans
- Insurance
- Compulsory purchase and compensation
- Lease extensions and enfranchisement
- Development appraisals
- Legal or regulatory requirements
- Litigation.

The valuer must select an appropriate valuation method for the purpose, specify the basis of value for the valuation, and include explicit assumptions upon which the valuation is based.

WHO CARRIES OUT VALUATIONS?

Since October 2010, following a full consultation process, the RICS has required valuers carrying out Red Book valuations to be registered with the RICS Registered Valuer scheme. Valuer registration is a quality assurance mechanism that monitors all registered RICS members carrying out Red Book valuations. Members are registered individually, and firms can also be registered for regulation or for sponsoring Registered Valuers. The scheme aims to ensure that standards are consistent, that all valuers are regulated and qualified professionals, who are experts in their field, and that all valuations produced are of high quality. Valuer registration also gives clients an easily identifiable designation to demonstrate that the valuations provided consistently apply the Red Book standards. A team of Regulatory Surveyors audits Registered Valuers to ensure that standards are being complied with, that best practice guidelines are being followed, and that appropriate processes and procedures are in place. Any areas for improvement will be highlighted in a report following the audit.

ARE ALL VALUATIONS REGULATED BY THE RED BOOK?

The regulations of the Red Book relate to all **written** valuations. However, all valuation advice provided by members, including wholly oral valuations, should still follow the principles set out in the Red Book as far as possible. There is however a diverse range of contexts within which valuations and valuation advice are provided so the Red Book distinguishes between full Red Book valuations, that must comply with all valuation standards, and those that may be exempt from some of them.

Examples of written valuations that may not comply with all the mandatory standards are estate agency, where providing advice on value in the course of an agency instruction, for either acquisition or disposal, will not need to follow all the standards within the Red Book. There is however an RICS global practice statement[9] that provides further advice on these valuations. When acting, or preparing to act, as an expert witness the member will have to follow the rules and procedures laid down by the judicial body before which the member is appearing. Again, there is specific RICS guidance concerning surveyors acting as expert witnesses[10] which should be consulted. Valuations in connection with the performance of statutory functions are usually governed by specific statutory provisions which will need to be followed, rather than the Red Book. Valuations provided purely for internal purposes, and without any communication to a third party, do not have to comply with all the Red Book standards although it is best practice to comply with them where possible. It should be explicitly stated, when the written advice is provided, that there is a prohibition on disclosure and that the valuation is for internal purposes only. Where valuers are acting in negotiations, or litigation, valuation advice may be provided as part of preparation for this. Any written report provided that does not comply with all the Red Book mandatory standards should include a specific statement that outlines why there has been a departure from them.

WHAT ARE TERMS OF ENGAGEMENT?

Prior to producing a written valuation report, it is essential that the Terms of Engagement are agreed between the client and the valuer. The Terms of Engagement should clearly set out the scope of the work including the format, purpose, and full details of the proposed valuation report. The valuer has a professional responsibility to explore their client's requirements and expectations of the valuation report and, where necessary, to guide the client towards the most appropriate advice. The Terms of Engagement should specify any actual, or anticipated, marketing constraints relating to the valuation. Most organisations will have their own standard Terms of Engagement, but the Red Book sets out suggested subheadings to assist valuers in ensuring all essential aspects are covered. These subheadings include:

- Identification and status of the valuer
- Identification of the client and any other intended users of the valuation
- Identification of the assets/liabilities to be valued
- Financial currency that the valuation is in
- Purpose of the valuation
- Basis of the value adopted
- Valuation date
- Nature of the valuer's work including the extent of investigations and the limitations
- Nature and sources of information used to compile the valuation
- Assumptions and special assumptions
- Format of the report
- Restrictions on use, distribution, and publication of the report
- Confirmation that the valuation is in accordance with the IVS
- The fee basis
- Reference to the complaints handling procedure for registered firms
- A statement that compliance with standards could be monitored by the RICS
- A statement on any limitations on liability agreed

WHAT MUST A VALUATION REPORT INCLUDE?

The Red Book contains mandatory requirements for valuers providing valuation reports. The report needs to be clear and unambiguous when stating the conclusions of the valuation. The Red Book provides a list of subheadings that must be included in a valuation report. These are like those outlined in the Terms of Engagement but exclude the format of the report and the fee basis. They additionally include the valuation approach and reasoning, the amount of the valuation and a commentary on any material uncertainty where appropriate. The valuation must be stated in both words and figures and the valuation date clearly stated. There is a requirement to comment on any material uncertainty in relation to the valuation. It is also essential that the basis of a valuation is stated and that this is appropriate for, and consistent with, the purposes of the valuation. The Red Book refers to four further bases of valuation, in addition to market value and worth (or investment value) outlined at the start of this chapter. These six bases of valuation are defined in the International Valuation Standards. The six bases are:

- Market value
- Investment value (or worth)
- Market rent
- Equitable value
- Synergistic value
- Liquidation value

The valuer has responsibility for ensuring that the basis of value is consistent with the purpose of the valuation. This is, however, subject to compliance with any mandatory requirements such as those imposed by statute. The basis of the valuation should be agreed with the client at Terms of Engagement stage. It is possible for two different bases of value to arrive at the same valuation, for example the investment value of a property to a specific party may be the same as the market value despite different assessment criteria being used.

Market rent is defined by the IVS, and adopted in the Red Book, in a similar way to market value. It is:

> the estimated amount for which an interest in real property should be leased on the **valuation date** between a willing lessor and a willing lessee on appropriate lease terms in an arm's length transaction, after proper marketing and where the parties had each acted knowledgeably, prudently and without compulsion.[11]

Market rent is directly dependent on the terms of the lease contract. Although lease terms will normally reflect current market practice, it is possible for there to be unusual lease terms that will need to be incorporated into the valuation. Aspects such as the lease term, frequency of rent reviews, responsibility for maintenance, and other statutory factors and contractual terms will impact a market rent. Valuers therefore need to set out the principal lease terms that have been assumed, or are in existence, when providing an opinion of market rent. Market rent should also take account of any letting incentives used when considering the comparable evidence (see Chapter 10).

Equitable value, previously defined by the IVS as fair value, is

> *the price that would be received to sell an asset or paid to transfer a liability in an orderly transaction between market participants at the measurement date.*[12]

Equitable value, in most cases, would be consistent with market value but there can, on occasion, be a difference between the valuation figures reported. Equitable value requires determination of the principal, or most advantageous, market for the asset or liability, and use of a valuation approach that uses the same assumptions that market participants would make when pricing the asset or liability. Equitable value, or fair value, is used by the International Accounting Standards Board (IASB) in the International Financial Reporting Standards (IFRS).

In certain cases, for example when assembling parcels of land into a larger development site, it is possible that this combination of individual ownerships will result in a higher value. This is known as **synergistic value** (known in the Red Book as marriage value) and this is defined by the IVS as:

> *the result of a combination of two or more assets or interests where the combined value is more than the sum of the separate values.*[13]

The Red Book definition is virtually identical simply deleting 'the result of a' and substituting 'An additional element of value created by the'. Synergistic, or marriage, value also commonly occurs where a freehold and a leasehold interest, if let at less than full rental value, is merged. If the owner of one of the interests purchases the other's interest, then the interest will merge by operation of law. The lease is extinguished, and the freehold becomes a freehold at full rental value which is highly likely, particularly in a rising market, to have a higher capital value than that of the two separate interests.

Finally, **liquidation value** refers to the value of assets that are sold separately usually with a view to satisfying the obligations of a company to its creditors and shareholders. Liquidation value is defined by the IVS as:

> *The amount that would be realised when an asset or group of assets are sold on a piecemeal basis.*[14]

Liquidation value is likely to be lower than market value as it tends to involve an unwilling seller, limited marketing, and an element of compulsion.

The Red Book is intended to enable valuers to provide high quality, transparent, consistent, objective, and ethical valuation advice. The global standards focus on professional, technical, and performance, or delivery, standards. This is aimed at providing clients with confidence that valuations produced will be undertaken to the highest professional standards. With these provisions in place, it is expected that the accuracy of valuations should have improved, however, there continue to be cases relating to negligent valuations.

CAN A VALUATION BE 'WRONG'?

The number of cases concerning negligent valuations, and the levels of damages awarded, would suggest that valuations can be 'wrong'. For example, in *Capita Alternative Fund Services [Guernsey] Limited and Matrix Securities Limited v Drivers Jonas 2011* a complex valuation, involving Enterprise Zone capital allowances and other tax implications, resulted in damages of over £18 million being awarded, although these were reduced to £11.86 million on appeal. Whether a valuation is 'right' or 'wrong' depends, largely, on the specific assumptions made to support it.

A value is derived from the demand for a particular property and the level of demand can change quite quickly. For example, the Covid-19 pandemic in 2020 had quickly impacted on all sectors of the real estate market. The rise in home working led to a desire for larger homes further away from transport networks and a reduction in the demand for central business district office space. There was an increase in the demand for warehousing and distribution units to service the further growth in Internet shopping and a reduction in the demand for student housing as many degrees went wholly online.

Valuers need to be precise about the assumptions that underpin their reported valuations and may provide a range of values rather than a precise figure, depending on the purpose, and basis, of the valuation. They must also provide the date of the valuation and the date on which the report is signed which will not always be the same. The Red Book even states that the time should be specified if the asset is one where its price is likely to change materially during a single day. This could happen, for example, where there is hyperinflation.

Real estate has historically been considered as a hedge against inflation when compared to other assets such as bonds, stocks, and shares. This is because as inflation rises, property values and rents also tend to rise, keeping pace with inflation. When purchasing, and holding, real estate, as an investment, investors will consider the return and yield on their properties.

WHAT IS MEANT BY THE RETURN?

The return on an investment refers to the change in value of a property over time. The total return will be made up of the income and the capital return. The income return comes from the rents received and any additional sums such as interest payable on late rent payment. The capital return relates to the change in value of the asset during a specific period. The return is based on historic data as it is a retrospective analysis of what the investment property has earned over a period. However, previous return bears little relation to future performance therefore investors will consider potential future returns when making investment decisions.

WHAT IS MEANT BY THE YIELD?

Whilst it is difficult to predict the capital return on an investment, as this depends on so many factors that are outside the control of the investor, it is easier to predict the income return. In the case of property, the income return is the rental income. At the time of purchase, the investor will know the passing rent, that is the rent payable specified in the lease. Based on comparable evidence in the area, they will be able to estimate what likely future rental levels will be. The income return is what is known as the yield of the investment. It is calculated as a percentage of the capital value of the investment. The yield is therefore a prospective way of identifying what an investment might earn, in relation to its capital value. It is a measure of anticipated return, but it is not guaranteed, and the yield applied will reflect the expectation of achieving the present, and future, rental income.

Yields can be expressed as:

> *gross* yields – which are simply rent received in relation to capital value, or *net* yields – which allow for the deduction of expenses in relation to the investment such as management, insurance, and repairs.

The most widely used expression of yield is what is known as the *all risks yield* (ARY). This yield represents the expectations of future rental income and capital growth. It is a simple calculation that involves dividing the rental income by the capital value of the property and then multiplying the result by 100 to arrive at a percentage. The ARY, as its name suggests, incorporates the investor's views on not only future growth but also all potential future risks relating to the property. The ARY is also sometimes referred to as the investment yield or market yield.

Not all properties, however, are let at market value. In this case, as discussed in the next chapter on valuation methods, when considering an investment property, two different yields will be applied.

INITIAL YIELD

The rent passing under the terms of the lease will be valued up to the next event when the rent changes. This will normally be a lease renewal or rent review. The adjusted ARY applied to this part of the income reflects both the additional security of this, already contractually agreed, income stream and the anticipation of its future growth. The initial yield expresses, as a percentage, the ratio of current income to capital value.

REVERSIONARY YIELD

When a rent is reviewed to market value, this next part of the income stream is then valued using an adjusted ARY reflecting the

additional risk relating to potential future income. The reversionary yield expresses, as a percentage, the ratio of future income to
capital value. This income is valued in perpetuity, which means
forever, based on the assumption that the property owner will want
to maximise their income from the property so will carry out whatever work is necessary to maintain the market rent during the life of
the investment. If they decide to sell, the interest will retain a value
that is reflected by valuing it forever.

EQUIVALENT YIELD

Having two different yields, applied to the two different parts of
the income stream, can make comparison with other investment
opportunities difficult. This is where the equivalent yield comes
in. The equivalent yield is a weighted average of the initial and
reversionary yields relating to an investment. It takes account of the
respective periods of time for which the yields are received giving a
total return for the life of the investment. It is similar to the ARY as
it also implicitly allows for growth, but it differs from the ARY as it
incorporates the timing of the income flows.

EQUATED YIELD

The equated yield is the average rate of return over the holding
period of the investment that explicitly allows for growth. The
equated yield is also known as the internal rate of return (IRR).
The IRR reflects the rate of interest at which all future cash flows
must be discounted to arrive at a net present value (NPV) of zero.
The IRR is calculated using a discounted cash flow (DCF) appraisal
which will be discussed in the next chapter. One main advantage
of the equated yield, or IRR, is that it makes real estate investment directly comparable with other investments such as stocks and
shares.

RUNNING YIELD

This refers to the changing yield over the life of the investment.
If, for example, a property is let at below market rent, the initial
yield is likely to be relatively low as it would reflect the security

of the income stream and the likely prospect of an increase in rent at the next rent review opportunity. The reversionary yield would probably be slightly higher to reflect the time until the revised rent could be received and the risk of it not occurring. The running yield would therefore change during the life of the investment. It is calculated by dividing the rental income received over a specified period, by the capital value at time. Although usually quoted on an annual basis, it can be calculated on a quarterly, or even a monthly, basis, depending on how frequently rent is received and the property is valued. Many REITs have quarterly valuations of their property holdings carried out and their analyses will show running yields on a quarterly basis. This is particularly important when it is an asset with frequently changing income streams such as multi-tenanted offices or shopping centres.

HARD AND SOFT YIELDS

Investment agents will often talk about yields hardening or softening. A hardening yield is one that is projected to fall over time and a softening one is the one that is projected to rise. This opinion will be based on the analysis of market trends and comparable evidence.

A hardening yield, that is one that appears to be falling, suggests a rising market with increased demand for properties in this asset class. This means that they will become more expensive for investors to buy. A hardening yield can also be referred to as yield compression.

A softening yield suggests a falling market. For example, the lockdowns in response to the Covid-19 pandemic caused a dramatic change in working and shopping patterns. It also reduced the number of real estate transactions. This pressure, together with the continued uncertainty surrounding Brexit, resulted in a considerable softening in yields. This had an impact on real estate valuations, one example being where the value of the UK's biggest real estate company, Landsec, dropped by 13.7% in a year as reported in its 2021 results.[15]

NOMINAL AND TRUE YIELDS

The difference between nominal and true yields is down to the assumptions made on the timing of receipt of the income. The *nominal yield* takes rent divided by capital value so, implicitly, is based on receipt of the income on an annually in arrears basis. In practice, however, most rents are receivable quarterly in advance. This enables the investor to reinvest the rents received over the course of the year making the *true equivalent yield* (TEY) slightly higher than the nominal yield.

EXIT YIELD

Finally, the exit yield refers to the yield to be applied at the end of a DCF appraisal. This will reflect expectations of the value of the interest at the end of the holding period.

Although not an exhaustive list, the above are the most commonly used yields in relation to investment properties.

WHAT FACTORS CAUSE CHANGES IN YIELDS?

Fundamentally, yields are driven by levels of demand for, and supply of, properties. A high level of demand and low supply levels are likely to lead to a hardening of yields – as prices rise, yields fall – reflecting the increased certainty of receipt of rental income. As a yield is measuring the potential future income from an investment other factors, both general and property specific, will have an impact on the yield. We have already mentioned the impact of the Covid-19 pandemic and Brexit on the demand for, and therefore yield from, real estate. Business confidence, based on economic performance, will also have an impact on yields. Property-specific factors impacting on yield include the location of the property; the quality of existing or potential tenants; lease terms; levels of borrowing; and the need for, and costs of, maintenance.

If, having read this chapter, you are still confused about yields, do not worry, this is not unusual. Many of our contemporaries, who have been in general practice for over 30 years, still get confused and need to double-check their definitions. When you read the next chapter on valuation methodology, it should help you to develop a deeper understanding of which yields are used in which valuation approaches, and why.

NOTES

1 The IVSC is an independent not-for-profit organisation that acts as an independent global standard setter for the valuation profession promoting consistency and professionalism in the public interest. www.ivsc.org

2 IVS (2020) Available (to members, sponsor organisations and subscribers) from: www.ivsc.org/standards/international-valuation-standards/IVS

3 See RICS, 2019: 55

4 RICS (2020) *Impact of COVID-19 on Valuation* Online. Available from: www.rics.org/globalassets/rics-website/media/upholding-professional-standards/sector-standards/valuation/covid19-practice-alert-supplement-14-09-2020.pdf

5 Valuation Office Agency (2017) *Inheritance Tax Manual* Online. Available from: www.gov.uk/guidance/inheritance-tax-manual/section-7-revenue-basis-of-market-value-general-principles

6 See RICS, 2019: 57

7 Mallinson, M (1994) *Report of the President's Working Party on Commercial Property Valuations* London: RICS

8 Carsberg, B (2002) *Property Valuations* Report of the RICS Committee London: RICS

9 RICS (2016) *Real Estate Agency and Brokerage Guidance* 3rd Edition London: RICS

10 RICS (2014) *Surveyors Acting as Expert Witnesses* 4th Edition London: RICS

11 See RICS, 2019: 56

12 See note 5

13 See IVS, 2020: 22

14 See IVS, 2020: 22

15 Landsec (2021) *Landsec Annual Report* Online. Available from: https://landsec.com/annual-report-2021

ESSENTIAL READING

RICS (2019) *RICS Valuation: Global Standards Incorporating the IVSC International Valuation Standards* London: RICS

REAL ESTATE VALUATION METHODS

As outlined in the previous chapter, all written valuations must be carried out by a Registered Valuer and in accordance with the provisions of the Red Book. Before considering the main methods of valuation the key steps involved in producing a valuation are explained.

WHAT DOES THE VALUATION PROCESS ENTAIL?

The valuation process requires several key steps that will generally follow a linear pattern although, on occasion, it may be necessary to go back and revisit a step, for example, to renegotiate the Terms of Engagement as additional factors come to light during the process.

CLIENT'S INSTRUCTIONS

The client will contact the valuer with a request for a valuation and the valuer will need to check that they are sufficiently qualified, experienced, and registered, certified, or licensed (depending on where in the world they are located) to carry out the valuation themselves, or to supervise the inputs into a valuation. In circumstances where the valuer does not have a sufficient level of expertise, it is possible, with the explicit agreement of the client, to commission other professionals to assist. The valuer may also work as part of a team where, across all team members, the required skills and knowledge are satisfied.

CONFLICTS OF INTEREST

The valuer will need to check for any conflicts of interest following the RICS professional standards and guidance.[1] A conflict of interest occurs where there is any possibility that the aims of the valuer and their client could be incompatible. The growth of global multi-disciplinary real estate consultancies has led to the need for robust internal procedures to check for any conflict. The valuer will need to be transparent about any factors relating to the potential conflict of interest and ensure that their client understands the situation. There are occasions where the client may be prepared to acknowledge the risk of an adverse impact from the potential competing interest but grant informed consent. This may be subject to conditions such as the provision of information barriers. It is important that the valuer formally records the agreement and satisfies themselves that they can carry out the valuation independently and objectively. This has been seen where, for example the firm appointed to carry out quarterly valuations for a REIT was then appointed to dispose of a property that the REIT was interested in purchasing. The installation of robust information barriers ensured that all parties were content to proceed despite the potential for a conflict of interest.

The valuer will also need to check that they have enough PII to cover any claims made by clients for valuations they have relied on, and acted upon, which have resulted in loss or damage should they be considered negligent.

TERMS OF ENGAGEMENT

Prior to carrying out a valuation, it is essential that the Terms of Engagement are agreed between the client and the valuer. This may require some discussion and negotiation to ensure that the appropriate basis of valuation is agreed for the required purpose. At this stage, although not required as part of the Terms of Engagement it would be sensible to agree timescales and arrangements for obtaining documentation and carrying out inspections.

LEGAL DOCUMENTATION

The valuer needs to obtain copies of all leases and other documentation relating to the asset to be valued as the legal interest in each asset or liability must be stated. It is essential to clarify the extent of the interest being valued prior to carrying out an inspection to ensure that all relevant areas have been inspected.

INSPECTION AND MEASUREMENT

The extent of the inspection should be explicitly stated in the Terms of Engagement if there are likely to be limitations in the extent of them. The scope of the inspection must, however, be sufficiently thorough to provide the valuer with enough information to carry out the valuation. The extent of the inspection will obviously depend on the purpose and basis of the valuation to be carried out. Checking the legal documentation before inspection enables the valuer to not only clarify the boundaries of the premises and their actual, and assumed, condition, but also, for example whether improvements are to be included or excluded from the valuation.

Inspection should include, in addition to the extent and condition of the premises, other aspects such as the presence of any sustainable features; the types of property and uses in the surrounding area; whether the area appears to be improving or declining; and any major transport or other infrastructure changes. It is a good idea to take photographs of the subject premises, and the surrounding area, as this provides evidence of the state of the premises at the time of valuation and can be added to the body of documentation that supports the valuation.

The premises will need to be measured in accordance with the appropriate standards. As discussed in Chapter 10, the RICS is gradually incorporating the IPMS into their professional statement, RICS property measurement.[2] At the time of writing mandatory requirements for registered firms are in place for the measurement of offices and residential property. The IPMS have published standards for industrial and retail property which are likely to be adopted in the next edition of RICS property measurement; until that time the Code of measuring practice[3] continues to be used. The IPMS Coalition is currently working on standards for the measurement of mixed-use properties. Again, it is essential that the valuer adopts the correct method of measurement for the purpose and basis of valuation adopted.

MARKET RESEARCH

The next step is to investigate the market for the property to include not only comparable evidence in relation to the asset but also information on the local area. Depending on the type of property, and the purpose of the valuation, the valuer should check public records such as the local plan for both existing and future implications, highways plans, and any other aspects likely to impact on value, both now and in the near future. The Land Registry and Valuation Office can also be accessed to provide information on values.

Comparable evidence concerning recent transactions, such as lettings and sales, in the area must be verified to ensure its accuracy and reliability. Any evidence coming from third parties will require thorough assessment and investigation and, ideally, corroboration from another party. If it is impossible to achieve this, then the evidence should not be used.

It is important for valuers to keep detailed records of all evidence, inspections, and investigations so that it is clear to both internal colleagues, and the client, what the valuer has relied upon to provide their opinion of value. Should there be any negligence claims in the future this evidence would also help to justify the approach and the valuation figure provided.

DATA ANALYSIS

This stage is where the skills and experience of the valuer are paramount. The valuer needs to analyse the data available to arrive at as objective a figure as possible for the valuation. Forty years ago, the only way to obtain comparable data was to talk to those personally involved with the transaction. Today there is a wealth of data available from various computerised systems, but this data needs to be thoroughly researched and analysed to ensure that it is reliable and valid. It may be necessary to qualify some of the data used and it is important to be transparent about this process. One of the difficulties with relying on evidence from comparable transactions is that all valuations are based on historic data. This may however begin to change as more data becomes available, and advances in technology make it easier to analyse, facilitating the identification of trends.

VALUATION

The valuer will select the appropriate approach and methods of valuation that are suitable for the subject premises; the purpose, and use, of the valuation; and any statutory or other mandatory requirements relating to it. The valuer must be able to justify their selection of valuation approach and methods and an overview of the main methods is provided later in this chapter.

Although the valuer should independently produce the valuation, it can be sensible to discuss the value with the client before producing the formal valuation report. This is not so that the client can influence the outturn figure but to ensure that the value complies with the parameters identified in the Terms of Engagement, that it reflects the agreed purpose of the valuation, and that all available evidence has been used. There are occasions where the client might have access to information that the valuer is not yet aware of. The discussion with the client should also agree any limitations or assumptions made to support the valuation that had not previously been covered in the heads of terms.

The valuation report should then be produced in accordance with the Terms of Engagement agreed at the outset and covering, as a minimum, all those items listed in Chapter 10.

Having considered the valuation process, the next section provides an overview of the five main methods of valuation.

WHAT ARE THE FIVE METHODS OF VALUATION?

As outlined earlier, real estate is a significant store of value and valuation is the process of measuring of that value. The basic premise underpinning this measurement of value is the time value of money. What this means is that the money we hold today is worth more than the same sum of money in the future. This is for two reasons:

- because we can save or invest the money, we hold today, to generate interest or capital gains in the future;
- because inflation means that you will be able to buy less in the future with your money than you can buy with it today.

For example, if you are given the sum of £100 and invest it in a fixed rate bond paying 2.5% for one year you will have £102.50 at the end of that year. If you hold it for five years and take out, and spend, the interest every year, you will earn £2.50 per year for five years; a total of £12.50. However, if you add the interest to the sum invested in each year, then the total interest earned, due to the power of compound interest, will be £13.14. Compound interest reflects the fact that you are not only earning interest on your initial investment, but you are also earning interest on the interest accumulating over the investment period.

The impact of inflation means that although today you would be able to buy your weekly groceries for say £100, those same groceries next year might cost £102 if inflation is running at 2%.

The core concept that money is worth more today than it is in the future, known as the time value of money, underpins all the valuation methods. The purpose of the valuation, agreed at heads of terms stage, and the type of interest being valued, will have an impact on the method selected. There are five main methods, or approaches, to valuation: the comparison method, the investment method, the profits method, the cost (contractor's or depreciated replacement cost) method, and the residual method. There is a wealth of valuation textbooks that provide detailed numerical examples of the valuation methods (see end list); therefore the basic approaches only are described.

THE COMPARISON METHOD

This is the most widely used method globally. It is used to assess the value of all asset types including residential, commercial, and land, for both capital and rental purposes. It is the easiest method to understand as it simply involves the valuation of a property based on a comparison with similar properties that have recently been let or sold. The comparison method is a standalone method, but it also feeds into all the other valuation methods.

Comparison is straightforward when dealing with an active and transparent market such as that for stocks and shares. Shares can be bought in seconds and prices are updated immediately after a sale or purchase has taken place. Comparison in the real estate market is more challenging due to the less active market, the wide range of assets with significant differences between them, and the relatively limited number of buyers and sellers, particularly for the more expensive assets. For example, Blackstone's purchase of a US$18.7

billion industrial portfolio from Singapore-based GLP in 2019[4] was reportedly the largest private real estate deal in history and the market for such a sizeable purchase, in terms of numbers of willing buyers, is likely to be fairly limited.

The globalisation of the real estate market, requiring valuations in developing markets and compliance with increased regulation, highlighted issues with the availability of, consistency in the use of, and relative importance of sources of, comparable evidence. In response to these issues, the RICS developed comparable evidence in real estate valuation,[5] to provide guidance on best practice in the identification, analysis, and application of comparable evidence to the valuation of real estate. This guidance note highlights the difficulties of the comparison method for real estate which include:

- The limited number of transactions available
- The lack of up-to-date evidence
- The existence of special purchasers
- The lack of similar or identical evidence, and
- The lack of transparency in the real estate market

The valuer's skills and experience are used to analyse and interpret the comparable evidence available, making appropriate adjustments, to arrive at their opinion of value. In some circumstances, such as where suitable comparable evidence is very limited, they might need to report material uncertainty.

The comparison method is particularly suitable for the residential sales and lettings market where there is an active market with many transactions and adjustments can be made to reflect differences in aspects such as location, size, and condition. Even apartments in a block, which seem might seem identical, are likely to be slightly different due to interior decoration or relative position in the block.

The commercial market can be more challenging, particularly in relation to, for example, sites for redevelopment where an alternative valuation method will be needed. Each asset class will have different aspects of comparison that need to be adjusted for. The values of warehouse and distribution units, for example, are impacted by the accessibility to transport networks, the size, condition, and format of the building. For retail units the location, footfall, tenant mix, car parking provision, and building quality are important. For offices, location, services, building quality, facilities, and extent of obsolescence are important. Whatever asset class is being valued, it is inevitable that some analysis and adjustment to the evidence will be required as no two real estate assets are identical.

There is a hierarchy of comparable evidence with the best, most heavily weighted, evidence coming from direct transactions in the open market. This is followed by publicly available evidence, such as the land registry and local rating lists, but these show headline values only without details of any incentives. The headline rent is the rent stated in the lease but there are often incentives such as rent-free periods, capital contributions, or capped service charges which mean the effective rent is lower than the headline rent reported. There are an increasing number of published databases that are often available on a subscription-only basis. Like publicly available lists, they do not show details of transactions so they are helpful to support an opinion of value but should not be used as a primary source of evidence. These lists are useful as a source of initial information that can then be checked directly with the agents involved. Asking prices are not a good source of comparable evidence but can be interpreted as an indication of the trends in value. If asking prices are regularly being exceeded, for example, it suggests there may be a rising market. All comparable evidence is historic but out-of-date evidence can be misleading so will need to be combined with knowledge of market trends between valuation date and comparable transaction date. Finally, market indices, from providers such as MSCI,[6] can be used for comparable evidence but valuers do need to be aware of their limitations which are, primarily, due to the assets included within the indices as these may not be representative of the premises being valued.

The comparison method involves comparing real estate assets with other similar assets and making appropriate adjustments to reflect the differences. Comparison can be used for both capital values and rental values and, as such, forms a vital element of the investment method of valuation.

THE INVESTMENT METHOD

Real estate investment is based on the opportunity it presents to purchase a future income stream in the form of rent paid by a tenant. To prepare an investment valuation, the valuer will require comparable evidence on two elements: the rent and the yield. The yield, as discussed in Chapter 11, refers to the annual return on the investment which is expressed as a percentage return on the capital value. The yield reflects the anticipated risk and return of the investment.

The traditional investment valuation approach involves the assessment of market rent and an appropriate yield. These can then be used to calculate capital value. Where a property is let at market rent, this is a simple calculation involving the multiplication of market rent by the yield. As the yield reflects the anticipated return on the investment, the mathematical calculation requires the conversion of the yield to a multiplier; this is achieved by dividing 100 by the yield.

It is, however, very rarely the case that a property is let at market rent; therefore the valuation becomes more complex requiring a two-part approach. The first part, known as the 'term', values the market rent at a yield that reflects the anticipated risk and return of that income stream. The second part, known as the 'reversion', values the market rent at an adjusted yield to reflect the different risk and return profile of a rent not received until a future date. The term runs until the first event where the rent will be reviewed to market rent. This is likely to be a lease renewal or a rent review. The reversion runs in perpetuity. This is because the underlying assumption is that real estate will always have some value, unlike, for example stocks and shares which can become worthless if the company fails.

In a falling market, the rent payable for the term may be higher than the market rent. In this case, the hardcore or top slice approach can be used. The difference with this approach is that the market rent is capitalised in perpetuity at a yield that reflects the security of that income stream. The top slice, that portion of rent that exceeds market rent, will then be capitalised at a yield that reflects the increased risk of that rent in excess of market rent continuing to be paid. During the Covid-19 pandemic in 2020, many retailers found that reduced shopper numbers and lockdowns meant that they were unable to pay their rent, so they either did not pay or renegotiated their rents with their landlords, leading to a downward pressure on market rents.

The yield applied in this traditional investment approach is known as the ARY. As outlined in Chapter 11, the ARY encompasses assumptions about future rental growth, void periods, capital expenditure, and any other anticipated future events. The ARY is therefore a growth implicit yield. This however means that it is impossible to distinguish between the impact of each of these separate elements resulting in a lack of transparency and precision. To overcome this limitation, the DCF approach, used in the financial markets, was adopted by the real estate industry. This is a growth explicit approach that sets out detailed information on the actual and predicted rental incomes and expenditures during the period the investment is held. This allows for a greater understanding of the inputs and precise identification of the assumptions the valuation is based on. Many different assumptions can be easily modelled, to demonstrate the impact of various changes, giving investors an ability to gauge the sensitivity of the valuation.

The basic premise behind the DCF approach is to bring back all future income flows to today's values. This uses a discount rate, which reflects the rate of return the investor requires, applied to the net cash flows for the period that the investor wishes to hold the investment. The discount rate selected is likely to be based on a combination of the rate of interest that might be received if the money were deposited elsewhere, plus a risk premium to reflect the relative uncertainty of the receipt of income invested in property, compared to interest on money in a deposit account. At the end of the holding period, the exit value of the investment is calculated using the same traditional investment valuation approach outlined earlier. The holding period will vary between investors. When working for a property fund, the standard time period applied was 15 years so that comparison of all real estate holdings was on the same basis. The longer the holding period, the lower the impact of the traditional valuation at the end of the cash flow.

The cash flow will have a net present value (NPV) which represents the balance of all cash flows, positive and negative, during the holding period. A positive NPV shows that the investment, at the discount rate applied, will make a profit. A negative NPV, at the discount rate applied, represents a loss. The NPV provides a method of comparing different investments, or projects, with each other.

Where the NPV is equal to zero, the discount rate that leads to this balance between positive and negative cash flows is known as the internal rate of return (IRR). As the cash flows are in balance the IRR represents the rate of interest being earned by the money spent on the investment. The IRR is a measure of performance, specifically profitability, that can be compared with other investments, or projects, to identify which should create the highest return.

An investment valuation, whether using the traditional or the DCF approach, is based on the expectation of a future income stream. As such, the terms of the lease that is generating the future income stream are important. Aspects such as the length of the lease and clauses relating to repairing obligations, use, ability to assign or sublet, breaks and others will have an impact on assumptions about future rental levels and yields. The strength of tenant covenant will also influence yields due to the impact this may have on the ability to pay the rent and maintain the premises. If there are vacant properties assumptions can be made concerning potential tenants, rental levels, and lease terms to arrive at an investment valuation. In some cases, the property may have development potential and here the residual method of valuation will be used.

THE RESIDUAL METHOD

Where a property has the potential for redevelopment or refurbishment, or for plots of land, the residual method is used. The residual method of valuation is used where redevelopment is needed to achieve the highest and best use, or where improvements are planned, or in progress, at the date of valuation.

The residual method calculates the gross development value (GDV) of a project based on comparable evidence of rents and yields. From this figure all the costs of development are deducted including building costs, fees, finance, letting fees, contingencies, and sale fees. The residual value will normally represent either land value or developer's profit; whichever of these is unknown. This method does, however, require many comparable evidence-based inputs and informed assumptions about costs.

A residual method valuation arrives at a precise figure for either land or developer's profit. This can then be extended into a residual, or development, appraisal. This is a financial appraisal that is similarly used to calculate either the residual site value or the residual developer's profit, it can however be used to calculate other outputs and can provide an indication of the viability of the scheme.

A difficulty with the residual method and development appraisals is that the resulting figures are very sensitive to the inputs used. A small change in yields, rental values, or building or finance costs can have a big impact on the output values. A development appraisal is therefore often accompanied by a sensitivity analysis which models the impact of changes in the input variables, in a series of calculations, to show what the impact of minor changes will be on the outturn figure. A development appraisal can achieve a greater level of precision, and transparency, by using the DCF approach outlined earlier as this accounts for the flows of cash in real time.

If arriving at a land value, this can often be checked against comparable evidence on land values for the specific use. The RICS guidance note, Valuation of development property,[7] states that relying on just one method of valuation for development property is 'rarely advisable' and that other methods should be used to cross-check the figures.

THE PROFITS METHOD

Another method of valuation that might require an additional method to cross-check the outturn figure is the profits method. This method is used where the value of the property is related to the business that is carried out in the property. The profits method is sometimes known as the accounts, or income and expenditure, method.

This method is used for unusual properties where it is difficult to use the comparison method due to the substantial differences between properties and their specialist nature. It is used for properties, generally known as trade-related properties, that change hands based on their trading potential. The value is assessed on the basis of the level of income they are likely to be able to generate. These include properties such as hotels, public houses, bars, nightclubs, theatres, cinemas, golf courses, petrol stations, care homes, and marinas. It can also be used for some restaurants, and data centres, where there are no directly comparable ones. These properties are usually constructed, or amended, for the specific use they are put to. This means that they tend to mainly be bought or sold as a part of the overall business.

The value of the property will depend on the profitability of the use at the time of the valuation and the potential for future trade. This method of valuation recognises the value that will be attributed by the current, or prospective, owner, that might be different from that of the general market. The valuation is based on an assessment of the fair maintainable turnover (FMT) that could be achieved at the property by a reasonably efficient operator (REO). This then leads to an assessment of the fair maintainable operating profit (FMOP).[8] The assessment of FMT reflects the assumption that the property is in good condition, fully equipped, and operating at capacity. The REO assumption acknowledges that the existing operator might not be maximising the potential of the property which could be due to lack of competency or to inefficiency. Rather than basing the valuation on existing accounts, it is therefore based on assumed trade. It is, however, sensible for the valuer to access the existing accounts over time to identify trends and compare them with the market norms for other similar operators. The FMOP should reflect all income and outgoings of the REO and include appropriate allowances for maintenance and repair. From the FMOP, finance costs and depreciation also need to be deducted. The FMOP is then capitalised at an appropriate yield, based on comparable evidence, to arrive at a capital value. For rental valuation, a sum is deducted from the FMOP to cover a return to the tenant on the capital they have invested in the property. The remaining sum, known as the divisible balance, is then divided between the landlord and the tenant on a basis that reflects the risks and rewards of the property. The landlord's share represents the rent to be paid by the tenant.

This is a specialist method of valuation that requires detailed knowledge of the specialist sub-market together with sufficient knowledge of accounting principles to be able to form an opinion on whether existing accounts, if available, provide an accurate and reliable picture of the trading potential for the property being valued. It is essential that a profits method valuation is supported by comprehensive assumptions that underpin the value arrived at.

THE COST METHODS – CONTRACTOR'S METHOD AND DEPRECIATED REPLACEMENT COST METHOD (DRC)

For some properties, none of the methods outlined earlier will be suitable. These are properties that very rarely change hands and cannot be compared with others due to their unique nature. Examples of properties that have been valued using cost methods include airports, oil refineries, major chemical works, steel works, shipbuilding yards, and other public sector buildings that cannot be valued by other methods.[9] Cost methods are widely considered the method of last resort as cost is not usually a reliable indication of market value. Market value is a product of the interaction of demand and supply and the cost methods take no account of this. It assumes that market value reflects the cost of buying the land and erecting a similar building.

The cost methods involve assessing the replacement cost of all structures on the site then making an adjustment to reflect the difference between the value of a new building and the condition of the existing building. The value of the land is then added and, again, an adjustment may need to be made, this time to reflect the impact that the buildings might have on the value of the land.

The contractor's method and the DRC method are widely used interchangeably but there is a subtle difference between the two. The basic approach is the same; they are both cost-based methods. They are, however, used for different purposes and therefore have slightly different approaches.[10] The contractor's method is used for rating assessments and the DRC method for accounting purposes. Both methods use building costs, which are adjusted to reflect age and obsolescence, then add land value. Both methods require specialist valuers due to the complexities of the adjustments to be made to reflect differences in the modern equivalent and the existing construction. The RICS guidance note[11] states that the DRC method alone is unsuitable for secured lending, although it can be used to help to support other methods.

WHICH VALUATION METHOD SHOULD BE USED?

Although this will obviously depend on the type of property, it is also dependent on the purpose of the valuation. For example, a property may have been valued for sale at one figure using the comparable method; it may then be valued at another figure for rating purposes using the contractor's method; and then, if capable of redevelopment for an alternative use, at yet another figure using the residual method.

The real estate market, as outlined in Chapter 3, covers a diverse range of property types and valuers tend to specialise in a particular asset class and geographical area so that they develop the expert knowledge needed. With experience, valuers can 'sense check' the valuation figure they arrive at based on previous valuations of other similar properties. If they find that the figure falls far outside their expected parameters, they may consider using other methods to support their opinions of value.

When selecting an appropriate valuation method, or methods, it is essential that the client is informed and understands the approach, and this should be clearly set out in the Terms of Engagement. It is also essential that the valuer states all assumptions made to support the valuation and keeps clear records of the evidence and approach used. This information not only makes it possible to understand and, if necessary, amend the initial valuation but will also provide essential evidence should the valuer later end up in court accused of negligence.

NOTES

1 RICS (2017) *Conflicts of Interest* Online. Available from: www.rics.org/globalassets/rics-website/media/upholding-professional-standards/standards-of-conduct/conflicts-of-interest/conflicts_of_interest_global_1st-edition_dec_2017_revisions_pgguidance_2017_rw.pdf]

2 RICS (2018) *RICS Property Measurement* 2nd Edition Online. Available from: www.rics.org/globalassets/rics-website/media/upholding-professional-standards/sector-standards/real-estate/rics-property-measurement/rics-property-measurement-2nd-edition-rics.pdf

3 RICS (2015) *Code of Measuring Practice* 6th Edition Online. Available from: www.rics.org/globalassets/rics-website/media/upholding-professional-standards/sector-standards/valuation/code-of-measuring-practice-6th-edition-rics.pdf

4 JLL (2019) *What the Largest Private CRE Transaction in History Means for Logistics* Online. Available from: https://www.jll.co.uk/en/trends-and-insights/investor/the-largest-private-cre-transaction-in-history-means-for-logistics

5 RICS (2019) *Comparable Evidence in Real Estate Valuation* 1st Edition Online. Available from: www.rics.org/globalassets/rics-website/media/upholding-professional-standards/sector-standards/valuation/comparable-evidence-in-real-estate-valuation.pdf

6 MSCI (Morgan Stanley Capital International) Online. Available from: www.msci.com/

7 RICS (2019) *Valuation of Development Property* 1st Edition Online. Available from: www.rics.org/globalassets/valuation-of-development-property-first-edition.pdf

8 RICS (2010) *The Capital and Rental Valuation of Public Houses, Bars, Restaurants and Nightclubs in England and Wales* 1st Edition Online. Available from: www.rics.org/globalassets/rics-website/media/upholding-professional-standards/sector-standards/valuation/capital-and-rental-valuation-of-public-houses-bars-restaurants-and-nightclubs-in-england-and-wales-1st-edition-rics.pdf

9 RICS (2017) *The Contractor's Basis of Valuation for Rating Purposes* 2nd Edition Online. Available from: www.rics.org/globalassets/rics-website/media/upholding-professional-standards/sector-standards/valuation/the-contractors-basis-of-valuation-for-rating-purposes-2nd-edition-rics.pdf

10 Scarrett, D and Osborn, S (2014) *Property Valuation: The Five Methods* 3rd Edition Abingdon, Oxon: Routledge

11 RICS (2018) *Depreciated Replacement Cost Method of Valuation for Financial Reporting* 1st Edition Online. Available from: www.rics.org/globalassets/rics-website/media/upholding-professional-standards/sector-standards/valuation/drc-method-of-valuation-for-financial-reporting-1st-edition-rics.pdf

FURTHER INFORMATION

SPECIALIST VALUATION TEXTS

Hayward, R (2008) *Valuation: Principles into Practice* 6th Edition Abingdon, Oxon: EG Books

Isaac, D and O'Leary, J (2012) *Property Valuation Principles* 2nd Edition Basingstoke: Palgrave Macmillan

Millington, A F (2000) *An Introduction to Property Valuation* 5th Edition London: Estates Gazette

Scarrett, D and Osborn, S (2014) *Property Valuation: The Five Methods* 3rd Edition Abingdon, Oxon: Routledge

Shapiro, E, Mackmin, D, and Sams, G (2019) *Modern Methods of Valuation* 12th Edition Abingdon, Oxon: Routledge

PUBLICATIONS

RICS (2019) *Valuation: Global Standards* London: The Royal Institution of Chartered Surveyors Available from: www.rics.org/uk/upholding-professional-standards/sector-standards/valuation/red-book/red-book-global/

WEBSITES

International Valuation Standards Council (IVSC) www.ivsc.org
The Royal Institution of Chartered Surveyors (RICS) www.rics.org

EFFECTIVE REAL ESTATE MANAGEMENT

WHAT IS EFFECTIVE REAL ESTATE MANAGEMENT?

Management is a skilled discipline and forms a significant part of real estate practice. Effective management protects the value and function of real estate as an asset, whether its purpose is to facilitate the operation of a business or to provide a home or a return on investment. It involves making the most of available resources to manage the asset efficiently, in order to achieve the client's objectives.

Proper management also protects against financial risk and legal liability. Poor management of a block of flats, for example, may diminish the value of the individual flats, result in arrears of rent and service charge, cause cash-flow problems, and expose the landlord to legal action. Effective management can, therefore, minimise the risk of a claim for negligence or breach of covenant, reduce the occurrence of complaints, and help resolve disputes if they do arise.

There are many different management arrangements available, depending on the type of property, the type of investor, and the type of occupier. Management may be of freehold properties; an estate of freehold houses with shared private roads, play areas, leisure facilities, and gardens, for example. These communal facilities need to be managed, even though the householders will be responsible for their own individual homes. Management may also be of a portfolio of freehold properties including both those used as a resource and those held as assets. Institutions, such as some universities, will require a property management service, either internal or outsourced, to deal with all repairs, maintenance, health and safety, and related issues.

DOI: 10.1201/9781003155256-13

It is more common, however, for property management to relate to leasehold properties. The need for effective management reflects the complexity of the relationship between landlord and tenant and their respective rights and obligations. In essence, effective property management is about ensuring compliance with lease terms, the law, professional guidance, and codes of practice.

Real estate management is a broad term that covers three different levels of management: asset management, property management, and building management. This chapter focuses on property management, that is the day-to-day management of the property. Asset management is discussed in Chapter 4 and building management in Chapter 6.

EFFECTIVE MANAGEMENT AND THE LAW

Real estate students and practitioners need an awareness and understanding of a wide range of laws in order to manage effectively. These include agency law, consumer protection legislation (see Chapter 10), company law, contract law, employment law, and negligence. This is in addition to land law and landlord and tenant law outlined in Chapters 7 and 8. It is not the purpose of this chapter to explain the law in detail, but we refer to some key legal matters, where relevant, and you will find sources of further information at the end of the chapter.

ASSET TYPES AND MANAGEMENT

It is important to recognise that different types of real estate have different management requirements, reflecting the asset's purpose and the nature of occupancy. Management needs and constraints vary considerably between the residential and commercial sectors; the occupiers have different needs – to provide a home as opposed to business premises.

Residential management may cover the private-rented sector, HMOs, social housing, shared ownership properties, long residential leases, freehold houses, student lets, holiday lets, and retirement homes. Commercial management could include industrial, retail, office, or leisure premises and many property managers will deal with mixed residential and commercial sites. We outline different asset types in more detail in Chapter 3. It is important to remember that whilst it is still necessary to sustain the value of the asset, the needs of, for example, a residential block of flats owned and managed by the leaseholders on a not-for-profit basis will differ from those of, for example a shopping centre, with rental levels, lease terms, and a tenant-mix policy that aim to generate an income for investors. However, there are still fundamental principles that apply to each, as you will see in this chapter.

WHAT TYPES OF MANAGEMENT STRUCTURES ARE THERE?

It is important to identify tenure in order to manage any type of real estate. Tenure structures can be complex, sometimes with tiers of ownership comprising freehold, headleases, and sub-leases. We are focusing on leasehold management in this chapter and most people will be familiar with bi-partite leases; a two-party agreement in which there is a landlord and there is a tenant. These are the most common types of lease in commercial properties. However, some leases will be tri-partite; a third party will be named as the manager in the lease. The third party may be, for example a residents' management company in which each resident has a share, or it may be a professional management organisation named as the manager in the lease. Commercial properties can be managed either in-house or outsourced. If outsourced, then the management will be dealt with under a separate management agreement.

For residential management purposes, the landlord may not mean the landlord named in the lease. The term 'landlord' may be broader than this, covering the person or organisation with the right to collect the service charge, which may differ from the landlord as owner. Section 30 of the Landlord and Tenant Act 1985[1] defines 'landlord' (for the purposes of those parts of the Act that relate to service charges) as:

any person who has a right to enforce payment of a service charge.

Thus, a residents' management company, which does not own the freehold, may still need to comply with the statutory obligations imposed on landlords when collecting service charges.

Leasehold management can be a burden on a landlord. For this reason, residential property developers will often choose to transfer the freehold to a residents' management company, which becomes the landlord, rather than to retain it. This is particularly the case with small residential developments in which leaseholders have paid a premium – they have bought their properties – and only pay a small ground rent each year. Once the development has been completed, and the units sold, there is limited value in it for the developer and this must be balanced against management responsibilities and liabilities. Alternatively, the developer may retain the freehold but transfer management responsibilities on to a residents' management company named as manager in the leases, or they may delegate management to an agent. Most commercial developers will delegate management to a professional managing agent. We discuss managing agents in a little more detail later on in this section.

Although we are focusing on leasehold management in this chapter, we have mentioned freehold houses; this type of management tends to extend only to the grounds and facilities shared with other properties on a privately owned estate. Typically, the estate will be owned and managed by a company set up for this purpose and each resident will have a share in the company and an obligation to contribute towards the running costs.

A commonhold block of flats will have a Commonhold Association with responsibility for management; the owners of each flat within the block will be members of the Association and the Association can decide whether to self-manage or to appoint an agent to manage on their behalf.

We have mentioned managing agents. It is very common for day-to-day management functions to be delegated to professional managers. The person or organisation appointing the manager is called the principal, and the manager becomes the agent of the principal. This means that the principal authorises the agent to carry out certain functions, for example to collect rent and service charges and to arrange repairs. The extent of the agent's authority will depend on what has been agreed between the landlord and the agent and recorded in the Terms of Engagement. The agent's authority will also vary according to the type of management. In the private-rented sector it is very common for landlords to appoint a letting agent to manage a single tenancy. Other agents may manage blocks of flats, or residential, commercial, or mixed-use estates. Large-scale landlords, such as social-housing providers or build-to-rent investors, may employ in-house managers rather than appointing an external agent. Most major commercial landlords will employ professional managers although a few may manage in-house.

MANAGEMENT TIMEFRAMES

Effective management should ideally begin at the planning and development stage, before acquisition of the property, whether it is a development site, a renovation property or an existing investment property that is changing hands. Key questions include:

- Is the intention to retain the property to generate an income or to sell it at a profit?
- How long does the investor intend to hold the property for?
- Does the developer or investor intend to retain control over the property?
- What management resources are required and who will pay for them?
- What steps can be taken to mitigate against management risks?

The decisions made in response to these questions will guide the management arrangements for the property. Advice from real estate professionals, including property managers and solicitors, at this early stage can aid the effective management of the asset from the outset.

Property management has a 'life cycle' in that some elements will recur annually, whereas some will recur less frequently and some aspects only occasionally. For example, service charges are usually managed on an annual basis; budgets are created, invoices issued, and annual accounts prepared. Maintenance may be cyclical, for example redecoration every five years, in which case the annual budget may need to include a contribution towards a reserve fund to save up for the redecoration before it becomes due. Large capital items, such as re-roofing or replacement of a lift, will occur only very occasionally, but the annual budget might include a contribution towards the sinking fund. This enables funds to be collected towards these substantial costs over a long period of time, which will make the work affordable for tenants. It also ensures that when there are changes of tenants, they are not faced with large costs incurred during a period when they might not have been in occupation.

Property managers need to understand this timeframe. They must ensure compliance with the lease and with the law, dealing with all necessary formalities when the lease is created and when it is terminated, and monitoring compliance with its covenants throughout its term.

KEY MANAGEMENT CONSIDERATIONS

Effective management involves proper use of resources. It can also require leadership; property managers will frequently be asked to advise their clients, and asset managers, to consider options available to them and to make recommendations based on those options. In this section we consider some of the key areas of expertise, essential to successful and efficient property management.

CLIENT CARE

A manager must manage a property in the best interests of their client. This involves providing good client care, understanding the client and their level of expertise, establishing the client's objectives, and managing the client's expectations to deliver a good service.

However, the end user is the occupier – typically a tenant – and the manager will be the point of contact for the tenant, liaising between landlord and tenant where necessary. It is important that managers understand the extent of their authority under the management contract and avoid conflicts of interest. This is part of professional, ethical conduct. However, it is also important to consider both points of view in order to understand a scenario fully and to advise the client. Transparency and integrity are key here. Managers who fail to recognise the importance of high standards of client care can find themselves breaching professional codes of practice (you can find these listed at the end of this chapter) and they may also breach consumer protection legislation.

CONTRACTUAL MATTERS

We have mentioned that managers must be clear about the extent of their authority: what decisions can they make without reference to their principal and when are instructions needed from the principal? This will be contained in the management contract, also called the Terms of Engagement, and will cover matters such as:

- The property to be managed;
- The duration of the management agreement;
- Management fees;
- Termination of the agreement;
- Management services to be provided;
- Additional services to be separately agreed and covered by an additional fee.

It is important that the Terms of Engagement are clear and reasonable. A lack of clarity and transparency from the outset can result in complaints, disputes, and a lack of cooperation, which drain management time and resources and hinder effective management.

You may find it useful to check RICS guidance on management agreements to familiarise yourself with typical management arrangements. It is usual for routine management tasks to be included within the management fee and for an additional fee to be payable in respect of other work, such as managing major repair projects. You can find links to RICS guidance at the end of this chapter.

DATA

As the use of technology grows, so does the need to protect personal data. This is now a valuable resource, but it can include information, which may be regarded as personal, private, and sensitive.

Property managers handle a wide range of data, much of which is clearly personal. For example:

- Tenant references may contain bank account information, income, and employment details;
- Right to Rent checks required under the Immigration Act 2014 require landlords (or managers on behalf of landlords) to verify a tenant's identity (and to keep a copy of the tenant's means of identification – a passport for example) to ascertain that they are not disqualified from renting in the UK;

- Financial records will display rental or service charge payments, arrears, and details of legal action taken against a tenant;
- A disabled tenant may have requested adaptations to the property or to procedures, in which case the property manager will hold information on health and disability.

The person to whom the data relates is called the data subject. Data subjects have rights under the Data Protection Act 2018; the right to be informed about what data will be held and why, and how it will be processed; the right to object to the use of data; the right to be forgotten (for data to be erased); and the right to access their personal data, for example. This Act implements the European Union's General Data Protection Regulation (GDPR). Effective data management begins with the provision of information to data subjects via privacy notices, so that they understand what data is being collected, why it is being collected, and how it will be used.

Property managers will usually have duties under the Data Protection Act 2018 as data controllers. The data controller is the person or organisation deciding how and why data will be used. They may provide information to a data processor – a third party who performs tasks for the data controller. For example, if a property manager asks for a tenant's telephone number as part of their management information, the manager will be the data controller. If the manager then engages a contractor to deal with an emergency and gives that telephone number to the contractor to arrange access direct, the contractor will be the data processor. Data controllers must register with the Information Commissioner's Office (ICO) and must pay an annual fee to the ICO. They are also responsible for ensuring that data processors comply with the law.

It is essential that property managers follow the principles of data protection, for example processing data securely, fairly and for legitimate purposes only and for a limited period of time. Effective data management therefore requires training of staff and suitable and secure data management systems. Some organisations may appoint a Data Protection Officer to oversee compliance. This became even more important during the Covid-19 pandemic with more people working from home. Personal data, which was previously only available in an office, may now be accessed from home, with less oversight from senior members of staff. Data confidentiality may be compromised if other household members have access to shared computers. This can increase the risk of deliberate, malicious, or accidental data breaches, risking enforcement action by the ICO, legal action by data subjects, and reputational damage for the property manager and their client.

The ICO website is an extremely useful resource – you will find more details at the end of this chapter.

HEALTH AND SAFETY

Health and safety are fundamental aspects of all types of business and property management. Failure to properly, and effectively, assess risks and to manage hazards can result in serious consequences, for the health, physical safety, and mental well-being of occupiers, visitors, service providers, and contractors. It can also have serious consequences in terms of legal liability and financial risk for the client and for the property manager. Health and safety considerations therefore extend to the property manager's own business premises and operations, and to their managed properties.

We are all familiar with risk assessment in that it is something we do every day, when crossing the road, for example, and when driving a car. The Covid-19 pandemic highlighted the need to react quickly to changes in the level and type of risk. The changes we all made – wearing facemasks, working, and studying from home, social distancing and shielding for example – were all forms of risk management; they were steps taken to reduce the risk of transmitting the virus in order to keep ourselves, our families and social networks and wider society safe.

Management of risk in the workplace and in the context of property management involves:

- Identifying hazards and who might be harmed;
- Assessing the level of risk: the likelihood of harm occurring and the likely severity of the harm;
- Identifying the existing measures in place to control the risk and how these measures could be improved;
- Recording the assessment (in writing if the business has five or more employees);
- Monitoring and reviewing the assessment.

Risk management needs to be proportionate, reducing risks as far as is reasonably practicable. There are many hazards associated with property management – lone-working, travel, asbestos, fire, working at height, legionella, slips, trips and falls, electricity, gas – to name a few. Some of these hazards are subject to additional legislation, including, for example:

- The Gas Safety (Installation and Use) Regulations 1998 require landlords to carry out annual gas safety checks on residential and mixed-use premises. Although not required on commercial premises, it may be considered best practice to do so;
- The Regulatory Reform (Fire Safety) Order 2005 covers requirements to carry out a fire risk assessment, of all non-domestic premises but also the communal areas of blocks of flats (fire safety is discussed further in Chapter 14);
- The Control of Asbestos Regulations 2012 impose a duty to manage asbestos in non-domestic premises, which includes the communal areas of blocks of flats.

The Health and Safety Executive (HSE) oversees health and safety compliance. The primary statute is the Health and Safety at Work etc. Act 1974. Section 2 of the Act imposes general duties on employers to ensure as far as reasonably practicable the health, safety, and welfare of employees. Employers with five or more employees must prepare and keep under review a written health and safety policy. Section 3 of the Act extends an employer's duty to ensure that persons, other than employees (e.g. visitors, contractors, clients, residents), are not exposed to health and safety risks. The Management of Health and Safety at Work Regulations 1999 impose a duty to carry out risk assessments to establish the health and safety risks to employees and to others who are not employees, but who may be affected by the employer's business.

In addition, the Occupiers' Liability Act 1957 imposes a duty on occupiers of premises to take reasonable care to ensure the reasonable safety of lawful visitors. The Occupiers' Liability Act 1984 extends the duty to persons other than visitors in certain circumstances; this can include trespassers. It is important, therefore, that property managers are aware of this legislation and that steps are taken to protect those on-site, whether they are present lawfully or otherwise.

Property managers can significantly reduce risk by selecting reputable contractors and service providers with appropriate professional accreditation, such as NAPIT, NICEIC, Fensa, and the Gas Safe Register. Works should not start until a risk assessment has been carried out and a safe method of working agreed. Contractors must have adequate public liability insurance and property managers must also be familiar with the Construction (Design and Management) Regulations 2015, which may apply to building and maintenance projects. This leads us on to the requirements regarding housing standards, which tend to be more stringent than those relating to commercial premises. Section 11 of the Landlord and Tenant Act 1985 imposes repairing obligations on landlords of some residential tenancies. This Act was amended by the Homes (Fitness for Human Habitation) Act 2018, which requires landlords to ensure that their properties, including any communal areas, are fit for human habitation at the start of the tenancy and throughout its duration. Defects that may contravene this legislation include damp, lack of natural light and ventilation, and drainage and sanitation issues.[2]

The requirements listed earlier are not exhaustive; there are others. The following RICS documents are useful sources of further information: Surveying Safely 2nd Edition November 2018, and Health and Safety for Residential Property Managers 1st Edition 2016. The laws that we have mentioned are long and detailed, so we also recommend that you explore the HSE website – see this and other links at the end of this chapter.

INSURANCE

Insurance is another means of managing risk and it protects against losses, which could otherwise be substantial and unaffordable. The person taking out the insurance – known as 'the Insured' – pays a premium to insure against specified risks, which might occur, and which might cause loss or damage.

Effective management requires insurance cover for the manager's own practice – for example PII to protect against negligence claims. Some types of insurance are a legal requirement (Employer's Liability Insurance is an example) and the RICS stipulates minimum PII insurance levels for regulated firms according to the turnover of the business.

Insurance cover will also be required in relation to the client's leases, properties, and businesses, to protect against property damage and legal liability, for example to tenants and visitors.

As regards building insurance, the lease should always be checked carefully. Typically, the lease will require the landlord to insure the building against insured risks, which will be defined in the 'Definitions' section of the lease. It will also require the landlord to use funds received in relation to an insurance claim to repair the damage caused. The lease may allow the rent to be suspended if it is not possible to occupy the property. It may even be possible for the lease to be terminated by the landlord and/or the tenant if the damage is not repaired within a specified period of time.

It is important to reduce the likelihood of damage by an insured risk occurring. This will help to minimise the number of insurance claims made, as claims histories will be reflected in insurance premiums and in the availability of affordable and suitable insurance cover. Property managers should carry out regular property inspections to identify and address hazards and repairs early. Using an insurance broker can help to ensure that the insurance policy is competitive and claims services provided by the broker or the insurer can help with the efficient handling of claims. Loss adjusters may need to be appointed to help negotiate a larger claim.

Building reinstatement cost valuations should be carried out periodically to check that the building is adequately insured to cover the full cost of rebuilding including demolition and professional fees. Rent insurance and costs of alternative accommodation may also be needed. Again, the property manager should check the lease to identify the insured risks and to check whether the premium is to be recovered from the tenant.

The distribution of insurance products is a regulated activity, and this may apply to real estate managers who receive remuneration, whether commission or fees in return for insurance activities such as claims handling or arranging insurance. There are different methods of compliance, including regulation by the Financial Conduct Authority, becoming an appointed representative of an insurance broker, or through regulation by a Designated Professional Body, such as the RICS. You will find more information at the end of this chapter. It is important to note that the policy holder themselves – the landlord or residents' management company for example – does not need to be regulated; it is the professional dealing with insurance on behalf of their client who has to be regulated.

ETHICS

Ethics are another fundamental aspect of professional management. Managers must be alert to potential ethical issues such as conflicts of interest, compliance with anti-money-laundering laws, the Bribery Act 2010, and the Equality Act 2010. We consider this in more detail in Chapters 10 and 14.

OTHER LEASE TERMS

You will find information on the main contents of a lease in Chapter 8. We do not go into this again in detail in this chapter to avoid duplication, but effective management requires a detailed understanding of the lease and prompt enforcement of any breaches of covenant. This will include key covenants and provisions, such as user, rent reviews, break clauses, alienation, repairs, and alterations. If the lease contains an error, it may be necessary to agree a deed of rectification between the landlord and the tenant(s) to correct the error. Defective residential long leases can also be rectified by application to the First-tier Tribunal (Property Chamber) under Section 35 of the Landlord and Tenant Act 1987 if specific grounds are met.

STRATEGY

'Strategy' refers to the policies and approaches adopted when managing a single asset or a portfolio comprising multiple assets in order to achieve the client's objective.

Portfolios, in particular, require dynamic and tactical management, whether the portfolio is international, national, regional, or local. Portfolios may comprise a diverse mix of residential and commercial properties or specialise in one or more specific property types. A portfolio may also diversify or be focused within an individual asset type – for example a residential lettings portfolio might focus on HMOs or student lets; a commercial portfolio might decide to focus on retail properties only.

Strategic property management, also known as asset management, involves monitoring and analysing the performance of the asset. In the case of a portfolio, it needs to consider the portfolio as a whole, as well as the individual assets within the portfolio. This includes checks on performance with regard to both capital value and rental return. The effective asset manager must monitor finances, costs, and compliance with legal obligations, consider the client's attitude towards risk, and the need for diversification or redevelopment of the asset or the portfolio. It may be necessary to invest in the individual asset (refurbishment for example), or in the portfolio at times, perhaps to expand it with the addition of new assets, perhaps to redevelop the assets within it to maximise the rental return or perhaps simply to maintain the physical structure to maintain its value (see Chapter 4). It is essential that the property manager and the asset manager communicate so that decisions by both parties are made with a rounded knowledge of the asset being managed. A simple, but essential, way to help maintain performance of the asset or portfolio is to carry out regular rent reviews, on a timely basis, to ensure rents do not fall below the market rate. A failure to invest in a property to keep pace with market demand and legal compliance – for example, energy efficiency improvements – will ultimately devalue the asset or the portfolio and result in a reduced income.

TECHNOLOGY

It is difficult to manage property in the modern world without the aid of suitable technology. This may be generic:

- Remote 'cloud' storage may be used for record-keeping;
- Spreadsheets can be useful for book-keeping and cash-flow forecasts;
- Many tenancy agreements now authorise the service of formal notices by email;
- Tablets aid mobile management, for example for inventories and property inspections.

Alternatively, software may be specialist. There are many sector-specific software products available for property managers to aid efficient record-keeping, tenancy management, financial management, maintenance, and legal compliance. We consider PropTech further in Chapter 14.

EFFECTIVE MANAGEMENT OF RESOURCES

We explained in Chapter 6 that real estate professionals must possess a combination of technical knowledge and 'soft-skills'. Effective time management is one of the key skills required of a property manager. Real estate management can be pressured due to the needs and demands of landlords and tenants, the need to be a good problem solver and the burden of ensuring legal compliance in a wide range of areas. In the residential sector, the working hours can be long as clients may need to hold evening meetings. In the commercial sector meetings may also be held out of hours to ensure confidentiality and not interfere with the running of the tenant's business. Dealing with emergency repairs is unplanned and reactive by its nature and can divert from other tasks.

The ability to plan ahead and to manage time and resources efficiently and consistently is therefore key to effective real estate management. Clear policies and procedures will assist here. Staffing levels must be appropriate to deliver the required service, systems and procedures must be suitable to support all aspects of management, and staff must be trained to carry out their roles and supported to work in a sector that is changing and developing. Team working is therefore also important, whether the team is entirely in-house or external advisers are brought in. An effective property manager should know to whom they would turn for advice or to delegate the many tasks required during the life cycle of real estate management.

FINANCIAL MANAGEMENT

Effective property management requires careful management of finances. This may involve ensuring that the landlord is able to meet maintenance and management costs if the landlord is non-profit-making (e.g. a residents' management company, a Right to Manage company or a charity) or it may need to ensure that the landlord achieves a sufficient return on their investment.

The property manager will first need to check the payments due under a lease. These may include:

- Market rent for a property for which no premium has been payable, for example an Assured Shorthold Tenancy or standard commercial leases;
- Ground rent payable in the case of a long lease, which has been bought at a premium;
- Service charges to cover contributions towards management and maintenance costs;
- Insurance rent – contributions towards insurance premiums not included in the service charge;
- Administration charges, for example for consents to sublet or to assign the lease;
- Interest charges on late payment.

The lease will prescribe payment due dates, when and how the sum is to be demanded, how the sum is calculated, by whom the payment is to be made and to whom, whether the sum is subject to review and what happens if the tenant is in arrears. The lease may stipulate intervals between rent reviews or in the case of ground rent, it may specify each increase for the term of the lease.

Service charge payments are likely to vary between financial years, as a service charge is a variable charge that reflects the costs incurred in relation to maintenance, management, and insurance.

Once the lease has been checked, the property manager must comply with the relevant legislation. In the residential sector, ground rent demands must comply with the format and timeframe prescribed by Section 166 of the Commonhold and Leasehold Reform Act 2002. Ground rent is not payable unless the landlord complies with Section 166. Section 47 of the Landlord and Tenant Act 1987 requires the landlord to include their name and address in rent and service charge demands; failure to do so will result in service charges (but not rent) not being payable until the information has been provided. Section 48 of this Act requires the landlord to serve notice on the tenant with the landlord's name and address for service of notices in proceedings. If this address is not in England and Wales, the landlord must notify the tenant of an address in England and Wales for service of notices in proceedings. If the landlord fails to comply with Section 48, neither rent nor service charge will be payable until the information has been provided.

Furthermore, Section 153 of the Commonhold and Leasehold Reform Act 2002 (CLRA) requires residential service charge demands to be accompanied by a Service Charge Summary of Rights and Obligations; failure to do so entitles the tenant to withhold payment. Similarly, Section 158 of the CLRA requires demands for administration charges to be accompanied by an Administration Charge Summary of Rights and Obligations. Again, failure to do so entitles the tenant to withhold payment.

The lease will also contain specific advice on aspects such as the process for rent reviews and the operation of break clauses. Failure to comply with the provisions of the lease can result in substantial costs.

Service charges, whether residential or commercial, will need to be apportioned between the contributing tenants. This means that each tenant will pay a proportion of the costs, usually reflecting the size of the demised premises. Sometimes this will also reflect the facilities that the tenant uses. The lease should state the proportion payable by the tenant, which might be a fixed percentage or fraction of the total costs, or it may be a fair proportion of the costs, which might be determined by the landlord or by the landlord's surveyor. Residential service charges are considered in more detail in the separate section later.

So far, we have considered how funds can be collected effectively. However, this is just part of the jigsaw. It is also important that rents are set at a market level and are reviewed and increased periodically, that service charge budgets are reasonable and sufficient to cover costs, and that costs are contained and cash flow monitored throughout the financial year. At the end of the financial year, service charge accounts must be prepared and issued to tenants in accordance with the lease. If the client is a limited company, the property manager may also need to arrange preparation of company accounts and ensure these are filed at Companies House within the required time period. Technical Release 03/11 issued by the Institute of Chartered Accountants in England and Wales in conjunction with other industry bodies provides guidance on residential service charge accounts. RICS professional statement Service charges in commercial property 1st edition 2018 contains useful information on accounting for commercial service charges and mandatory requirements for RICS members and regulated firms.

The property manager will also need to consider tenant incentives – common in commercial leases – such as rent-free periods, as these will affect cash flow.

Of critical importance is the recognition that client money belongs to the client. This means that funds received by the property manager on behalf of the client must be paid into a client account and not the property manager's business account and must be used for authorised purposes only. The RICS professional statement Client money handling 1st Edition 2019 provides information on requirements. Residential surveyors holding client money must take out client money protection insurance to protect against the loss of client funds.

RESIDENTIAL SERVICE CHARGES

Residential service charges are affected by legislation to a considerable degree; key aspects are outlined in this section. Remember that these provisions do not apply to commercial leases.

Section 42 of the Landlord and Tenant Act 1987 imposes a trust over service charges paid by residential tenants. This means that the landlord collecting the service charges is trustee, holding the funds for the tenants as beneficiaries. The money must only be used as authorised by the leases and will ultimately benefit the tenants through the effective management, insurance, and maintenance of the property. The Landlord and Tenant Act 1985 (LTA 1985) also impacts upon management to a considerable degree; all residential managers should have regard to this Act as failure to comply can have serious consequences for the client landlord, as we will see later.

REASONABLENESS OF SERVICE CHARGES

Section 19 of the LTA 1985 stipulates that costs included in service charges must be a reasonable amount and they must be reasonably incurred, so, for example the cost must be reasonable in relation to the standard of the work carried out. Under Section 27A of this Act, application can be made to the First-tier Tribunal (Property Chamber), by either the landlord or the tenant, to determine whether a cost is reasonable. It is quite common for managers to represent their clients at the Tribunal in an application regarding the reasonableness of service charges. A decision by the Tribunal that a cost is unreasonable can leave the landlord unable to recover some or all of the cost from the tenant.

THE 18-MONTH RULE

Section 20B of the Act – 'the 18-month rule' – stipulates time limits for charging costs to tenants via a service charge. A landlord intending to recover their costs from the tenant via a service charge must demand payment from the tenant within 18 months of those costs being incurred. Alternatively, the landlord must notify the tenant in writing within 18 months of the costs being incurred, that the costs will be included in a subsequent service charge demand. This improves transparency and avoids the tenant receiving unexpected service charge bills years after the costs have been incurred, and if the landlord fails to comply, the tenant will not have to pay for those costs.

CONSULTATION WITH TENANTS

Section 20 of the Act (amended by Section 151 of the Commonhold and Leasehold Reform Act 2002) and the Service Charges (Consultation Requirements) (England) Regulations 2003 form a significant part of the work of a property manager in this sector. It requires landlords to consult with leaseholders before the landlord can charge the tenant for certain costs above the cost threshold set by the legislation.

There are three basic types of consultation:

- Qualifying works (repairs, maintenance, or improvements) the cost of which will exceed £250 for any one leaseholder;
- Qualifying long-term agreements (e.g. a contract for cleaning, or to service a lift) the cost of which will exceed £100 for any one leaseholder in an accounting year;
- Qualifying works under long-term agreements (e.g. the company contracted to service the lift carries out major repairs to the lift) the cost of which will exceed £250 for any one leaseholder.

Failure to follow the formal consultation process may result in the landlord being unable to recover from each leaseholder, more than £250 for those works, or £100 for the service. However, it is possible to apply to the First-tier Tribunal (Property Chamber) for dispensation from consultation, for example in an emergency, when there may not be time to consult.

In the commercial sector, although the legislation is not as extensive, the RICS self-regulates by way of its publication Service charges in commercial property 1st edition 2018, which sets out mandatory requirements for commercial service charges. Failure to comply with the contents of the professional statement may give rise to claims for negligence.

REGULATION OF PROPERTY MANAGERS

You will find more information on the regulation of property managers in Chapters 6 and 14.

WHAT HAPPENS IF THINGS GO WRONG?

Real estate management, as we have seen, involves dealing with complex situations and on occasion things can go wrong. The manager may face a claim of negligence or a complaint about their service. Litigation is costly and time-consuming and even alternative forms of dispute resolution such as mediation will take up valuable time and resources. Furthermore, poor handling of issues when matters do go wrong can cause significant damage to the reputation of the manager and their organisation.

It is therefore important that the manager has a suitable complaints-handling procedure and that this procedure is followed diligently. Good communication and transparency can enable a dispute to be resolved informally; understanding the complainant's perspective and resolving the issue in a timely manner can even help to build relationships and to repair any reputational damage.

However, if the complaint or dispute cannot be resolved within the manager's own firm, it may be necessary to escalate the matter to a third party, such as an ombudsman, which provides dispute resolution services. In the event of serious complaint, the client may decide to terminate the management contract, or the manager may face a negligence claim. The terms of the manager's PII should be checked in the event of a complaint, as it is likely to require notification to the insurer and the insurer may decide to take over the management of the matter.

In the residential sector, banning orders prevent the banned person from letting or managing residential property, or from holding an HMO (House in Multiple Occupation) licence. They are made if a landlord, agent, or manager is convicted of a specified offence, including unlawful eviction or harassment, managing an unlicensed HMO, breach of gas safety regulations and breach of the right to rent provisions of the Immigration Act 2014.[3]

Leaseholders with long residential leases have significant legal rights available to them to enable them to change the management if they wish. We consider these briefly in the next section.

CHANGING THE MANAGEMENT OF RESIDENTIAL LONG LEASEHOLDS

APPOINTMENT OF A MANAGER

Part II of the Landlord and Tenant Act 1987 enables leaseholders to apply to the First-tier Tribunal (Property Chamber) to appoint a new manager in place of the existing manager (or in place of the landlord if the landlord self-manages). The application may be made by one or more leaseholders, who may nominate a replacement manager. Once appointed, the new manager reports to the Tribunal, not to the landlord. There is no change of ownership in this scenario, but it is important to note that the right to appoint a manager is fault-based. The Tribunal will consider whether the landlord or existing manager has complied with the covenants in the lease, with the law and with the relevant codes of practice.

RIGHT TO MANAGE

The Commonhold and Leasehold Reform Act 2002 introduced the Right to Manage, enabling leaseholders to take over the management of their block of flats without needing to prove that the landlord is at fault. The leaseholders and the building must qualify, and the proper procedure must be followed. The right is exercised by a majority of the leaseholders, who must set up a Right to Manage company (RTMCo) to manage the block. All qualifying leaseholders and – importantly – the landlord, are entitled to become members of the company.

An RTMCo can only manage one qualifying building, so if an estate has more than one building, each needs to set up a separate company.[4] The company takes over the landlord's management role, managing the communal areas, arranging repairs, maintenance, and insurance, granting consents to assignments and alterations, collecting service charges and enforcing leaseholders' covenants in the leases. If the landlord had contracted with third parties – for example with property managers and maintenance contractors – these contracts will end and the RTMCo can enter into new contracts if the leaseholders wish to do so.

The current situation whereby an RTMCo may only manage one block can make it difficult to efficiently manage a large multiblock estate via the Right to Manage. Due to teething problems with the Right to Manage and case law generated since the creation of the right, it is under review by the government (see Chapter 14).

Finally, residential leaseholders may have the right to enfranchise – to acquire the freehold – if they wish to do so (see Chapter 8).

In the commercial sector, management is more straightforward. The property owner will select a firm of managing agents and decide on the extent of their duties. Should the owner believe that the managing agent is not performing their duties to a satisfactory standard they are normally able to terminate the agreement and appoint another firm. It is considered good practice to periodically re-tender management of portfolios to benchmark costs and to see if there is a need for new ideas and approaches.

CONCLUSION

As we have seen in this chapter, real estate management is a diverse and challenging area of practice. We have introduced you to key aspects and the general principles that we outline have a wide application. In addition, the specific topics covered in relation to residential leases should be considered when studying or dealing with this type of asset. Most importantly, remember that the manager may not only be dealing with valuable real estate but will also be impacting upon their client's income, and managing a home or a key business asset. Hence the importance of effective real estate management.

Do refer to the other chapters in this book and to the sources of further information listed below to develop your knowledge of this topic.

NOTES

1 Landlord and Tenant Act 1985, London: The Stationery Office
2 Ministry of Housing, Communities and Local Government (2019) *Guide for Landlords: (Fitness for Human Habitation) Act 2018* Online. Available from: www.gov.uk/government/publications/homes-fitness-for-human-habitation-act-2018/guide-for-landlords-homes-fitness-for-human-habitation-act-2018
3 Shelter (2021) *Banning Orders against Landlords and Letting Agents* Online. Available from: https://england.shelter.org.uk/legal/housing_options/private_rented_accommodation/banning_orders
4 Ninety Broomfield Road RTM Co Ltd v Triplerose Ltd [2015] EWCA Civ 282; [2016] 1 WLR 275

FURTHER INFORMATION

ARHM (2016) *Private Retirement Housing Code of Practice: England* London: Association of Retirement Housing Managers Available from: www.arhm.org/publication-category/code-of-practice/

Card, R, Murdoch, J, and Murdoch, S (2011) *Real Estate Management Law* 7th Edition Oxford: Oxford University Press

ICAEW, ACCA, ARMA, ICAS, and RICS (2011) *ICAEW Technical Release Tech 03/11 Residential Service Charge Accounts* London: ICAEW, ACCA, ARMA, ICAS, RICS Available from: www.icaew.com/technicalfinancial-reporting/accounting-for-specific-sectors/service-charges-and-service-charge-accounts

RICS (2011) *Commercial Property Management in England and Wales* 2nd Edition London: Royal Institution of Chartered Surveyors Available from: www.rics.org/uk/upholding-professional-standards/sector-standards/real-estate/commercial-property-management-in-england-and-wales/

RICS (2015a) *Commercial Property Service Charge Handover Procedures* 1st Edition London: Royal Institution of Chartered Surveyors Available to isurv subscribers from: www.isurv.com/downloads/download/1332/commercial_property_service_charge_handover_procedures

RICS (2015b) *Private Rented Sector Code of Practice* 1st Edition London: Royal Institution of Chartered Surveyors Available from: www.rics.org/

uk/upholding-professional-standards/sector-standards/real-estate/private-rented-sector-code-1st-edition/

RICS (2016a) *Health and Safety for Residential Property Managers* 1st Edition London: Royal Institution of Chartered Surveyors Available from: www.rics.org/uk/upholding-professional-standards/sector-standards/real-estate/health-and-safety-for-residential-property-managers/

RICS (2016b) *Real Estate Management* 3rd Edition London: Royal Institution of Chartered Surveyors Available from: www.rics.org/uk/upholding-professional-standards/sector-standards/real-estate/real-estate-management/

RICS (2016c) *Service Charge Residential Management Code and Additional Advice to Landlords, Leaseholders and Agents* 3rd Edition London: Royal Institution of Chartered Surveyors Available from: www.rics.org/uk/upholding-professional-standards/sector-standards/real-estate/service-charge-residential-management-code/

RICS (2018a) *Guidance for the Designated Professional Body Rules* London: Royal Institution of Chartered Surveyors Available from: www.rics.org/uk/upholding-professional-standards/regulation/regulatory-support/dpb-scheme-for-general-insurance-distribution/

RICS (2018b) *Service Charges in Commercial Property* 1st Edition London: Royal Institution of Chartered Surveyors Available from: www.rics.org/uk/upholding-professional-standards/sector-standards/real-estate/service-charges-in-commercial-property-1st-edition/

RICS (2018c) *Surveying Safely: Health and Safety Principles for Property Professionals* 2nd Edition London: Royal Institution of Chartered Surveyors Available from: www.rics.org/uk/upholding-professional-standards/sector-standards/building-control/surveying-safely/

RICS (2019) *Client Money Handling* 1st Edition London: Royal Institution of Chartered Surveyors Available from: www.rics.org/uk/upholding-professional-standards/standards-of-conduct/client-money/client-money-handling-1st-edition/

RICS (2020) *Professional Indemnity Insurance Requirements Version* 7 London: Royal Institution of Chartered Surveyors Available from: www.rics.org/globalassets/rics-website/media/upholding-professional-standards/regulation/professional-indemnity-insurance-requirements-version-7.pdf

Scarrett, D and Wilcox, J (2018) *Property Asset Management* 4th Edition Abingdon, Oxon: Routledge

WEBSITES

Association of Residential Managing Agents https://arma.org.uk
Association of Retirement Housing Managers www.arhm.org
Health and Safety Executive www.hse.gov.uk/index.htm

Information Commissioner's Office https://ico.org.uk

Institute of Residential Property Management www.irpm.org.uk

Isurv www.isurv.com

Leasehold Advisory Service (LEASE) www.lease-advice.org

The Property Ombudsman www.tpos.co.uk

The Property Redress Scheme www.theprs.co.uk

Propertymark www.propertymark.co.uk

RICS Client Money Protection Scheme www.rics.org/uk/upholding-professional-standards/standards-of-conduct/client-money/cmp-scheme/

RICS Designated Professional Body Scheme for General Insurance Distribution (UK) www.rics.org/uk/upholding-professional-standards/regulation/regulatory-support/dpb-scheme-for-general-insurance-distribution/

CONTEMPORARY ISSUES IN REAL ESTATE

WHY DO WE NEED TO BE AWARE OF CONTEMPORARY ISSUES?

This chapter introduces some contemporary issues of relevance to students and property professionals. Students need to be aware of what is happening in the world and how this is relevant to their studies. Some issues may be directly applicable to scenario-based assignments. Real estate professionals need to adapt to the legal, political, environmental, economic, and social issues affecting the sector.

The Covid-19 pandemic is a recent example of an issue that impacted upon property markets. Brexit similarly created some uncertainty in the UK property market. Those of you already working as real estate professionals may have seen your roles affected by Covid-19 restrictions and we mention the effect of the pandemic in some of the sections later. We do not provide an exhaustive list of issues in this chapter, and you may be aware of others, so when you read this chapter, think about your local issues and those you read about in the mainstream news and in trade publications. How might these be relevant? Perhaps, for example HS2 is affecting your local property market. You may be aware of a proposed development affecting nearby house prices or creating pressure on infrastructure and services. Keeping up to date with contemporary issues is an expectation of a real estate professional in practice and its importance is reflected in requirements to complete annual Continuing Professional Development (CPD).

Some contemporary issues are also reflected in the RICS competencies, and particularly in the mandatory competencies, which

DOI: 10.1201/9781003155256-14

all APC candidates must satisfy. This reflects the need for professional practice to keep up with changes in society. Ethics, Rules of Conduct and Professionalism, Client Care, Diversity and Inclusion, Inclusive Environments, Health and Safety, Sustainability, and Data Management are all examples of current RICS APC competencies, which assess understanding of contemporary issues in real estate.

Awareness of contemporary issues can lead to active engagement with them. Government and professional organisations often consult with stakeholders and the public before making changes to professional standards and the law. These enable individuals to have an impact on policy (and even on legislation) and to influence contemporary issues in practice.

The purpose of this chapter is not to provide detail, as this can change rapidly; rather we aim to alert you to topics about which you need to be aware. Many of the issues included here are interconnected, as you will see. The issues we mention will evolve during the course of your studies and your careers and other pressing problems will arise.

Finally, awareness of contemporary issues also helps real estate professionals to understand the client, their motivation, and some of the factors influencing decision-making. This in turn may affect the advice that you provide, whether to a client, either verbally or in a written report, a colleague, another professional, or to the assessors in your APC interview.

CONTEMPORARY ISSUES IN REAL ESTATE

ADAPTING TO CHANGE

Change is a fundamental aspect of the issues that we consider in this chapter. We may react to change, or we may proactively create change; sometimes our actions are a combination of the two. The Covid-19 pandemic created sudden and unexpected change for many students as face-to-face teaching ceased, and students returned home. This was an unprecedented event and whilst some students did receive refunds for their accommodation, many others were not released from their tenancy obligations. Reactions to this change can be seen in the 2020 petition to Parliament demanding rent refunds. The government approach was to encourage universitie and private providers to act fairly in their decisions about rents.[1] Under the Coronavirus Act 2020 the government also banned forfeiture of commercial leases for non-payment of rent. At the time of writing in 2021, this continues to be an issue for students, universities, and landlords of both residential and commercial premises.

Another example of the need to adapt is the rise in online shopping fuelled by technological and social change. Innovation by some retailers, and the effects of the Covid-19 pandemic, has forced other retailers to react and adapt to this changing market. This has an impact on the real estate market, and, in turn, on other drivers such as planning policy. The growth of flexible office and remote working requires businesses to reconsider their real estate requirements and individuals to consider the requirement for space and Internet connection at home. Workplace behaviour, once regarded as normal, might now be considered unacceptable. The issues outlined beneath therefore reflect the need to adapt to a changing political, economic, social, technological, environmental, and legal context.

DIVERSITY AND INCLUSION

Diversity means variety and it recognises the range of characteristics encountered amongst individuals and communities. Inclusion, as a concept, values these differences and requires the removal of barriers to participation and progression within our society. Diversity and inclusion therefore relate to people and to the physical environment; in other words, they apply to real estate and to the people who occupy or access it.

The concept of discrimination needs to be considered here. Discrimination means treating someone differently due to a characteristic they possess. Discrimination can be positive – intended to promote or support – or it can be prejudicial to that person. For example, retirement housing imposes a minimum age on occupiers to create a community that shares similar characteristics and needs. Social housing, with below market rents, reflects the income of its residents. Discrimination might, however, exclude certain individuals. Gender-based discrimination is a barrier that we have encountered early in our careers, but female real estate professionals are now frequently represented in senior roles, demonstrating progress over the past 30 years. There are still groups underrepresented in the real estate sector, such as ethnic minorities and the disabled. Diverse teams are now generally accepted as conferring business advantage as they offer differing perspectives and experience.

The Equality Act 2010 protects some characteristics that make up a diverse population. Section 4 of the Act lists these:

- Age;
- Disability;
- Gender reassignment;
- Marriage and civil partnership;
- Pregnancy and maternity;
- Race;
- Religion or belief;
- Sex;
- Sexual orientation.[2]

Discrimination – the unfavourable treatment of a person or a group of people in comparison to others – can be direct (e.g. an express policy of refusing to let a property to a person due to a particular protected characteristic) or indirect (a policy or practice that has the effect of discriminating against a person with a protected characteristic). The Equality Act prohibits direct and indirect discrimination against listed protected characteristics. Victimisation and harassment are also prohibited by the Act. These are all examples of conduct contrary to diversity and inclusion as they alienate and exclude people.

An inclusive environment is a physical environment that can be used and enjoyed by all regardless of ability. In our experience, inclusive environments are commonly confused with diversity and inclusion. This is understandable, as they are interconnected. Real estate that is accessible to all and addresses the needs of all will help to create a physical environment that welcomes a diverse range of users and occupiers.

The Equality Act applies to inclusive environments and may require reasonable steps to be taken to avoid disadvantage to a disabled person caused by a physical feature. Examples of reasonable adaptations that we have encountered in practice include the installation of wet rooms, access ramps, handrails, emergency call systems and stairlifts. Adaptations may also need to be made to policies, such as landlord's consent to adaptations.

Inclusive environments are recognised by planning policies and building standards. Section 8 of the NPPF[3] states that:

> Planning policies and decisions should aim to achieve healthy, inclusive and safe places

The importance of design to inclusive environments is apparent. For example, the Design Council has created an Inclusive Environments Hub as a resource for real estate professionals and RIBA held an Inclusion by Design Festival in 2020. Approved Document M of the Building Regulations relates to accessibility, including facilities for disabled people. Inclusive environments can encompass other broader obligations, such as fire safety. Evacuation procedures that consider disabled occupiers and fire safety notices in different languages are examples.

We have mentioned retirement housing. Interestingly, under Section 32 of the Equality Act, discrimination on the basis of age is not prohibited in relation to housing; hence it is common to see age-restricted retirement housing.

ETHICS

Ethical practice is a critical aspect of a real estate practitioner's professional duty. In the case of the RICS, and most other professional bodies, this is evidenced by requirements to undertake regular training in ethics and to comply with ethical standards. Ethics underpin practice and there is much legislation applicable to this area. We cover some within this chapter – the Equality Act 2010, for example, seeks to achieve a fair society, which prevents or counters disadvantage in relation to protected characteristics. Concepts such as integrity – doing the right thing – underpin good business practice and personal conduct. This is important: ethical conduct is not limited to professional life but applies to personal life also, and this is reflected in RICS ethics training and guidance.

Other aspects such as providing a good service are enshrined in consumer protection legislation. For example, the Consumer Rights Act 2015 requires businesses to provide their services with reasonable care and skill, at a reasonable price and within a reasonable timescale. These legal requirements are reflected in professional standards. Real estate professionals should have regard to proper standards of service and have clear Terms of Engagement and effective complaints handling procedures (see Chapter 10).

Ethics cover a range of issues, all of which are current and many of which have become increasingly important in recent years. Some examples of ethical considerations in professional practice are:

- Anti-money laundering measures. Money laundering is the processing of money obtained from criminal activities so as to appear to be from a legitimate source. Investment in property is one way of laundering money. Property professionals therefore need to be alert to this and carry out risk assessments and due diligence checks as required. They must also report any suspicions to the National Crime Agency or HM Revenue and Customs. Relevant laws include the Proceeds of Crime Act 2002 and the Money Laundering, Terrorist Financing and Transfer of Funds (Information on the Payer) Regulations 2017;
- Bribery – a bribe is an advantage conferred as an incentive or reward for improper conduct. The Bribery Act 2010 is the key piece of legislation here and we recommend that you familiarise yourself with it. Offences include bribing another person, agreeing to receive or accepting a bribe, and bribing a foreign public official. In the case of commercial organisations, there is also an offence of failing to prevent a bribe. It is a defence to the latter if the organisation can prove that it had adequate procedures in place designed to prevent bribery;[4]
- Conflicts of interest – these compromise the ability to act in the best interests of the client. The RICS identifies three types of conflict of interest:
  - Own-interest conflict
  - Party conflict
  - Confidential information conflict;[5]

- Competence – it is important that real estate professionals only carry out work that they are trained and competent to do. Failure to recognise the limits of expertise can lead to a negligence claim and breach of professional conduct rules;
- CSR is the assimilation of socially responsible policies into business practice. For example, a company may raise funds for charity

or allow employees time off for voluntary work. CSR may often be associated with environmental sustainability policies, for example replacing company vehicles with electric versions;

- Environmental, social, and governance (ESG) standards may influence investors' willingness to invest in an organisation or asset;
- Modern slavery and human trafficking involve the abuse and exploitation of the workforce through slavery, servitude, and forced or compulsory labour, as defined by Section 3 of the Modern Slavery Act 2015.[6] Examples of abusive practices can include retention of passports by an employer, payment of wages to a supervisor, and deduction from wages of excessive charges for food and accommodation.[7] The Gangmasters and Labour Abuse Authority (GLAA) licenses gangmasters and investigates exploitation of the workforce. Real estate professionals may encounter this abuse through forced labour in the construction industry. Potential victims include immigrants and individuals with mental health issues. Higher risk activities include hand car washing, hospitality, and horticulture, so real estate professionals need to be vigilant when, for example letting or inspecting premises or when paying contractors and they must report suspicious activity to the GLAA.

In 2020 the RICS consulted on changes to its ethical standards and conduct rules, with the intention of making them clearer for members and regulated firms. As a result, in October 2021 the RICS announced new ethical standards and conduct rules, with effect from February 2022.

Ethical behaviour involves the use of judgement and may depend on context. For example, a modest gift given in recognition of good service may be acceptable after a contract has concluded. However, this is likely to differ from an extravagant gift given by a contractor before the awarding of a major contract. In this instance, the gift could be seen as an inducement for the contract to be awarded to the donor contractor – in other words, bribery.

A 2021 report into forced labour in the solar panel supply chain illustrates the interconnected nature of some ethical issues. 'In Broad Daylight: Uyghur Forced Labour and Global Solar Supply Chains' describes coercion of indigenous workers in China tantamount to enslavement, which pervades the polysilicon raw material supply chain and the international market for solar panels. As a consequence, manufacturers demanding an ethical supply chain must check that their polysilicon is not sourced from companies involved in forced labour practices. In this instance, the price of green energy is the abuse of human rights.[8]

The example of Uyghur forced labour demonstrates the global reach of some ethical issues. The International Ethics Standards Coalition (IESC) has published International Ethics Standards aimed at the real estate sector, with a view to creating consistent global standards to serve the public interest. Membership of the IESC includes the RICS, the Royal Institute of British Architects, and the Royal Town Planning Institute. The RICS's own ethical standards and mandatory competencies, with which all surveyors need to be familiar, reflect these international standards.

HEALTH AND SAFETY

When we first started work in the real estate sector, the Health and Safety at Work etc. Act 1974 was in effect, but attitudes were often very relaxed. Risk assessments were not generally carried out and it was still legal to use asbestos in construction. Property management did not have regard to safety in the way that it now does, and we remember cleaners climbing out of third floor windows, holding on to the frames and balancing on the sills without any protection or safety measures, to clean the windows.

Awareness has changed since we started work in the late 1980s and property professionals must be familiar with their obligations and with essentials such as the need for risk assessments, method statements, and compliance with the many regulations that apply. The Construction (Design and Management) Regulations 2015, The Regulatory Reform (Fire Safety) Order 2005, and The Control of Asbestos Regulations 2012 are just a few examples.

The following are some of the key risks to health, safety, and well-being that real estate professionals need to be aware of:

- Asbestos;
- Covid-19;
- Electrical safety;
- Fire safety;

- Gas safety;
- Legionella;
- Lone working;
- Manual handling;
- Mental health;
- Structural failure;
- Working at heights.

Fire safety has received considerable media attention in recent years, particularly since the Grenfell Tower tragedy in 2017, in which 72 people lost their lives when a fire broke out in a flat and quickly spread through the tower block. The presence of combustible aluminium composite materials in the external cladding was a major contributor to the spread of the fire. The ramifications of the fire are wide-reaching and include building design and construction, Building Regulations, responsibility for fire safety and the cost of fire safety measures, evacuation procedures, and attitudes towards residents' safety concerns. One consequence of the fire is that many leaseholders are now struggling to sell or mortgage their flats due to problems valuing high-rise flats, fire safety concerns, and compliance costs. Fire safety is a huge topic, but key sources include the review by Dame Judith Hackitt following the Grenfell Tower fire, the Building Safety Programme, The Regulatory Reform (Fire Safety) Order 2005, and the Fire Safety Act 2021.

You may also find the HSE website helpful; we have included a link at the end of this chapter. The RICS also produces guidance, in particular Surveying safely: health and safety principles for property professionals 2nd edition 2018. Other sector and risk-specific guidance is available, for example RICS Health and safety for residential property managers 1st edition 2016.

Health and safety also relate to living standards. The Homes (Fitness for Human Habitation) Act 2018 stipulates that rented dwellings must be fit for human habitation. Legislation – for example Section 11 of the Landlord and Tenant Act 1985 – places an obligation on landlords to maintain their properties.

At the time of writing in 2021, the Building Safety Bill was progressing towards becoming law. This Bill is intended to improve building safety through measures such as a new Building Safety Regulator and the regulation of building inspectors.

HOUSING CRISIS

In the UK, it is generally acknowledged that we have a housing crisis. We have a shortage of homes in some areas, home ownership is unaffordable for many people, and in recent years there has been a failure to achieve house-building targets. The extent of the issue varies regionally, reflecting factors such as supply and demand and local economies. This is illustrated by differing average house prices. For example, property portal Rightmove reports an average price for a terraced house in Middlesbrough, North Yorkshire of £74,894[9] compared to £1,204,958 in Battersea, London.[10]

It is suggested that reform of housing policy is needed to address the crisis, to include building in areas of highest demand, the introduction of more flexible planning policies (including in relation to greenbelt development), and changes to subsidies for home buyers and to the tax treatment of housing transactions.[11] Other measures include brownfield regeneration and taxation policies to discourage investment in the private-rented sector. The planning aspect is considered further in the section later.

Solutions need to involve a wide range of stakeholders. In Chapter 4 we mention the Church Commissioners' housing commission which reported that a significant proportion of their approximately 200,000 acres of land could be used to build affordable housing.[12] This could help with the housing crisis if restrictions around charity law can be overcome.

The issue is not just a matter of the volume of houses; there is a concept of 'right-sizing'. Changes in a population need changes to the housing stock, but this can be slow to achieve, as housing takes time to plan and construct. In the UK, in common with many developed countries, we have an aging population, which requires provision of suitable and affordable retirement housing, which in turn can release family homes for a new generation of occupier. It is not only housing that is impacted on by the aging population, but also the provision of health care, accessibility, modes of transport, and leisure facilities. Real estate developers and investors need to be aware of these trends to ensure that they are meeting the needs of the market. Similarly, the student population has grown considerably since we were at university. Many more towns and cities need suitable student accommodation in a greater volume. Much of this will be in purpose-built halls of residence, which are another relatively new area of real estate. Although it was common for universities to construct their own accommodation, there are now specialist investors and developers of student housing. Much student housing is still, however, former family housing let to groups of students leading to 'studentification'[13] of certain areas.

The housing crisis is not limited to the UK. In other regions, geography may restrict opportunity to develop new housing. This, combined with high population density, can result in a shortage, pushing up house prices and making even modest housing unaffordable for many. Barcelona, the capital of Catalonia in Spain, provides us with an example of a city affected by issues of affordability. La Borda is a social housing cooperative created in response to housing problems in the city.[14] The development is located in a former industrial area and combines flexible modular housing units with shared facilities and sustainable design features such as solar energy,[15] a timber structure, and an atrium roof that opens and closes to assist with ventilation and temperature control.[16]

'Beehive housing' is another attempt to address housing affordability. This is the use of tiny sleeping pods, inspired by Japanese 'capsule' hotels, with a shared kitchen and bathroom, let at a low rent with occupiers limited according to age and income. Attempts have been made to adopt beehive housing in Barcelona. Its supporters argue that it is preferable to a hostel or life on the streets, but its opponents counter that the pods are illegal, as they do not meet minimum housing standards.[17] In Austin, Texas housing charity New Story have partnered with ICON, a construction technology company, to produce 3D printed homes, creating 400 sq. ft. homes for the chronically homeless in Austin. They are now creating further communities in Mexico to replace existing shacks. These homes were estimated to take 24 hours to print and cost merely $4,000 each in 2018.[18]

PLANNING AND DEVELOPMENT

Planning affects the use of all real estate. Chapter 3 highlights changes to planning Use Classes in 2020, which reflect the need for real estate use to diversify and adapt. This topic is also closely linked with the housing shortage mentioned earlier. In 2020, the UK government consulted on changes to the current planning system, including:

- Assessing the local housing need;
- A temporary raising of the threshold below which developers do not need to contribute to affordable housing;
- Permission for housing without needing detailed plans.[19]

One method of addressing the housing shortage is to convert commercial premises to residential. This is also relevant to the changing commercial and retail sectors, and we discuss this further in the 'Struggling high streets' section later. In England, The Town and Country Planning (General Permitted Development etc.) (England) (Amendment) Order 2021 permits certain development without planning permission. The 2021 Regulations introduce a new permitted development Class MA in relation to the conversion of commercial and service premises to residential.[20] This may become increasingly apparent in high streets and business districts in years to come.

The Town and Country Planning (Permitted Development and Miscellaneous Amendments) (England) (Coronavirus) Regulations 2020 created a permanent permitted development right to create new homes on existing purpose-built blocks of flats. This, again, is intended to help address the housing shortage and also forms part of the government's Covid-19 economic renewal package.[21] Similarly, The Town and Country Planning (General Permitted Development) (England) (Amendment) (No. 2) Order 2020 permits existing houses to be extended upwards to create additional living space. Additional storeys can also be built upon some commercial and mixed-use buildings to provide new homes.[22]

In May 2021, the government announced proposals for a new Planning Bill with the purpose of updating planning laws to support increased home building. As at March 2021, local plans allowed for 192,725 new homes in England, significantly below the government's target of 300,000 new homes per year.[23] The shortage of supply in relation to demand is reflected in high prices, so planning policies that increase supply are an attempt to address this issue.

RESIDENTIAL LEASEHOLD REFORM

Leasehold can be a controversial tenure in that owners of a legal estate in land are tenants and may lack the degree of control and security enjoyed by freeholders. These tenants may have to pay ground rent in addition to the premium they paid for their property. They are also likely to pay service charges, which can be significant. Leaseholds have been the focus of media and government attention in recent years due to reported abuse of the system, such as excessively high ground rents. It does seem likely that the leasehold sector is on the cusp of change, with extended and simplified rights for leaseholders and possibly an increase in the number of commonhold properties, as an alternative to leasehold.

In 2016 the Law Commission launched its 13th Programme of Law Reform, which included research and reports into the residential leasehold sector. Following the publication of the Commission's reports on leasehold enfranchisement, commonhold and the right to manage, in 2021 the Ministry of Housing, Communities and Local Government announced proposals for leasehold reform and the intention to reinvigorate commonhold. This announcement followed an earlier announcement that leasehold was to be banned for new houses.

Recommendations and proposed reforms in the long residential leasehold sector include:

- Measures to simplify commonhold to encourage its use as an alternative to leasehold;
- Zero ground rents for new leases;
- A ban on new leasehold houses, so with limited exceptions, all new houses will be sold as freehold;
- Extension and simplification of the leasehold enfranchisement process;
- A right for leaseholders of flats and houses to extend their leases by 990 years;
- Changes to the Right to Manage to extend and simplify it;
- Regulation of managing agent firms and licensing of individuals carrying out certain roles in the sector, within a requirement for a minimum level of qualification, a single code of practice, and an independent external regulator.

There are also proposals for change in the short-term lettings sector, including:

- The proposals to regulate firms and license individual agents that we mention earlier also apply to letting agents, including the requirement for minimum qualifications, a single code of practice, and the creation of an independent external regulator;
- Abolition of Section 21 of the Housing Act 1988 notices procedure to terminate tenancies, as part of a review of landlords' rights to regain possession.

These proposals may change the face of the residential sector in the future. It is possible that, over time, there will be fewer long leasehold properties and property managers may increasingly be managing estates of freehold houses and commonhold flats. Implementing change will require legislation and plans to improve long leaseholder rights may become less important over time if the long residential leasehold sector does shrink. We are already seeing changes with the growth in numbers of build-to-rent properties where both established, and new, real estate investors and developers are constructing good quality residential blocks purely to rent to tenants.

The May 2021 Queen's Speech announced proposals to enhance the rights of renters and a Leasehold Reform (Ground Rent) Bill. If this Bill becomes law in England and Wales, it is expected to limit new ground rents to a peppercorn, which means that the rent will have no financial value.[24] At the time of writing in 2021, legislation to implement other proposals for leasehold reform has not yet been announced.

STRUGGLING HIGH STREETS

We mention changes in shopping habits in recent years, exacerbated by the Covid-19 pandemic. The consequences of these issues are visible in high streets, shopping centres, and retail parks, with empty units detracting from many previously thriving areas. Some locations, including our local shopping centres, have lost their anchor tenants The list of major brands that have gone into administration is long Others are still trading but with a reduced number of outlets. Thi can result in a downward spiral, as areas become less attractive to consumers, footfall reduces, contributing towards further decline. The pandemic also reduced the opportunity to spend in physical shops during the lockdowns that were imposed. High business rates have been blamed for creating an additional burden on struggling businesses.

These issues all have an impact on real estate and on investors in this type of real estate, which include REITs and pension funds. Empty units mean no rent and continuing costs such as insurance premiums and security measures. In other cases, struggling tenants may try to renegotiate their rents; a landlord wishing to avoid vacant units may need to agree to rent reductions, even if only temporarily. Landlords may need to offer incentives (see Chapter 10), such as rent-free periods, to help attract new tenants.

A reference to the 'high street' is usually a reference to town and city centres. These are not just shopping areas; they are also workplaces, leisure destinations, and residential areas. Government initiatives designed to help high streets to adapt include the Future High Streets Fund. At the time of writing in 2021, funding had been allocated to 72 high streets for projects such as transport improvements, new homes, hospitality and performance venues, and repurposing vacant retail space.[25] This issue will continue to evolve over the coming years, but a solution may be in diversification; less reliance on retail combined with development of residential, leisure, commercial, and service premises in order to attract people to these areas.

SUSTAINABILITY

Climate change and sustainability impact significantly on the real estate sector in many ways. In this chapter we aim to highlight some key points and some political milestones to help develop your awareness of these issues. Global warming has been a growing concern for several decades now, and you are probably already aware of some measures to reduce greenhouse gas emissions to combat global warming.

However, sustainability is not limited to climate change. To sustain means to endure, to last and also to support, nurture, or nourish. Sustainability therefore also relates to ethics; for something to be sustainable, it needs to be justifiable in relation to economic, social, and environmental concerns, with the aim of creating fair and just societies whilst protecting our planet. Sustainability relates to the conservation and responsible use of resources. It also relates to the development of clean, safe, desirable environments in which to live, work, and relax. Critically, sustainable development avoids future problems. For example, asbestos is a naturally occurring mineral, which was widely used in construction due to its fire-resistant properties. However, we are now aware of the health risks associated with asbestos and its use in construction is now banned. Yet, many properties still contain asbestos, which may be safe whilst in good condition but if it deteriorates, it poses a serious risk to health. This is an example of poor sustainability; we have created a hazard, which must now be managed. In some parts of the world, sustainable development may require buildings to be earthquake proof or flood resilient. Other environmental issues linked to land use include desertification and deforestation. Whilst new developments can incorporate sustainability into their design, retrofitting existing properties can be difficult and expensive. It may also change the appearance of a property to a degree considered unacceptable.

Action to address climate change and to improve sustainability requires collaboration and cooperation between governments, organisations, and individuals to be effective. Measures can therefore be seen on a global, national, local, and individual scale:

- In 1987 the World Commission on Environment and Development published its report 'Our Common Future' (known as the Brundtland Report).[26] The report eloquently defines sustainable development as development which:

  > meets the needs of the present without compromising the ability of future generations to meet their own needs

- In 1997 the Kyoto Protocol created the first international greenhouse gas emission reduction obligations, focused on industrialised nations as major polluters;
- The Paris Agreement is a 2015 treaty with the goal of limiting global warming to below 2 degrees Celsius and to pursue efforts towards 1.5 degrees Celsius in comparison with pre-industrial levels. In April 2021, the UK government announced plans to

reduce greenhouse gas emissions by 78% by 2035 compared to 1990 levels, consistent with its Paris Agreement obligations. The overall aim is for the UK to become net zero by 2050;[27]

- The United Nations has created Sustainable Development Goals, which include climate action, sustainable cities and communities and affordable and clean energy, with the aim of protecting the planet and addressing inequality and injustice;[28]
- The NPPF provides that planning decisions should apply a presumption in favour of sustainable development;[29]
- Government green initiatives aim to support sustainability in the built environment. In recent years, these have included the Green Deal and the Green Homes Grant. However, these can be problematic because, for example of the inability of the sector to meet demand;
- Other government policies impose minimal energy efficiency standards. Properties rented as dwellings must have a minimum energy performance rating of E unless an exemption applies; this may rise to a minimum C rating by 2025. With effect from 2023, all non-exempt commercial lettings must also have a minimum EPC rating of E;
- Proposed changes to Part L of the Building Regulations (conservation of fuel and power) and Part F (ventilation) to improve the energy efficiency and ventilation standards of residential properties (The Future Homes Standard[30]) and non-residential buildings (The Future Buildings Standard[31]);
- Green leases are leases in which the tenant has sustainability responsibilities, such as energy and water efficiency and waste management;
- Green mortgages reward owners of energy-efficient homes with lower mortgage rates and other incentives;
- In Chapter 3, we mention wind farms. These increasingly apparent features of the landscape and seascape provide green energy. Energy supplier SSE plans to build the world's largest offshore wind farm at Dogger Bank;[32]
- Other 'green' technologies such as ground source heat pumps, solar power, and recycling of grey water are being designed into new properties or retrofitted to older ones;
- On an individual basis, we can recycle, improve the insulation of our homes, choose green energy, and walk or cycle where possible.

Sustainability and technology go hand in hand; we saw during the Covid-19 pandemic how technology enabled many people to work from home and reduced the need for meetings to take place face to face. It is possible that this could alter working patterns in the longer term and reduce demand for office space, perhaps releasing commercial premises for residential use. Retail premises have been affected by online shopping, enabled by technology, so premises suitable for a 'click and collect' service and storage and distribution units may see increased demand. Real estate will need to adapt to provide millions of charging points as petrol vehicles are phased out in favour of electric vehicles. This may be straightforward in some circumstances, such as a detached house with adjacent parking. However, it will be far more difficult to achieve in a block of flats with limited parking spaces or in on-street parking.

Sustainability can sometimes be measured, and we mention minimum energy efficiency ratings above. BREEAM is the world's first sustainability assessment method for planning, infrastructure and building construction, use, and refurbishment. This applies standards to assess environmental, social, and economic performance. These three pillars of sustainability reflect in environments that enhance occupier well-being, whilst protecting natural resources and creating desirable investments.[33] The RICS owns an environmental assessment system for retail and office premises, called SKA. This comprises good practice measures for energy, carbon dioxide emissions, waste, water, materials, pollution, well-being, and transport, giving a percentage score and a Bronze, Silver, or Gold Standard.[34]

TECHNOLOGY IN REAL ESTATE

Technology has transformed working practice in many sectors, including real estate. We can remember 30 years ago properties for sale or to let would only be in agents' windows and advertised once a week in the property section of the local newspaper. Lease negotiations required a paper draft, which passed between solicitors in the post with the addition of comments and amendments in coloured pen. This was a laborious task that slowed the progression of transactions. These processes have been transformed by modern information technology.

In the UK, land registration is an example of how technology can change a sector. As more and more properties become registered, information on ownership, that was once private, is now publicly available online at very low cost, making conveyancing more efficient and transparent.

In recent years we have seen other changes, some of which gained further momentum as a result of the Covid-19 pandemic. Online meetings, virtual viewings, and use of social media to market properties are just a few examples. Whilst some workers need to be onsite to carry out their roles, the pandemic demonstrated that many roles can be carried out remotely, potentially affecting population location and demand for commercial premises.

Examples of the use of technology in the real estate sector include:

- Building information modelling (BIM) is a three-dimensional computer model of a building that includes information, such as safety features and the specification of the building's component parts. This information can assist with the management of all aspects of the building's lifespan, including construction and management through to demolition;
- Information and communications technology (ICT), for instance mobile phone applications (apps), computer software, and cloud computing. When we began practising in the real estate sector, it was only possible to create records manually, so they existed only on paper and there were no computers in our offices. There were no mobile phones in general use, so we could not be contacted when out on site. This is difficult to imagine now, and the sector relies heavily on information technology, which continues to develop. Technology is used in every aspect of real estate practice: property management software, cloud storage and data management systems, electronic signatures, safety 'alert' devices, laser measuring devices, mapping software, property platforms listing premises for sale or to let and providing historical price data, to list just a few;
- Drones are another creative application of technology to assist real estate practitioners. They can reduce risk in that they can access and film areas of a building that may be unsafe or costly for a surveyor to physically inspect;

- Virtual tours of properties became more popular during the pandemic when inspections could not be carried out in person. These are likely to continue to be used as they can save time and allow agents to reach a larger number of people simultaneously;
- Smart buildings use technology to gather data on how a building functions. Analysis of that data can then improve efficiency – so this technology relates also to sustainability – as well as the experience of the building's occupiers. For example, occupancy data can help manage resources and energy efficiency. Sensors monitor occupancy rates and patterns, which can then be used to increase site capacity through efficient use of workspace and to reduce energy use;
- Unique Property Reference Numbers (UPRNs) identify every individual property capable of having an address. These include buildings and other structures such as bus shelters, electricity substations, or telephone boxes. UPRNs help to avoid errors when identifying properties as postcodes relate to areas or clusters of premises, rather than to individual properties. UPRNs assist with the efficient identification of properties, by, for example emergency services and the Environment Agency to produce flood plans;[35]
- Automated Valuation Models (AVMs) provide property valuations based on mathematical modelling using databases of property transactions.

Technology can influence real estate at a fundamental level, making challenging environments more conducive to human habitation and activity. For example, the invention of air conditioning has been associated with a population increase in the American 'sun belt' (the warm southern states from Florida to California), from 28% to 40% of Americans in the second half of the 20th century.[36] Technology also influences the type of real estate that is constructed. For example, when we started in the profession data centres did not exist and nor did solar farms, or serviced offices. Real estate professionals need to try to keep abreast of changes to ensure that they are planning to build real estate that will be in demand.

The use of technology brings new challenges, in particular regarding data security and privacy. We discuss data management in Chapter 13, so we do not go into detail here. However, it is mentioned because it is so relevant to the rapid growth of technology throughout our lives. Balancing the widespread use and benefits of technology with data security risks and the right to privacy is not always an easy task and it is important to understand the parameters around which data is obtained, used, and stored. Data protection laws are important, whether national or international. For example, does domestic legislation permit the storage of data on cloud-based systems overseas, where different laws will apply?

Data use is also connected with ethics – how is personal or commercially sensitive or private data ethically used? As technology evolves, so does the need for good data management. There has been a number of high-profile data security breaches in recent years and cyber-crime or simple human error are real risks to the data security of businesses and individuals.

The Real Estate Data Foundation has created six data ethics principles for real estate organisations.[37] You may find it helpful to look at their website and the website of the ICO, both listed at the end of this chapter.

Data management is also a mandatory competency for APC candidates, so it is important to familiarise yourself with this area, to keep up to date and to ensure that you comply with all legal requirements.

Technology continues to evolve, and it is likely that AI may be used for various functions currently carried out by individuals such as managing calls concerning repairs and maintenance or identifying suitable properties for applicants. Blockchain and tokenisation might be used as a way of overcoming the challenges of raising funds for investing in real estate and of opening it to a wider market. 'Smart cities', that is those with excellent ICT networks and connections will become prevalent which should help to promote sustainable development.

CONCLUSION

We have identified and outlined some key contemporary issues in real estate based on our own experiences. It is important to remember that this list is not exhaustive, and you may be able to think of more. Change is inherent in this topic, so it is essential to keep up to date and to be ready to adapt. There are many professional resources available, such as the Estates Gazette and isurv, which you may be able to access through your employer or educational institution. Social media and professional forums can also be useful sources of information, due to the speed at which commentators can react on these platforms.

However, it is also important to read mainstream media, as this will help you to interpret how wider society regards the issues that affect your studies and professional practice. Wider reading will help you to develop your awareness and understanding. We also recommend that you follow political developments and events such as the Queen's Speech (in which the Queen sets out the government's programme for legislation) and the budget, as these often directly affect real estate.

Students need to develop an awareness of contemporary issues and may be directly affected by them from an early stage. As practitioners, and even as students, you may be able to make a useful contribution. We have been involved in real estate policy, which is a rewarding activity and a direct way of becoming involved in, and potentially influencing, contemporary issues in real estate. It is important that we continue to be aware of these issues, and to search out and investigate new ones that emerge, beyond the parameters of our own profession. This will enable us to provide advice on how real estate can contribute towards making the world a better place in which to live and work.

NOTES

1 UK Government and Parliament (2020) *Refund University Rent and Tuition Fees Due to Coronavirus* Petition Online. Available from: https://petition.parliament.uk/petitions/304855

2 The Equality Act 2010, London: The Stationery Office

3 Ministry of Housing, Communities and Local Government (2012) *National Planning Policy Framework* Online. Available from: www.gov.uk/guidance/national-planning-policy-framework/8-promoting-healthy-and-safe-communities

4 Bribery Act 2010, London: The Stationery Office

5 RICS (2017) *Conflicts of Interest*. Available from: www.rics.org/uk/upholding-professional-standards/standards-of-conduct/conflicts-of-interest/

6 Modern Slavery Act 2015, London: The Stationery Office

7 RICS (2018) *Persistent Vigilance: Ending Forced Labour Stamping Out Slavery* Online. Available from: www.isurv.com/info/390/features/11718/persistent_vigilance_ending_forced_labour

8 Murphy, L and Elimä, N (2021) *In Broad Daylight: Uyghur Forced Labour and Global Solar Supply Chains*. Sheffield, UK: Sheffield Hallam University Helena Kennedy Centre for International Justice. Available from: www. shu.ac.uk/helena-kennedy-centre-international-justice/research-and-projects/all-projects/in-broad-daylight

9 Rightmove (2021) *House Prices in Middlesbrough* Online. Available from: www.rightmove.co.uk/house-prices/middlesbrough.html

10 Rightmove (2021) *House Prices in Battersea* Online. Available from: www. rightmove.co.uk/house-prices/battersea.html

11 Centre for Cities (2021) *Housing* Online. Available from: www.centrefor cities.org/housing/

12 The Commission of the Archbishops of Canterbury and York on Housing, Church and Community (2021) *Coming Home: Tackling the Housing Crisis together Full Report February 2021* Online. Available from: www. archbishopofcanterbury.org/sites/abc/files/2021-02/COE%204794%20% E2%80%93%C2%A0HCC%20Full%20Report%20%E2%80%93%20V6.pdf

13 Smith, D (2005) 'Patterns and Processes of "Studentification" in Leeds' *The Regional Review* 12, 14–16

14 La Borda (2016) Online. Available from: www.laborda.coop/en/project/ funding-structure/

15 La Borda (2016) *Architectural Project* Online. Available from: www.laborda. coop/en/project/architectural-project/

16 Gomez-Moriana, R (2018) *Into the Woods* Roca Gallery Online. Available from: www.rocagallery.com/into-the-woods

17 BBC News (2018) *Barcelona Blocks Tiny "Haibu" Living Pods* Online. Available from: www.bbc.co.uk/news/world-europe-45450238

18 Bendix, A (2019) 'These 3D-Printed Homes Can Be Built for Less Than $4000 in Just 24 Hours' *Business Insider* Online. Available from: businessinsider.com/3d-homes-that-take-24-hours-and-less-than-4000-to-print-2018–9?r=US&IR=T

19 Ministry of Housing, Communities and Local Government (2021) *Government Response to the Local Housing Need Proposals in "Changes to the Current Planning System"* Online. Available from: www.gov.uk/government/ consultations/changes-to-the-current-planning-system/outcome/ government-response-to-the-local-housing-need-proposals-in-changes-to-the-current-planning-system#next-steps

20 The Town and Country Planning (General Permitted Development etc.) (England) (Amendment) Order 2021, London: The Stationery Office

21 Ministry of Housing, Communities and Local Government (2020) *Explanatory Memorandum to the Town and Country Planning (Permitted Development and Miscellaneous Amendments) (England) (Coronavirus) Regulations 2020* Available from: www.legislation.gov.uk/uksi/2020/632/memorandum/contents

22 Ministry of Housing, Communities and Local Government (2020) *Explanatory Memorandum to the Town and Country Planning (General Permitted Development) (England) (Amendment) (No. 2) Order 2020* Available from: www.legislation.gov.uk/uksi/2020/755/memorandum/contents

23 Prime Ministers Office (2021) *Queen's Speech 2021: Background Briefing Notes* Policy Paper Online. Available from: www.gov.uk/government/publications/queens-speech-2021-background-briefing-notes

24 Prime Minister's Office (2021) *Queen's Speech 2021: Background Briefing Notes* Policy Paper Online. Available from: www.gov.uk/government/publications/queens-speech-2021-background-briefing-notes

25 Ministry of Housing, Communities and Local Government, Jenrick, R (2021) 'More High Streets Set for Funding Boost as Reopening Accelerates' *Press Release* Online. Available from: www.gov.uk/government/news/more-high-streets-set-for-funding-boost-as-reopening-accelerates

26 World Commission on Environment and Development (1987) *Our Common Future* Online. Available from: https://sustainabledevelopment.un.org/content/documents/5987our-common-future.pdf

27 Department for Business, Energy & Industrial Strategy, Prime Minister's Office, Kwarteng K, Sharma A and Johnson B (2021) 'UK Enshrines New Target in Law to Slash Emissions by 78% by 2035, *Press Release* Online. Available from: www.gov.uk/government/news/uk-enshrines-new-target-in-law-to-slash-emissions-by-78-by-2035

28 RICS (2020) *UN Sustainable Development* Online. Available from: www.rics.org/en-hk/about-rics/responsible-business/un-sustainable-development/

29 Ministry of Housing, Communities and Local Government (2021) *National Planning Policy Framework* Online. Available from: https://assets.publishing.service.gov.uk/government/uploads/system/uploads/attachment_data/file/810197/NPPF_Feb_2019_revised.pdf

30 Ministry of Housing, Communities and Local Government (2021) *The Future Homes Standard: Changes to Part L and Part F of the Building Regulations for New Dwellings* Online. Available from: www.gov.uk/government/consultations/the-future-homes-standard-changes-to-part-l-and-part-f-of-the-building-regulations-for-new-dwellings

31 Ministry of Housing, Communities and Local Government (2021) *The Future Buildings Standard* Online. Available from: www.gov.uk/government/consultations/the-future-buildings-standard

32 Department for Business, Energy & Industrial Strategy, Prime Minister's Office, Sharma A and Johnson B (2020) 'UK Sets Ambitious New Climate Target Ahead of UN Summit' *Press Release* Online. Available from: www.gov.uk/government/news/uk-sets-ambitious-new-climate-target-ahead-of-un-summit

33 Building Research Establishment (undated) *What Is BREEAM?* Online. Available from: www.breeam.com

34 RICS (undated) *SKA Rating* Online. Available from: www.rics.org/uk/about-rics/responsible-business/ska-rating/

35 GeoPlace LLP (2021) *The Power of the UPRN* Online. Available from: www.geoplace.co.uk/addresses-streets/location-data/the-uprn

36 Harford, T (2017) *How Air Conditioning Changed the World* 50 Things That Made the Modern Economy BBC World Service Online. Available from: www.bbc.co.uk/news/business-39735802

37 Real Estate Data Foundation (undated) *Data Ethics Principles* Online. Available from: www.theredfoundation.org/dataethics

FURTHER INFORMATION

RICS (2016) *Health and Safety for Residential Property Managers* 1st Edition London: Royal Institution of Chartered Surveyors Available from: www.rics.org/uk/upholding-professional-standards/sector-standards/real-estate/health-and-safety-for-residential-property-managers/

RICS (2018a) *Environmental Risks and Global Real Estate* 1st Edition London: Royal Institution of Chartered Surveyors Available from: www.rics.org/globalassets/rics-website/media/upholding-professional-standards/sector-standards/land/environmental-risks-and-global-real-estate-1st-edition-november-2018.pdf

RICS (2018b) *Surveying Safely: Health and Safety Principles for Property Professionals* 2nd Edition London: Royal Institution of Chartered Surveyors Available from: www.rics.org/uk/upholding-professional-standards/sector-standards/building-control/surveying-safely/

RICS (2019) *Implementing the UN Sustainable Development Goals* London: Royal Institution of Chartered Surveyors Available from: www.rics.org/globalassets/implementing-un-sustainable-development-goals-rics.pdf

RICS (2020) *The Futures Report 2020* London: Royal Institution of Chartered Surveyors Available from: www.rics.org/uk/news-insight/future-of-surveying/

World Commission on Environment and Development (1987) *Our Common Future* Available from: https://sustainabledevelopment.un.org/content/documents/5987our-common-future.pdf

WEBSITES

BREEAM www.breeam.com

Building Safety Programme www.gov.uk/guidance/building-safety-programme

Centre for Alternative Technology https://cat.org.uk

Centre for Cities www.centreforcities.org/our-focus-in-2020/

The Design Council www.designcouncil.org.uk/what-we-do/built-environment/inclusive-environments

Gangmasters and Labour Abuse Authority www.gla.gov.uk

GeoPlace www.geoplace.co.uk/addresses-streets/location-data/the-uprn

Health and Safety Executive www.hse.gov.uk

Information Commissioner's Office https://ico.org.uk

International Ethics Standards Coalition https://ies-coalition.org

Law Commission www.lawcom.gov.uk/project/leasehold-enfranchisement/

Leasehold Advisory Service www.lease-advice.org

Planning Portal www.planningportal.co.uk/info/200135/approved_documents/ 80/part_m_-_access_to_and_use_of_buildings

Real Estate Data Foundation www.theredfoundation.org

RICS Diversity and Inclusion www.rics.org/uk/about-rics/responsible-business/ diversity-and-inclusion/

RICS SKA Rating www.rics.org/uk/about-rics/responsible-business/ska-rating/

RICS Sustainability www.rics.org/uk/news-insight/future-of-surveying/ sustainability/

Shelter Legal https://england.shelter.org.uk/legal/courts_and_legal_action/ discrimination_and_housing

United Nations Framework Convention on Climate Change *The Paris Agreement* https://unfccc.int/process-and-meetings/the-paris-agreement/ the-paris-agreement

INDEX

Printed in the United States
by Baker & Taylor Publisher Services